THE COMPLETE ALASKAN MALAMUTE

Admiral Byrd Memorial Plaque to Antarctic Dogs.

THE COMPLETE
Alaskan Malamute

by MAXWELL RIDDLE
and EVA B. SEELEY

ILLUSTRATED

FIRST EDITION . . . Fifth Printing

1981

HOWELL BOOK HOUSE INC.

230 PARK AVENUE
NEW YORK, N.Y. 10169

"Please don't eat the daisies" might be a
proper warning to these puppies.

Library of Congress Catalog Card No. 75-43221
ISBN 0-87605-009-7

Printed in U.S.A.

Contents

Ch. Alaskaland's American Pie, owned by Patti Colcord, bred by Sheila Land. *Photo by Nick Pruyn.*

Acknowledgments

MANY PEOPLE have helped to make this book possible. We would like to thank Mrs. Nancy C. Russell, president of the Alaskan Malamute Club of America; Jeanne Olbrich; Mary Ann Breen; Dr. Kenneth Bourns; Sheila M. Fletch, D.V.M.; Dr. Henry W. Dodd, Jr.; Mrs. Linda Dowdy; Beth Harris; Mr. and Mrs. Earl Norris; Robert Zoller; Mrs. Phyllis Castleton; Mark Mooty and William Stifel, secretary and executive secretary respectively of the American Kennel Club; Norman Brown of the Canadian Kennel Club; and Ben Ogburn.

We acknowledge the help of the Cleveland Public Library and the University of Alaska Library. Our grateful thanks go to Mrs. Paul Nystedt who aided Mrs. Seeley by typing the manuscript and to Ms. Patricia Colcord who also helped.

—*The Authors*

7

Head study of an early Alaskan Malamute owned by Mrs. Louise Lombard, wife of the famed racing driver, Dr. Roland Lombard. The dog's name was Tin City.

Bernice B. Perry

Preface

THIS BOOK reflects a fine collaboration between Eva B. (Mrs. Milton J.) Seeley, founder of The Alaskan Malamute Club of America, and Maxwell Riddle, the international dog authority, judge and writer.

Eva Seeley, known among her friends by the nickname "Short," was born into an animal-loving family who owned race horses, dogs, cats, fancy pigeons and a pet lamb. In 1924 she married Milton Seeley, professor of chemistry and physics at Oregon State College where Eva was a member of the Physical Education staff. They settled in Wonalancet, N.H., the home of the famous dog Chinook. As a wedding gift, Mr. Seeley gave Eva a son of Chinook. "Short" later wrote *Chinook and His Family,* published by Ginn and Co.

Interested in all sled dogs, Eva also organized the second Siberian Husky Club of America after the first club was dissolved. In fact, the Seeleys were instrumental in setting up the standards for both the Malamute and Siberian Husky.

Mrs. Seeley also founded the Yankee Alaskan Malamute Club, the Yankee Siberian Husky Club and the all-breed Carroll County Kennel Club of North Conway, N.H. She is eligible as an American Kennel Club judge of the three Arctic sled dog breeds including Samoyeds.

As THE COMPLETE ALASKAN MALAMUTE will attest, the breed has had no stauncher supporter and no greater contributor to its growth and development than Eva B. Seeley.

Her co-author, Maxwell Riddle, has long been a friend and student of the Alaskan Malamute. Mr. Riddle has judged all breeds in America, Canada, Australia, Africa and South America. His weekly columns on dogs have been syndicated for many years in America's leading newspapers. He is Associate Editor of *Dog World* Magazine and a contributor to other periodicals. He has written eleven dog books, contributing more than half the articles in *The International Encyclopedia of Dogs,* and has won *all* the awards for excellence in writing from The Dog Writers' Association of America which he has served as a past President.

He was President of the Ravenna and Western Reserve Kennel Clubs in Ohio.

This book contains chapters by other outstanding breed authorities: Robert J. Zoller, Natalie Norris, Nancy C. Russell, Roger Burggraf and the eminent veterinarian, Dr. Kenneth Bourns.

It gives us great pleasure to bring this fascinating and authentic work to all fanciers of the noble Alaskan Malamute.

—Elsworth Howell

1

The Eskimos

THE ALASKAN MALAMUTE is an Eskimo dog. It gets its name from a particular group of Eskimos known as the Malamutes. If one is to appreciate the remarkable qualities of the dog, one ought to know something about the remarkable people who owned and developed them. The partnership between man and dog was a vital factor in making life possible in a land generally considered too inhospitable for human beings.

The Eskimos are a fairly homogeneous race of people who occupy nearly all the Arctic Coast from the Bering Sea north to Point Barrow, then all the way across the continent, and then across the sea to Greenland. It is an inhospitable land, desired by no one until the white man found it a rich source of fur, minerals, and now oil. It is a land without trees and with very little vegetation except lichens. There are long periods of darkness for six months of the year, and for six to nine months each year, the land is covered with snow and ice.

Anthropologists are constantly pushing back the date of man's entrance into the world, just as astronomers are steadily adding to the age of the universe. Once it was believed that North America was populated by Asiatics who crossed the Bering Strait about a thousand years ago. Today it is believed that men inhabited our plains states 15,000 to 25,000 years ago. There is also a report of the ashes of a man-made fire in a cave near the southern extremity of South America. That little pile of ashes has been dated by carbon 14 to be about 29,000 years old.

Anthropologists differ in opinions of where human life began. Once it was thought to be Asia Minor. Now some believe the site was in Central Africa. A few feel that the races of mankind might have developed simultaneously in various areas of the globe. Those who believe the former, also believe in the radiation theory.

The radiation theory is a means of explaining population migrations. As culture advances in a given center, population and industry also advance. Peoples living on the outskirts are then forced farther from the center. On the whole, these peoples will be more primitive than those at the center. They will continue the old ways, perhaps by necessity, and will not adopt the new ways of the center.

Based on the radiation theory, most anthropologists believe that both North and South America were populated by successive migrations across a land bridge at the Bering Straits. However, many of the migrations may have come after the land bridge had disappeared into the sea. Those people on the fringes would be forced farther and farther south. The Isthmus of Panama would be a temporary barrier, less for the human beings than for the animals. It is noteworthy that, except for cats, no North American animals ever made it to South America.

The radiation theory presumes that the Eskimos came from Asia. If so, they turned north into a land which could only support a people of their hardihood and their genius. All others, with one possible exception, turned south into the fertile forests below the tree line.

It is true that Eskimos have certain features which could indicate Mongol origin. Attempts to link their language with any of the Asiatic tongues, however, have not generally been accepted by linguists. Blood type is a fairly stable genetic characteristic. The Eskimo blood type is "B," and this type was unknown among the Indians who are also supposed to have come from Asia. Apparently there was never any mixture of the two until quite modern times. And there is probably more mixture of Indian-white blood than of Eskimo-Indian blood.

Eskimos have some remarkable and distinguishing features. For example, they have unusually small hands and feet. One could hardly expect this in a race forced to live under such difficult conditions. Their dentition is slightly different from that of Asiatics, Indians, and Caucasians. They have "shovel shaped" incisors, and such strong jaws and teeth that they use them for tasks which those of other races could not do without destroying the teeth. They have very narrow nose bridges and, as the authors have observed, have less nasal discharge than other people in frigid weather.

Modern anthropologists have evidence that an unknown race of people inhabited the Arctic coast line before the arrival of the Eskimos. Some have given a tentative date of several thousands of years before Christ for the time of these people. If one were to accept the theory that human life began independently in North America, then one could combine this with the radiation theory. Eskimos could have been forced north from internal America and, if the unknown Arctic people still lived, have destroyed them and taken over the land.

In any case, the date at which the Eskimos entered the Arctic is not known. We do know that they began a gigantic migration about a thousand years ago. That migration took them eastward until they at last reached Greenland. It is believed that they arrived there at about the same time as the Vikings. These people are called the "Thule People." Between 400 and 500 years ago, many of them returned across the Arctic to Alaska.

Since there was so little vegetation other than lichens, the Eskimos had to adjust to an all meat diet. In the short summers, they caught and dried fish. Summer travel was difficult and often impossible along the low lands because of melting ice and snow. When the freeze set in, the Eskimos could hunt for caribou, musk oxen, and other animals. To a certain extent, they got vegetable matter by eating the stomach contents of these animals. They were sometimes able to get polar bears, and they hunted for seals, walruses, and even whales.

Clothing had to be made from skins and pelts. Summer tents also had to be made from skins. In winter, ice houses or igloos were made. Utensils and hunting weapons had to be made from bones. Heat and light had to come from seal oil or other animal fats, including whale oil.

Men and women were so dependent upon each other that wife sharing was sometimes practiced. Women had to make the clothes, and they had to use their strong teeth and jaws to soften skin boots which had hardened during a day's hunt. Because of their many responsibilities, mothers could only handle one young child at a time and infanticide was sometimes practiced. All the evidence indicates, however, that Eskimos were unusually fond of children. They were, and they still are.

A more or less communistic society existed. The successful hunter and his family often had to share food with less successful hunters, for the successful one had to look ahead to the time when he and his family would be hungry.

Present knowledge indicates that the dog became a domestic animal about 6,000 years ago. It is difficult to imagine that the Eskimos could have survived without the dog. The reindeer was used in Asia but seems not to have been known by even those Eskimos living on the Asiatic side of the Bering Sea. There is some evidence that at least some of the early Eskimos did not own dogs but pulled their sleds and sledges by hand. They lived in low lying coastal areas.

Those Eskimos living more inland, or in rougher country, must have found it impossible to haul sleds by hand, and certainly not the heavier and larger sledges. The so-called Spitz, or Arctic type of dog is a strongly dominant one, and thus it is possible that the Eskimo dog may represent the oldest of all domestic animals.

"Sledge for burden in Kamtchatka," an 1809 print.

2

Arctic Explorers Tell
of Their Great Dogs

PEOPLE who own Alaskan Malamutes, or for that matter any of the Arctic breeds, ought to know something of the proud record their dogs have made in the service of the Arctic peoples. All the Arctic breeds share much in common—their ability to work under near killing conditions, their hardihood in the Artic cold and their willingness to work even on near starvation diets. Many of their great services were rendered to Arctic explorers, and so here we tell something of those explorers.

The search for a Northwest Passage to Asia began in the early 1700s, but the great age of Arctic exploration is roughly dated from 1740 to 1890. Most of the explorers went north from Europe and tried to go west. Others, the Spanish for example, went around Cape Horn and then began to explore the Pacific Coast of America northward. The great George Vancouver did the same for England.

Meanwhile, the Russians moved across Siberia. In 1728, Vitus Bering ₋₋ssed through the straight which bears his name. Three years later, Girondeff sighted the American coast. In 1741, Bering and Alexei Chirikov also located the American coast. Bering's ship was wrecked on the shore of the island that bears his name, and he died there Dec. 8, 1741. By 1775, the Russians had set up a series of trading stations along the southern coast of Alaska.

In one of history's greatest land trips, Alexander Mackenzie crossed

15

along the Arctic shores to Cape Menzies and returned. The great river bears his name, and one sometimes reads of dogs called Mackenzie River Malamutes. His journey was in 1792–93.

The first explorers to reach the north coast of Alaska, however, were the Englishmen, Sir John Franklin and Capt. F.W. Beechey. They had been sent in 1826 to map the coast west of the Mackenzie River. John Simpson, a ship's doctor, wintered at Barrow which was then, as now, the largest Eskimo village in the world. Point Barrow is the northernmost tip of the continent. This John Simpson is not to be confused with George Simpson, a Hudson's Bay Company employee who walked 1,910 miles from Fort Confidence to the Red River settlement from Sept. 26, 1839 to Feb. 2, 1840.

John Simpson describes in his journal four great Eskimo trade centers, and one of these is important to our story. It was near Kotzebue where the inland Eskimos and Indians of the Noatak and Kobuk River areas came to exchange furs for goods of Asiatic origin and dogs.

With this background, let the explorers themselves tell about their dogs. In 1824, *The Privtae Journal of Captain G.F. Lyon* was published. Capt. Lyon had commanded one of the ships of Capt. Parry on his 1821–1823 trip. The ships were the Hecla and the Fury. Here are excerpts from his journal:

> "They bear young at every season and seldom exceed five at a litter. In December, with the thermometer at 40 degrees below zero, the females were in several instances in heat. (My dogs) at the ship had no shelter, but lay alongside with the thermometer at 42–44 degrees (below zero), and with as little concern as if the weather had been mild.
>
> "I found, by several experiments, that three of my dogs could draw me on a sledge weighing 100 pounds, at a rate of one mile in six minutes; and as proof of the strength of a well grown dog, my leader drew 196 pounds singly, and to the same distance in eight minutes.
>
> "At another time, seven of my dogs ran a mile in four minutes, 30 seconds, drawing a heavy sledge full of men. . . . Afterwards, in carrying stores to the Fury, one mile distant, nine dogs drew 1611 pounds in the space of nine minutes. My sledge was on wooden runners, neither shod nor iced; had they been the latter, at least 40 pounds might have been added for every dog."

Writing of their marvelous ability to find their way, and their "homing instinct" he wrote: ". . . I have often returned home from the Fury, a distance of near a mile, in pitchy darkness, and admidst clouds of snow drift, entirely under the care of those trusty servants who, with their noses down to the snow, have galloped on board entirely directed by their sense of smelling. Had they erred, or even been at all restive, no human means could have brought us on board until the return of clear weather."

The dogs were, of course, hungry all the time, and Capt. Lyon remarks that "the dogs ate at least two dead Eskimos". These were bodies exposed on the ice when burial was impossible. Other accounts tell of the curious sense of conscience possessed by some of the dogs.

There is an Eskimo saying that when a marooned Eskimo starts to eat his dogs, he is doomed, for he is destroying his only means of transportation. But it has been noted that some dogs will ravenously devour a dead comrade, sometimes before he is quite dead. Others will not touch the body until it has been frozen for a day or so. Still others will not touch it at all, and prefer to starve to death.

Franz Boas had some interesting comments on the character of the dogs, as reported in *The Central Eskimo* in the sixth annual report of the Bureau of Ethnology, Smithsonian Institute, in 1888:

> "If any dog is lazy, the driver calls out his name and he is lashed, but it is necessary to hit the dog called, for if another is struck he feels wronged and will turn upon the dog whose name has been called; the leader enters into the quarrel, and soon the whole pack is huddled up in one howling mass, and no amount of lashing and beating will separate the fighting team. The only thing to do is to wait until their wrath has abated and clear the traces."

One of these authors had an experience worth mentioning at this point. It happened at Point Barrow. Heavy polar winds had broken up the ice and had piled huge cakes as large as the sides of houses upon the shore. The weather had calmed and the ocean beyond was again frozen over. The temperature was 35 degrees below zero.

In searching for a passage to the ocean, a comparatively round mound was found, but as the leading dogs went over the mound, they disappeared. Three of them had fallen into the carcass of a whale. They hung by their harness and tried to fight, and those outside set up their own fight.

The driver and the author had to jump into the carcass, take the dogs out of harness, and then haul them out. But not until the other dogs had stopped their own brawl.

One thinks of the Arctic Ocean ice as being as flat and smooth as on a pond, but the winds often break up the ice floes, leave open water areas and pile blocks upon blocks. Nor is the going always smooth on land. The gentle naturalist, John Muir, in the *Cruise of The Corwyn* gives several excellent descriptions of both the driving, and the way in which the Eskimos kept their dogs:

> ". . . we found the dogs, nearly a hundred of them, with eleven sleds, making, as they lay at their ease, an imposing picture among the white ice. Three teams were straightened out . . . the Captain and I were taken on behind the other two; and away we sped over the frozen ceiling of the sea, two rows of tails ahead.

17

"The distance to the village . . . was about three miles, the first mile very rough and apparently hopelessly inaccessible to sleds. But the wolfish dogs and drivers seemed to regard it all as a regular turnpike, and jogged merrily on, up one side of a tilted block or slab and down the other with a sudden pitch and plunge, swishing round sideways on squinted cakes, and through pools of water and sludge in blue, craggy hollows, on and on, this way and that, with never a halt, the dogs keeping up a steady jog trot, and the leader simply looking over his shoulder occasionally for directions in the worst places. My sled was not upset at all, the captain's only twice . . . (the dogs) are as steady as oxen, each keeping its trace line tight, and showing no inclination to shirk."

These Eskimos were Chukchis, living on the Siberian coast, and Muir tells how they lived:

"Three or four families live in one (hut), each having a private polog of deerskins of which there are several thicknesses on the floor. We were shown into one—the snuggest storm nest imaginable and perfectly clean.

"The common hut is far otherwise; dogs mingle with food, hair is everywhere, and strangely persistent smells that defy even the Arctic frosts. The children seemed in fair ratio to adults. When a child is to be nursed, the mother merely pulls out one of her arms from the roomy sleeve of her parka and pushes it down until the breast is exposed. The breasts are pendulous and cylindrical like those of the Tlingits.

"The dishes used in domestic affairs are of wood, and in the smallest of these the puppies, after licking them, were often noticed to lie down. They seemed made specially for them, so well did they fit. Dogs were eagerly licking large kettles, also, in which seal meat had been boiled."

Again: ". . . while puppies and nursing mother dogs and children may be seen scattered here and there, or curled snugly in the pots and eating troughs, after they have licked them clean, making a squalor that is picturesque and daring beyond description.

"In all the huts, however, there are from one to three luxurious bedrooms. The walls, ceilings, and floor are of soft reindeer skins, and (each polog) has a trough filled with oil for heat and light. After hunting all day on the ice, making long, rough, stormy journeys, the Chukchi hunter, muffled and hungry, comes into his burrow, eats his fill of oil and seal or walrus, then strips himself naked and lies down in his closed fur nest, his polog, in glorious ease, to smoke and sleep."

Muir has this description of summer travel:

". . . eight canoe loads of Eskimos, with all their goods, tents, children, etc., passed close along the shore going toward Icy Cape; all except one were drawn by dogs—from three to five to each canoe—attached by a long string of walrus hide, and driven by a woman or half-grown girl, or boy. 'Ooch, ooch, ooch' they said while urging them along. They dragged the canoe with perhaps two tons altogether at two and one half miles per hour. When they came to a sheer bluff, the dogs swam and the drivers got into the canoe until the beach again admitted of tracking. The canoe that had no dogs was paddled and rowed by both men and women. One woman, pulling an oar on the starboard bow, was naked from the waist. They came from Point Hope."

John Muir wrote this journal in 1881 as the Corwin searched for the remains of the lost explorer De Long and his ship, the Jeannette. We have quoted from the Houghton-Mifflin edition of 1917, edited by W.F. Badé.

By far the greatest and most tragic description of the Arctic dogs was written by Lieutenant Commander George Washington DeLong. His cruise in the Jeannette began at San Francisco July 8, 1879. He kept a daily log, until he died of cold and starvation early in October, 1881. The Jeanette was trying to reach the North Pole via the Western Arctic. On Aug. 25, 1879, George DeLong in command wrote that he was at St. Lawrence Bay, Siberia, and that he had forty dogs and nine sleds.

"They are all good sized and strong, and thus far roam around the deck in a happy go lucky kind of way, fighting every five minutes and seemingly well contented. . . . The nature of these dogs is to fight at all times, and unless they are beaten well, they will not keep the peace at all."

When four of the dogs had to be rescued from an ice floe, DeLong wrote: "The remaining dogs were very indignant at the absent but returning ones, and had they not been prevented would have given them a fight as a celebration, looking no doubt on the enforced separation as some new dodge for shirking work."

At one point, the dogs had to be fed frozen food, and DeLong observed that some had rotting teeth and some none at all. "These, while trying to get the frozen food down, are frequently robbed by the more vigorous dogs who have good jaws, and who can, if necessary, reduce an iron bar to proper size for their stomachs."

The Jeannette was locked in ice, and Lieut. DeLong took the time to write an incomparable description of his dogs:

"The weather is gloomy, depressing, and disagreeable. Velocities ranging from 10 to 23 miles drive the snow from the face of the floe in clouds, and other snow falling makes distant objects, say 100 yards, invisible. Here and there alongside the ship a little white lump indicates that there is a dog beneath it, and even the regular and irregular dog fights are discontinued until the weather gets clearer and friend can be distinguished from foe.

". . . Why they fight, how they fight, and whom they fight, seem to be purely abstract questions with them, so long as it is a fight. For

19

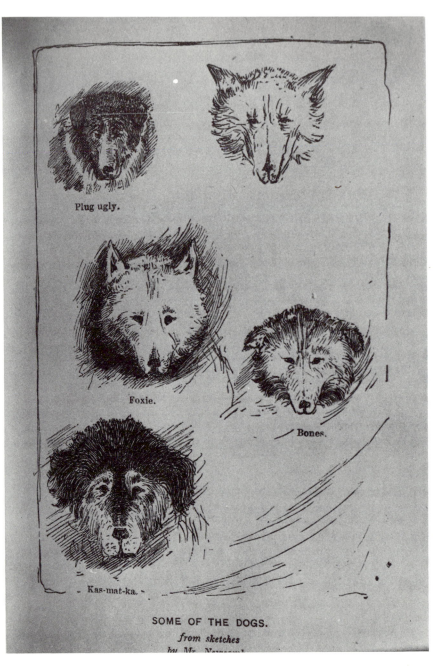

Plug ugly.

Foxie.

Bones.

Kas-mat-ka.

SOME OF THE DOGS.
from sketches

Sketches of dogs on the Jeannette by
Raymond L. Newcomb, naturalist.

instance dogs one and two will see dog three in a good position, perhaps enjoying a meat can that has been empty for months and has, of course, no nutriment. As if by concerted plan one and two will spring on three, roll him over, and seemingly tear him to pieces. Fortunately the wool is so long and thick that an attacking dog gets a mouth full of hair before his front teeth reach the flesh, so no great damage is generally done. The vulnerable places are the ears, and the belly.

"I have seen an attacked dog run, and, lying on his stomach, shove his head into a snow bank with impunity, while his foes are choking over the hair they tore from his back. However, this is a long digression. Suddenly dog three will turn on dog two and be promptly aided by dog one, his previous foe. By this time the whole pack has gathered as if by magic, and a free and indiscriminate fight occurs, until the advent of the quartermaster, and a merciless application of the whip breaks up the row.

"They divide up into little gangs of three or four, and in these friendly cliques they also fight. For days everything may go on smoothly, when one of the set does something offensive to his mates, and one of them (or sometimes all of them) administers a thrashing, and the offender is sent to Coventry until their feelings calm down. It is a common occurrence to see a dog on the black list, a quarter of a mile from the ship, all alone and afraid to come in until his time is up.

"He then approaches fawningly, wagging his tail deprecatingly to become reconciled, and is either welcomed with wagging tails or snarling teeth, in which latter case he retires to his isolated position for another spell.

"Another peculiarity is, that though they make no demonstration at any dog singly, or a team, going away, except the most doleful howling in concert, they seem to consider it a terrible indignity that he, or they, should presume to come back. The remainder of the pack scent the arriving one, several hundred yards off, and gather awaiting him. If the team comes in, a rough-and-tumble fight commences between the harnessed and the free, which requires two or three men to stop. As soon as the harness is off, they are all smooth and quiet again, the cliques reassembling and moving off to their usual haunts.

"If a single dog, so much the worse luck for him. As soon as he appears, they are all on him. Let him be never so wary, and slink around the hummocks to reach the ship unobserved, some one dog sees his head, or his tail, gives the signal, and away they go. It is then a question of speed, for if the single dog but reaches his usual sunning or stopping place, he is safe; for, by some rule always observed, the getting to home base restores him to the full rights of citizenship. The cautious approach, and the great speed on the last stretch, are worthy of much higher intelligence than we usually give to dogs.

"The care they bestow on each other in distress or trouble, arising from disability, has a marked exhibition in the case of Jack and Snuffy. Snuffy had his nose bitten into in a fight at St. Michael's last summer, and in consequence his head is twice the natural size, by swelling and diseased bone. Jack is seemingly Snuffy's brother, and he is devoted to him beyond much human fraternal affection. He stays by Snuffy, cleans him, sees that he is not molested by other dogs, follows him into enemies' camps, leads him through in safety, and guards his retreat. Let Snuffy get a tid-bit, like an old moccasin or a piece of hide, Jack sees him secure it, stand by him while he chews it, and if he leaves it, chews it for him until he seems to want it again, when it is promptly surrendered. So accustomed have the pack become to this sort of thing that they permit many liberties with their food which they would resent with a well dog.

"Their cunning is extraordinary. Going out the other night at 12 for meteorological observations, about a dozen of them came around me in great excitement about something or other. Looking around for a cause, I observed a good-sized dog head first in a barrel at an angle, with only his tail and flanks sticking out.

"He had gone in for some walrus meat at the bottom, and no dog had driven him out, because his stern view was not recognizable as belonging to a bully or not. Anxious to save the meat, I went to the barrel and drove him out, when half of the gang recognizing him as no great fighter, pitched into him, while the other half fought among themselves for entry into the barrel. For fear of catching a Tartar, they had waited for some one to solve the conundrum 'Who is in the barrel?' "

In another entry in his log, DeLong writes:

"Having great difficulty in getting any work out of our 'hoodlum gang,' Jack, Tom, and Wolf, a method of punishment had to be devised. Ordinarily they lie around on ash-heaps all day in the sun, blinking lazily, and ready to head an attack on some wandering dog in search of a bone, or more particularly sallying out to meet some dog returning with the hunters, who has incurred their grave displeasure by assisting at any work. The sight of a harness, merely, reminds them of a pressing engagement elsewhere; and the moving of a dog sled in their range of vision seems suggestive of the advisability of a change of base.

"Accordingly, each morning, when the ice has to be dragged in for melting, these three are occupied surveying the work from a distance until it is completed, and then they unite in an attack on those dogs who did the dragging. They were caught by strategy today, however, and harnessed up; but Tom slipped his harness quietly and bolted, while Wolf chewed his through and escaped. When caught they were securely tied to a rope over the stern, and kept there until 10 p.m. when, in order that their howls might not keep everybody awake, they were anchored with an ice-claw some distance off. This disgusted them. Tom took his punishment solemnly and quietly, but Wolf yelled incessantly, so much so that Tom got provoked and thrashed him twice into silence."

Toward the end of June, 1881, the Jeannette was crushed by ice and sank. The men left in two boats but got separated in a storm. The DeLong boat was wrecked and the men began a long overland trek in search of some habitation, food, and shelter. Their food ran out, and one by one, the dogs had to be killed for food. And one by one the men began to die. On the 113th day, the last dog was killed. And on the 140th day, the last entry was made in Lieutenant DeLong's log. It said: "Boyd and Gortz died during the night. Mr. Collins dying." His own death came shortly after.

Men And Dogs At Little America, Antarctica.

KOTZEBUE SOUND MALEMUT MEN AND WOMEN WITH LABRETS

Malemut Men and Women With Lip Labrets—1881.

24

3

The Malamutes and Their Dogs

THE WORD ALASKA is a corruption of the Aleut word, A-la-as-ka, meaning "great country" or vast land. Alaska has also been spelled Alyeska, and Alyeshka. The language of the Eskimos is one with an almost endless number of suffixes, each carrying a subtle grade of meaning. One suffix is "miut." It has been translated in two ways: "the people" and "inhabitants of."

One group of Eskimos called itself the Mahlemiut. The meaning of "Mahle" is not known, but we can translate the full term as "the people of Mahle". Most Eskimos are rather small in size, a factor permitting greater endurance under Arctic conditions. E.W. Nelson, who was on the Corwin in 1881, wrote as follows:

"The Malemut and the people of the Kaviak Peninsula, including those of the islands in Bering Strait, are tall, active, and remarkably well built. Among them it is common to see men from five feet ten inches to six feet tall, and of proportionate build. I should judge the average to be nearly or quite equal in height to the whites.

"As a race, the Eskimos are very hardy and insensible to cold. While the Corwin was at anchor in Hotham Inlet, during the fall of 1881, I found a Malemut woman with two little girls, one about two years and the other about five years of age, lying fast asleep on the deck of the vessel, clothed only in their ordinary garments. A very raw wind was blowing at the time, and it was very difficult for us to keep warm even while moving about in heavy garments.

Malemut Family With Dog Sled—1881.

Malemut Family From Shaktolik—1881. Drawing is from a photograph.

"While I was at the head of Norton Sound during February, when the temperature stood at minus forty degrees Fahrenheit, a boy ten years of age, with a sled and three dogs, was sent back several miles along the previous day's trail to recover a pair of lost snowshoes. He started off alone and returned a few hours later with the snowshoes, his cheeks glowing red from the cold, but without other indication of the effect of the temperature."

In 1877, Nelson was commissioned to make a collection for the U.S. National Museum in Alaska. His report, published in the 18th annual *Report of The Bureau of American Ethnology,* has much to say about the Malamutes:

"The Shaktolik people told me that in ancient times, before the Russians came (Authors: 1765 and later), the Unalit occupied all the coast of Norton Sound from Pastolik northward to a point a little beyond Shaktolik. At that time, the southern limit of the Malemut was at the head of Norton Bay. They have since advanced and occupied village after village until now the people of Shaktolik and Unalaklit are mainly Malemut, or a mixture of Malemut and Unalit. They added that since the disappearance of the reindeer along the coast, the Malemut have become much less numerous then formerly."

Nelson is not writing here of the domesticated reindeer used in Asia for food, milk, skins, and transportation, but of the American reindeer, called the caribou. The latter move in vast herds on long migrations, and they appear to have changed their migration route for unknown reasons. The Malamut population dropped as its food supply lessened.

"Various Russians," Nelson continued, "and others, who were living in that region in 1872 and 1873, informed me that at that time there were about 200 people living in the village of Kigiktauik, while in 1881 I found only about 12 to 14. At the time first named, the mountains bordering the coast in that neighborhood swarmed with reindeer, and in addition to the Unalit, many Malemut had congregated there to take advantage of the hunting.

"During November, 1880, I found a family of Malemut living in a miserable hut on the upper part of the Anvik River. As stated elsewhere, these people have become spread over a wide region."

Dr. John Simpson, the ship's doctor, who had wintered at Barrow in 1827, was one of the first white men to reach that point. He wrote of four great Eskimo trading centers, one of which was on the shores of the Kotzebue Sound. This was the land of the Mahlemiuts, or as we now spell it, Malamutes.

Two great rivers empty into Kotzebue Sound, the Kobuk and the Noatak. Indians and inland Eskimos could bring their furs down to the trading center and sell them for goods of Asiatic origin, and they could buy dogs.

Lieutenant George M. Stoney, who took part in a naval exploration of Alaska in 1900, reported seeing 40 Kobuk Eskimos, 50 dogs, and 12 sleds. They were returning to the mountains after trading with the Malamutes. These Eskimos were probably also Malamutes. For in 1887, Lieutenant John C. Cantwell had reported that the Kobuk River Eskimos spoke the "Malamiut dialect of the coast."

Lieutenant Stoney reported that some sleds were drawn by men, women, and dogs all hitched up together. And he noted one woman with a child in her parka, dragging a sled while her husband pushed and guided from behind. A single dog helped the woman pull. Lieutenant Stoney observed that the inland Eskimos seldom used many dogs. Food was scarce so they used only one or two as helpers.

The Malamute dogs of that time were heavy freighting dogs and they were probably as nearly purebred as an Eskimo society could manage. But in 1896, gold was discovered on Bonanza Creek in the Klondike. The massive rush of the gold miners put a demand for Malamutes which could not be met.

Outside dogs were brought in by both the miners and other fortune hunters. Among others, St. Bernards were used. They were great "pullers," as the miners said. All these dogs were crossed with Malamutes and other Arctic dogs. Good dog teams could bring as much as $1700.00, and an individual dog might cost as much as $500.00.

From that time on, people began to boast of wolf crosses and even of harnessing purebred wolves which had been captured as puppies. Probably very little of this was true, but what was true was that the fame of the Malamutes caused all of these dogs to be called Malamutes.

What was also true was that the cross-breds quickly began to return to the so-called Spitz type to which all the northern breeds belong. This Arctic type has been dominant for more centuries than man can unearth. So even the first generation of cross-breds tended to look more like the Spitz dogs than the other half of their breeding. Within three generations there would be no sign of outside blood.

There would, of course, be slight variations within the Arctic type, since dogs in isolated communities would be inbred. These differences can partially account for slight variations found in modern Alaskan Malamutes. They do not indicate any impure breeding in present day dogs, nor any departure from pure type.

4

The Beginning

as told by Eva "Short" Seeley

THE FIRST international sled dog race was held at Berlin, New Hampshire in 1922. It was this race which gave national prominence to sled dogs and to sled dog racing. The race was won by Arthur Treadwell Walden, a veteran of the Alaskan freighting trails, as well as of racing. At the time, Walden was living at Wonalancet, New Hampshire, at Wonalancet Farm. His wife, Kate Sleeper Walden, had converted a very old and fashionable boarding house into an inn. Walden had named his kennels after his lead dog, Chinook, meaning "Warm Winds," and the kennels were behind the Inn. Chinook was an exceptionally strong dog, massive in body for his 90 pounds of weight, and with drop ears.

In February, 1920, Gorham, New Hampshire held a winter carnival, and Walden and his team had taken part. In the early winter of 1923 I was returning from Florida to help organize the winter carnival in my home city of Worcester, Massachusetts. I happened to see a newspaper article about Walden and his great team, and it occurred to me that a dog sled team mght be a great attraction. The newspaper article, incidentally, called the dogs "wolf dogs" of the north.

I called Walden, talked to the carnival chairman and to the Worcester parks superintendent. All liked the idea, and as it turned out, we had two teams. At the carnival, Walden took me for my first dog sled ride. The trails were on a golf links. At one point, a cat scooted across the trail immediately in front of the dogs, and disappeared into a clump of trees.

Ch. Gripp of Yukon, first champion in the breed. Bred by Mr. and Mrs. Milton Seeley.

Chinook and his eight team mates immediately took off after the cat. Walden quickly overthrew the sled. This probably saved me from serious injury, but Walden did injure severely one hand. I was thrilled by this ride, and I began immediately to make plans to visit Wonalancet.

The winter of 1923 held its snow, and upon my arrival at the railroad station, 11 miles from Wonalancet, Walden met me or, I should say "us." I was a physical education director, and I had brought along two others. All three of us enjoyed winter sports. Walden took us for a "moonlight supper" ride during which he personally cooked a "mushers' meal" for us. We then continued the ride. The dogs were adorned with pom poms and bells which rang merrily. My future in sled dogs began right there.

Milton Seeley, then my fiancé, had come up to Worcester at the time of the winter carnival. He, too, was impressed by the dogs. Thus, in May, 1924, we decided to spend our honeymoon at Wonalancet. There we would do some mountain climbing, and we could learn more about the dogs. We returned to live at Nyack-on-Hudson, and we took with us a son of Chinook which we named "Nook." He was a tawny, gentle puppy, and he was very friendly. Later we returned him to Walden for training.

Milton worked at a chemical laboratory. After a trip to Europe, it became apparent that the strain was seriously affecting his health. He was ordered to take a winter's rest. Meanwhile, Walden had come to New York, along with Chinook, to take part in a charity sponsored by a humane organization. The event was held on the roof area of the old Waldorf-Astoria Hotel. Walden called us and brought Chinook to our home. Walden urged us to come to Wonalancet. We agreed, and shortly thereafter we moved into a cottage across from the Inn. That was the real beginning for us. It was January, 1927, and Walden was collecting dogs for the first Byrd Antarctic Expedition. He was busy training dogs and drivers as well. Among the highly skilled drivers which he had brought to Wonalancet was A.A. "Scotty" Allen, a veteran of the famed Alaska Sweepstakes races.

Commander, later Admiral, Byrd visited Wonalancet several times. His instructions were simple: "These dogs must be the best, and the best trained. Never has any Antarctic or polar expedition been successful without these faithful animals. And without them we could never accomplish our mission."

There was a need for 50 more dogs than those already assembled at Wonalancet and in February they arrived by train and were trucked the 11 miles from the station to the kennels.

One dog was a beautiful 80 pound, double coated, broad headed, and very gentle, male. Scotty Allen held him and called me over. "This is what the large sled dog of Alaska should look like," he said. And then he added: "From what I learned from the All-Alaska Sweepstakes drivers, I realized I had all too few of them in my kennels. He is without a name, so you name him."

People had long been influenced by Jack London and James Oliver Curwood's stories of "wolf dogs" of the North, but here was one who wagged his tail, stuck his muzzle into your hands, and never seemed to enjoy rough house or fighting with other dogs. So, in complete contrast to his disposition, I named him "Rowdy." Scotty suggested that I call him officially Rowdy of Nome, since that is where he had originated. Rowdy joined the team of Edward Goodale.

Arthur Walden had started the New England Sled Dog Club, and races had been held since 1924. But the racing schedule had declined, and it became necessary for someone to carry on after Walden left for the Antarctic. Walter Channing, a wealthy sportsman from Boston, had been president of the club, but he felt that the press of business made it necessary for him to resign. However, he agreed to stay on until we could reorganize the club. I became his secretary. Later, my husband joined me, and we carried on until the sport had been fully revived.

Leonhard Seppala had imported a Siberian Husky team from Alaska, and through Mrs. Elizabeth Ricker of the Poland Springs, Maine, Hotels, he had established his Seppala kennels at Poland Springs. Seppala knew that we were looking for a large Alaskan dog. Seppala had decided to train and race only the Siberians. So he turned over to us a large, handsome animal.

Mrs. Ricker had invited us to Poland Springs where we rode behind her team of 18 Siberians. It was there that we first saw the dog, Yukon Jad. A couple who had toured Alaska bought Jad from Frank Gough of Dawson, Yukon Territory. Jad became their pet, but they asked Seppala to take him when they planned an extensive European tour.

Mrs. Ricker had applied for registration of Siberian Huskies with the American Kennel Club. The idea then occurred to us that we might develop and register a true American breed, the Alaskan Malamute. To strengthen this resolve, we had acquired a lovely female named Bessie. The former owner of Bessie had brought her to Walden, saying that he wanted to move south and did not wish to take her along. He said he had purchased her from an Alaskan. Walden presented her to us. She had a fondness for chasing chickens, and we always suspected that that was the reason the owners had brought her to Walden.

In 1929, Yukon Jad and Bessie delivered four sons. This was the first litter from our breeding of similar stock. These males were named Gripp of Yukon, Tugg of Yukon, Kearsarge of Yukon (after some of the mountains) and Finn of Yukon. Gripp of Yukon became the first American Kennel Club Alaskan Malamute champion, and the leader of my Olympic team at Lake Placid. He once saved my life while sled-dogging through the mountains. Finn of Yukon was the "canine broadcaster" from Little America in the Antarctic.

Because my husband was unable to return to his Nyack chemistry labo-

Finn of Yukon (left) and Kearsarge of Yukon resting after
a race. *Harold Orne*

ratory, we became residents of Wonalancet. The first Byrd Antarctic Expedition, called BAE I, returned. Commander Byrd, now Admiral Byrd, asked us to assemble and train men and dogs for a second expedition. We had moved from the Wonalancet Farm and had built our own kennels on 50 acres of land. We had erected log cabin buildings, pens, shelters, and shade for the dogs, and we had made trails on our own property.

We had also been breeding both Alaskan Malamutes and Siberian Huskies, thus we were able to supply Admiral Byrd with some dogs of our own breeding. In addition, we assembled Eskimos and cross breeds. The balance of the story belongs to the chapter on recognition of the breed.

Immortal Leonhard Seppala stands between two immortal ladies at the world championship Laconia, N.H. Derby in 1962. Left: Mrs. Lorna Demidoff; right Eva "Short" Seeley.

Chinook Kotzebue Gripp; breeder-owner, Eva Seeley.

Eva Seeley (right) points to the brake as a woman driver prepares to drive a team.
Arthur Griffin

5

Recognition by the American Kennel Club

FOLLOWING the departure of the first Byrd expedition, BAE I, Mr. Seeley and I began an intensive study of the Alaskan dogs. We had already produced a uniform litter. Now we wished to continue and to expand. Through A.A. "Scotty" Allen, we began extensive correspondence with owners and breeders in the Pacific Northwest, Alaska and the Yukon Territory.

Frank Gough sent us pictures of his dogs and explained his breeding plans. Gough had not previously considered asking for breed recognition by either the American or Canadian Kennel Clubs. He was merely trying to produce uniform large freighting dogs.

Among those with whom we corresponded, and who helped us in our concept of a pure Alaskan Malamute breed, were Bishop Bentley, who traveled by dog sled over much of Alaska; the famed Glacier Priest, Rev. Father Hubbard; and Frank DuFresne, the Alaskan judicial chief, and one of the most noted sportsmen of Alaska. He had owned a team of pure white Siberian Huskies.

We had produced a lovely home-bred bitch, and we obtained another, Holly, when she returned from BAE I. A Coast Guard captain who cruised the Pacific Arctic seas brought us a male which he had obtained on St. Lawrence Island. This dog was named St. Lawrence Mukluk. Mukluk was a great worker, and he was noted for both his strength and intelligence. Mukluk was bred to a bitch of good type, and the mating produced some uniform pups. In 1932, during BAE II, our stock had been used for breeding, and seven uniform gray dogs were produced. They were called the Admiral Byrd Grays. Our correspondents had also told us where we might find other dogs of similar type and character, and after seven years we felt we were ready to apply for recognition by the American Kennel Club.

Milton and I had been showing some of our Siberians at dog shows. We explained our aims to George Foley, who had founded the Foley Dog Show Organization and who had helped many clubs and even many breeds. Foley made an appointment for us to meet Charles Inglee, president of the American Kennel Club. Foley accompanied us to the meeting.

The American Kennel Club policy is to give a breed only tentative recognition at first. Dogs must be shown in the miscellaneous class until sufficient numbers have been registered to merit opening up the full facilities of the stud book to them.

Mr. Inglee explained that the dogs to be shown had to be uniform else he could not say how long it might take to grant full recognition. He also warned us against those fringe people who are a curse to every breed since they breed poor dogs to poor dogs, hoping merely to cash in on the upward going popularity of the breed. He suggested that we ought to enter at least six dogs at shows, so that judges could get a chance to study them and to check them for uniformity.

In those days, Mrs. Geraldine Rockefeller Dodge conducted the fabulous Morris and Essex show. It was the largest and most famous of American shows, and it was held on Mrs. Dodge's great estate Giralda in Madison, New Jersey. Mrs. Dodge, and her manager, McClure Halle, invited us to exhibit seven Alaskan Malamutes, seven Siberian Huskies, and seven Samoyeds. Our exhibit was placed in a special tent, and it created a great deal of interest and enthusiasm. For one thing, people came to realize that these dogs were gentle and had no wolf-like characteristics.

The American Kennel Club also sent several well known judges to visit our kennels and to study both our older dogs and our puppies. Among those who came were Clarence Gray and William Cary Duncan. Other judges, such as Charles Hopton, also became interested. The original standard was based on their studies and upon their conferences with Milton and me. At this time, Volney Hurd, a *Christian Science Monitor* editor, helped the breed immensely. Dr. Hurd had spent a week in the area, much of it in studying the Alaskan Malamutes. Later he wrote a full-page article describing the breed.

Many of our own Kotzebue dogs were lost in the Antarctic. Some were lost in accidents. Others were left behind and were destroyed either by time bombs or by starvation. In the meantime, the number of Alaskan Malamute breeders and owners was increasing rapidly.

Breed recognition came in 1935. In the years that followed, many dogs were brought from Alaska or the Yukon Territory. And these dogs, along with our own, formed the foundation stock for final approval by the American Kennel Club of the breed.

On April 17, 1935, the Alaskan Malamute Club was organized. It later became the Alaskan Malamute Club of America. The organizational meeting was held at the Seeley home at Wonalancet, N.H. The charter members were breeders, some breeders from other breeds, and sled dog enthusiasts.

Milton Seeley was elected president; Volney Hurd of the *Christian Science Monitor,* Boston, vice president; Miss Grace Hight (now Mrs. Samuel Kirkwood of Beirut, Lebanon, where her husband is president of American University), treasurer; and Mrs. Milton (Eva) Seeley, secretary.

Here we must explain AKC registration policies which existed at that time. Many dogs were of unknown ancestry. Those which appeared to be purebred would be used for breeding. Sometimes the puppies did not conform, and would be weeded out, or their parents would not be used further.

When final recognition came, there were many dogs of unknown pedigree. At one time, the American Kennel Club would grant such dogs a stud book number, that is, registration, provided they could win a certain number of championship points.

Later, the rules were tightened. A dog of unknown or defective pedigree had to win a championship. It could still not be registered but if bred to a registered dog, its offspring could be. The American Kennel Club continued this policy as it related to certain foreign breeds, but later cancelled it for American breeds. This brought protests from some Alaskan Malamute breeders and for a time, the American Kennel Club excepted certain dogs from the application of the rule. This explains why Alaskan Malamute pedigrees go back to "unknown" ancestors in so few generations.

The first recorded American Kennel Club registrations came in July of 1935. The first was Gripp of Yukon, born August 24, 1929. He was sired by Yukon Jad out of Bessie and he was wolf gray in color. Gripp also became the first champion in any country. Rowdy of Nome also was registered, as was Taku of Kotzebue.

The next year, Finn of Yukon, Kearsarge of Yukon, Patsy of Kotzebue, and Sheila of Kotzebue were registered. In 1938, Kobuk of Kotzebue, sired by Gripp out of Taku, was registered, as were his litter mates Kotlag, Navarre, and Wanda. The Chinook name did not appear until February, 1944, with the registrations of Chinook's Karluk of Kotzebue, and Chinook's Sheila of Kotzebue.

In the history of North American sled dog racing, no name is as well known as that of Dr. Roland Lombard. In 1946 he registered Igloo Pak's Gripp, sired by Jiffy of Kotzebue out of Tanana of Igloo Pak. But Dr. Lombard's amazing career had begun in 1930 when he won a race against the best drivers in the world at that time. The story of that race is told in another chapter. Since then he has won more races than he can remember. Among them are eight victories in the world championship Fur Ren-

Rowdy Of Nome, born at Nome, 1927: the dog that began it all.

Artist's head study of the immortal champion and sire,
Ch. Toro of Bras Coupe, owned by Earl and Natalie Norris.

dezvous race at Anchorage. In half a dozen other famous races he has lost by less than a second. Dr. Lombard was a founding member of the Alaskan Malamute Club of America, and for a time was its representative at the American Kennel Club.

In 1950, Earl Norris registered Klutina of Kobuk, a son of the Norris champion, Toro of Bras Coupe. Earl and Natalie Norris have played a continuing part in the progress of the breed. Earl won the Anchorage world championship race in 1947 and 1948, and Natalie won the women's race in 1954. Toro of Bras Coupe was one of history's greatest Alaskan Malamute sires, and he worked in harness for seven years before being shown to his bench championship.

We now come to the names of Paul Voelker, Robert Zoller, and Ralph and Marchetta Schmitt. They were developing and registering a different strain of Alaskan Malamutes. This is a story to be told by Robert Zoller of Husky Pak.

The Byrd Antarctic Expeditions and World War II had haken a heavy toll of registered Alaskan Malamutes and of others which were not registered but which in the course of time might have been. By 1947, it was estimated that there were only 30 registered "base stock" dogs left. It was therefore determined to reopen the stud book in order to accept new foundation blood.

One effect of this was to bring about the development of the M'Loot and Husky Pak strain. Another was to spread interest in the breed into the Midwest, the Pacific Coast, and even into Canada and Alaska itself.

Until this time, the Alaskan Malamute Club was essentially made up of Northeastern United States fanciers. Now interest was national in scope. And this brought about the organization of the Alaskan Malamute Club of America. On October 5, 1953, a formal application was made by the Alaskan Malamute Club of America for membership in the American Kennel Club. The following officers were listed upon the application: President: Mrs. Eva B. Seeley, Chinook Kennels, Wonalancet, N.H.; First Vice President: Mrs. Delta Wilson, 1681 Friar Tuck Rd., Atlanta, Ga.; Secretary: Mrs. Edna C. Lawler, 71 Concord Rd. Weston, Mass.; Treasurer: James W. Dawson, Box 165, RFD #3, Manassas, Virginia; AKC Delegate: Dr. Roland Lombard.

On December 15, 1953, Miss P.B. Everett, then secretary of the American Kennel Club, sent the following notification to Mrs. Lawler: "We are pleased to inform you that at the meeting of the American Kennel Club on December 8, the Alaskan Malamute Club was elected a member of the AKC." Mrs. Lawler enclosed a list of the current members of the club. There were 76 active members, including husbands and wives. They were divided into the following groups: New England, 22; Eastern States, 21; Midwest, 20; South, 5; Pacific Coast, 6; and Alaska, 2. Because they were the founding members of a great national club, we are listing them here.

Alaskan Malamute Club Membership Oct. 1, 1953

New England States

Paul A. Pelletier—34 Spring Street, Penacook, N.H.
Freeman and Margaret Frost—Jackson, N.H.
Harry and Gloria Hall, 3rd—Ellis Farm Lane, Melrose, Mass.
Arthur and Betty Hodgens—Wilton, N.H.
Mrs. Samuel Kirkwood—8 Swan Road, Winchester, Mass.
Jean Lane—Holman Street, Lunenburg, Mass.
Norman LeClair—14½ Cedar Street, Waltham, Mass.
Dr. and Mrs. Edward F. Lawler—71 Concord Road, Weston, Mass.
Dr. and Mrs. Roland Lombard—2285 Commonwealth Ave., Auburndale, Mass.
Mrs. Elwyne Smith—Rt. 1, Wilton, Maine
L.B. Dalton—7 Lynn Falls Parkway, Melrose, Mass.
Elizabeth Z. Aninger—48 Michigan Street, Indian Orchard, Mass.
Eva B. Seeley—Chinook Kennels, Wonalancet, N.H.
Mrs. Augustine Francis—Laconia-Glendale, N.H.
Joan Cowie—81 Concord Rd., Weston, Mass.
Mr. and Mrs. Nelson Butler—Unionville, Conn.

Eastern States

Mrs. Elnora Ferber—43 Lambert's Lane, Staten Island, N.Y.
Mrs. C.W. Cramer—Willow Brook Farm, Munnsville, N.Y.
Mrs. and Mrs. Robert Spawn—Rt. 1, Newark Valley, N.Y.
Robert Thompson—Rt. 2, Hamburg, N.Y.
John Hofft—Oak Ridge, N.J. (Gen. Del.)
Mrs. Roy Truchon—Stelton, N.J.
J.J. Lynn—Churchville, Buck's County, Pennsylvania
Robert E.P. Hoover, Sr.—1415 N. 2nd St., Harrisburg, Pennsylvania
Robert J. Zoller—Blue Ridge Summit, Pennsylvania
Franklin Martin—Lundy's Lane, Pennsylvania
Mr. and Mrs. J.W. Dawson—Rt. 3, Box 165, Manassas, Virginia
Mr. and Mrs. W.R. Gormley—Box 127, Barberton, Ohio
Wesson Seyburn—1827 National Bank Bldg., Detroit, Michigan
Joseph Wehrer—1372 Weston Court, Willow Run, Michigan
Duane Creller—501 June St., Endicott, N.Y.
Florence Lawrence—59 Hillcrest Ave., Nixon, N.J.
Kim Johnson—Central Ave., Stelton, N.J.
Barbara T. Sykes—East Chatham, N.Y.
Anthony Panther—N. Clinton Ave., Bayshore, N.Y.

Junior Drivers at the New England Sled Dog Club races in 1962.   *C.G. Bricket*

Midwest

Ralph and Marchetta Schmitt—RFD, Pewaukee, Wisconsin
A.P. Diel—3955 N. 46th St., Milwaukee, Wisconsin
R. Vale Faro—104 S. Michigan Ave (Rm. 1605), Chicago, Ill.
J.W. Wolfe—396 Prairie Ave., Elmhurst, Ill.
Albert Starcich—RD 3, Mt. Vernon Rd., S.E., Cedar Rapids, Iowa
J.J. Nemecek—Tabernash, Colorado
Jane Nygren—Rt. 3, Box 123, Hales Corner, Wisconsin
Doris A. and Emil F. Knorr—Rt. 3, Box 47A, Sheboygan Falls, Wisc.
Jon Palmer—Hartland, Wisc.
Elmer and Stella Springer—3522 S. 33rd St., Milwaukee, Wisc.
Lois and Eugene Faegles—27277B. West Michigan St., Milwaukee, Wisc.
Janita Reharst, Pewaukee, Wisc.
Mr. and Mrs. J.W. Millar—Tarku K's, Rt. 3, Box 482, Pewaukee, Wisc.
William Kugelman—7312 Elmira St., Des Plaines, Ill.

South

Mrs. Delta Wilson—1681 Friar Tuck Rd., Atlanta, Georgia
E. Blalock, Jr.—Jonesboro, Georgia
Cecil Allen—Fayetteville, Tennessee
H.W. Cox, Jr.—1863 Naylor St., Dallas, Texas
H.B. Pearson, Jr.—Rt. 7, Chattanooga, Tennessee

West Coast

Mrs. Dorothy DeMack Dillingham—1717 Lincoln Blvd., Anaheim, Calif.
Mr. and Mrs. Conrad Scalet—6612 Highland St., Buena Park, Calif.
Sam Maranto—11616 Hoxie Ave., Norwalk, Calif.
Dan W. Williamson—119 Mauna Loa Drive, Monrovia, Calif.
Robert Hammond—156½ E. Verdugo Ave., Burbank, Calif.

Alaska

Earl and Natalie Norris—P.O. Box 91, Anchorage, Alaska

Head study of Ch. Kotzebue Kanuck Of Chinook, owned by Marilyn P. Prouty. Mrs. Seeley considers this a superb type.

Now let us return to 1935. For it was during that year that the first breed standard was approved by the American Kennel Club. We give it here in full. It remained the standard of the breed until April 12, 1960 when, during the presidency of Robert Zoller, the present standard was adopted.

DESCRIPTION AND STANDARD OF POINTS

(As Adopted by The Alaskan Malamute Club, April 17, 1935 and Approved by The American Kennel Club)

Origin.—The Alaskan Malamute is a native sled-dog of Alaska and is the oldest native dog known to that country. It was originally named "Mahlemut" after a native Innuit (Mahlemut) Tribe.

General Appearance and Characteristics.—A large size dog with a strong, compact body, not too short coupled; thick dense, coarse coat and not too long; stands well over pads and has appearance of much activity; broad head, ears erect and wedge shaped; muzzle not too pointed and long, but not too stubby (other extreme); deep chest, proud carriage, head erect and eyes alert—Face markings are a distinguishing feature and the eyes are well set off by these markings which consist of either cap over head and rest of face solid color, (usually greyish white) or face marked with appearance of a mask, thus setting off eyes; tail is plumed and carried over back when not working, but not too tightly curled, more like a plume waving. Malamutes are of various colors, but usually wolfish grey or black and white. Their feet are of the "snowshoe" type with well cushioned pads giving firm and compact appearance; front legs straight and with big bone; hind legs well bent at stifles and without cowhocks; straight back gently sloping from shoulders to hips; endurance and intelligence are shown in body and eyes; the eyes have a "wolf-like" appearance by position of eyes, but expression is soft; quick in action, but no loss of energy in moving; affectionate dispositions.

Head.—The head should indicate a high degree of intelligence—it should be in proportion to the size of the dog so as to not make the dog appear clumsy or coarse. Skull—Broad between ears, gradually narrowing to eyes; moderately rounded between ears, flattening on top as it approaches eyes, rounding off to cheeks, which should be moderately flat; there should be a slight furrow between the eyes; the top line of skull and top line of muzzle showing but little break downward from a straight line as they join.

47

Muzzle.—Large and bulky in proportion to size of skull—diminishing but little in width or depth from junction with skull to nose—lips close fitting—nose black—upper and lower jaws broad with large teeth—the front teeth meeting with a scissors grip, but never "overshot."

Eyes.—Almond shaped—dark in color—moderately large for this shape of eye—set obliquely in skull.

Ears.—Medium—upper half of ear triangular in shape—slightly rounded at tips—set wide apart on outside back edges of top of skull with lower part of ear joining the skull on a line with the upper corner of eye; giving the tips of the ears the appearance when erect of standing off from the skull; when erect, ears are pointed slightly forward, but when at work the ears are usually folded back on the skull.

Body.—Chest should be strong and deep; body should be strong and compactly built, but not too short coupled; the back should be straight and gently sloping from shoulders to hips. Loins well muscled, but no surplus weight.

Shoulders, Legs and Feet.—Shoulders moderately sloping; forelegs heavily boned and muscled—straight to pasterns, which should be short and strong and almost vertical as viewed from the side; feet large and compact, toes well arched, pads thick and tough; toe nails short and strong; protective growth of hair between toes. Hindlegs must be broad and powerfully muscled through thighs; stifles moderately bent; hock joints broad and strong and moderately bent and well let down—as viewed from behind the hindlegs should not appear bowed in bone, but stand and move true and not too close or too wide. The legs of the Malamute must indicate unusual strength and powerful propelling power—any definite indication of unsoundness in legs and feet, standing or moving constitutes practically disqualification in the show ring.

Coat.—Thick, dense, coarse coat, but not long; undercoat is thick, oily and woolly, while outer coat is rather coarse and stands out. Thick fur around neck. (This allows for protection against weather.)

Color and Markings.—The usual colors are wolfish grey or black and white. Markings should be either cap-like or mask-like on face. A variation of color and markings is occasionally found.

Tail.—Well furred and carried over back when not working, but not too tightly curled to rest on back, a "waving plume" appearance instead.

Height.—Of male dog averaging from 22 to 25 inches; of bitch averaging from 20 to 23 inches.

Weight.—Of male dog averaging from 65 to 85 pounds; of bitch averaging from 50 to 70 pounds.

48

SCALE OF POINTS

	Points
General appearance	20
Head	20
Body	20
Legs and feet	20
Coat and color	10
Tail	10
Total	100

Official breed standards are not changed without a great deal of soul searching, arguments, and internecine battles among the fanciers. The present standard was adopted after years of debate 15 years ago. Today there is widespread demand for additional standard changes. These are being discussed with somewhat less heat than were the changes incorporated in the present standard. People within and without the breed are being asked for suggestions. These include those who judge Alaskan Malamutes and who must do so against dogs of other breeds. What changes, if any, will be made cannot be predicted. In the meantime, we present the standard as it now exists.

Patricia Colcord's Kotzebue Tango of Chinook shows a proper head in dome, muzzle, and lips, as well as top line.

Ch. Chinook Kotzebue Gripp, breeder, owner, handler, Mrs. Eva Seeley, AMC Specialty Best of Breed, 1951, Mrs. Edward Renner, judge. *Evelyn M. Shafer*

Official Standard for the
Alaskan Malamute

General Appearance and Characteristics—The Alaskan Malamute is a powerful and substantially built dog with a deep chest and strong, compact body, not too short coupled, with a thick, coarse guard coat of sufficient length to protect a dense, woolly undercoat, from 1 to 2 inches in depth when dog is in full coat. Stands well over pads, and this stance gives the appearance of much activity, showing interest and curiosity. The head is broad, ears wedge-shaped and erect when alerted. The muzzle is bulky with only slight diminishing in width and depth from root to nose, not pointed or long, but not stubby. The Malamute moves with a proud carriage, head erect and eyes alert. Face markings are a distinguishing feature. These consist of either cap over head and rest of face solid color, usually grayish white, or face marked with the appearance of a mask. Combinations of cap and mask are not unusual. The tail is plumed and carried over the back, not like a fox brush, or tightly curled, more like a plume waving.

Malamutes are of various colors, but are usually wolfish gray or black and white. Their feet are of the "snowshoe" type, tight and deep, with well-cushioned pads, giving a firm and compact appearance. Front legs are straight with big bone. Hind legs are broad and powerful, moderately bent at stifles, and without cowhocks. The back is straight, gently sloping from shoulders to hips. The loin should not be so short or tight as to interfere with easy, tireless movement. Endurance and intelligence are shown in body and expression. The eyes have a "wolf-like" appearance by their position, but the expression is soft and indicates an affectionate disposition.

Temperament—The Alaskan Malamute is an affectionate, friendly dog, not a "one-man" dog. He is a loyal, devoted companion, playful on invitation, but generally impressive by his dignity after maturity.

Head—The head should indicate a high degree of intelligence, and is broad and powerful as compared with other "natural" breeds, but should be in proportion to the size of the dog so as not to make the dog appear clumsy or coarse. **Skull**—The skull should be broad between the ears, gradually narrowing to eyes, moderately rounded between ears, flattening on top as it approaches the eyes, rounding off to cheeks, which should be moderately flat. There should be a slight furrow between the eyes, the topline of skull and topline of the muzzle showing but little break downward from a straight line as they join. **Muzzle**—The muzzle should be large and bulky in proportion to size of skull, diminishing but little in width and depth from junction with skull to nose; lips close fitting; nose black; upper and lower jaws broad with large teeth, front teeth meeting with a scissors grip but never overshot or undershot.

Eyes—Brown, almond shaped, moderately large for this shape of eye, set obliquely in skull. Dark eyes preferred.

Ears—The ears should be of medium size, but small in proportion to head. The upper halves of the ears are triangular in shape, slightly rounded at tips, set wide apart on outside back edges of the skull with the lower part of the ear joining the skull on a line with the upper corner of the eye, giving the tips of the ears the appearance, when erect, of standing off from the skull. When erect, the ears point slightly forward, but when the dog is at work the ears are sometimes folded against the skull. High-set ears are a fault.

Neck—The neck should be strong and moderately arched.

Body—The chest should be strong and deep; body should be strong and compactly built but not short coupled. The back should be straight and gently sloping to the hips. The loins should be well muscled and not so short as to interfere with easy, rhythmic movement with powerful drive from the hindquarters. A long loin which weakens the back is also a fault. No excess weight.

Shoulders, Legs and Feet—Shoulders should be moderately sloping; forelegs heavily boned and muscled, straight to pasterns, which should be short and strong and almost vertical as viewed from the side. The feet should be large and compact, toes, tight-fitting and well arched, pads thick and tough, toenails short and strong. There should be a protective growth of hair between toes. Hind legs must be broad and powerfully muscled through thighs; stifles moderately bent, hock joints broad and strong, moderately bent and well let down. As viewed from behind, the hind legs should not appear bowed in bone, but stand and move true in line with movement of the front legs, and not too close or too wide. The legs of the Malamute must indicate unusual strength and tremendous propelling power. Any indication of unsoundness in legs or feet, standing or moving, is to be considered a serious fault. Dewclaws on the hind legs are undesirable and should be removed shortly after pups are whelped.

Tail—Moderately set and following the line of the spine at the start, well furred and carried over the back when not working—not tightly curled to rest on back—or short furred and carried like a fox brush, a waving plume appearance instead.

Coat—The Malamute should have a thick, coarse guard coat, not long and soft. The undercoat is dense, from 1 to 2 inches in depth, oily and woolly. The coarse guard coat stands out, and there is thick fur around the neck. The guard coat varies in length, as does the undercoat; however, in general, the coat is moderately short to medium along the sides of the body with the length of the coat increasing somewhat around the shoulders and neck, down the back and over the rump, as well as in the breeching and plume. Malamutes usually have shorter and less dense coats when shed out during the summer months.

Color and Markings—The usual colors range from light gray through the intermediate shadings to black, always with white on underbodies, parts of legs, feet, and part of mask markings. Markings should be either caplike and/or mask-like on face. A white blaze on forehead and/or collar or spot on nape is attractive and acceptable, but broken color extending over the body in spots or uneven splashings is undesirable. One should distinguish between mantled dogs and splash-coated dogs. The only solid color allowable is the all-white.

Size—There is a natural range in size in the breed. The desirable freighting sizes are:

Males—25 inches at the shoulders—85 pounds.

Females—23 inches at the shoulders—75 pounds.

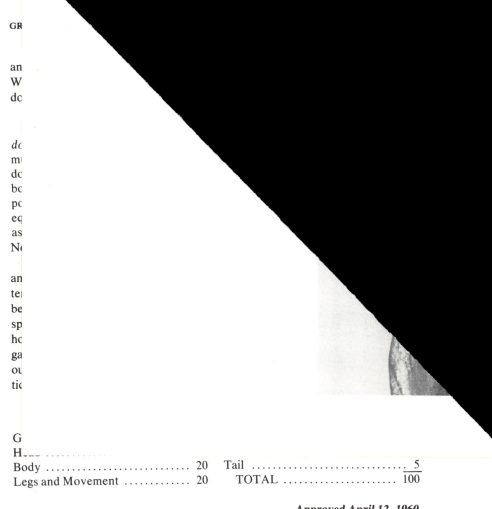

GR

an
W
do

do
m
do
b
p
e
as
N

an
te
be
sp
h
ga
o
ti

G
H
Body 20   Tail 5
Legs and Movement 20   TOTAL 100

Approved April 12, 1960

Sled Dog Team at Lake Chocorua, 1938.

Earl Norris, a pioneer Alaskan Malamute breeder, is shown hauling supplies up Muldrow Glacier on the slopes of Mt. McKinley in 1947.   *Bradford Washburn*

Ch. Apache Chief of Husky-Pak, handled by Robert Zoller, a great winner and sire, was Best of Opposite Sex at the 1953 National Specialty, to his kennel-mate, Ch. Arctic Storm of Husky-Pak.

6

The Beginning

as told by Robert J. Zoller

ALMOST EVERYONE agrees that the Alaskan Malamute is a product of canine development in a particular region of the Arctic. But there are many differing opinions as to where the registered Malamutes of today began. You can go back to a certain point in the 1930s and 1940s to fifty or fewer individual dogs and suddenly you get to "unknown."

I am sure that here and there people had been bringing a few dogs out of Alaska for generations, but it all began to add up to a breed perhaps in the 1930s, but mainly in the 1940s, when several people began to breed and sell these dogs. And they began to give the people who bought them a pedigree with "Alaskan Malamute" written across the top.

At the starting point, who really knew what a Malamute was, or whether this dog or that one was purebred? Obviously nobody knew. There was no Eskimo Kennel Club keeping track. So the selections and the labelling were all based on opinion, and opinions varied. That is why there were so many "Alaskan Malamutes" of widely varying type.

I'm convinced a lot of mistakes were made. I've seen a number of dogs claimed to be Malamutes that weren't even close including a 150 pound part timber wolf in Iowa and a huge blue-eyed cross-bred that was apparently half St. Bernard. The latter was actually shown in Baltimore in 1947. I know that neither of these dogs appears in the pedigree of any present day Malamute. But it seems logical that some questionable early dogs do.

It is important, however, to understand that we owe no apologies to any other breed. In Malamutes you finally get back to the unknown; in most other breeds you can get back to known dogs of other breeds.

What of the Malamutes of today, and where did they come from? The early major contributors were Arthur Walden, who assembled a number of sled dogs in New England, some of which were ancestors of many registered Malamutes today; Milton and Eva Seeley, who developed the Kotzebue line and who got them recognized and registered by the American Kennel Club; and Paul Voelker, who developed the M'Loot line. Voelker never registered his dogs but sold them to people who eventually did.

The logical next question is where did Walden and Voelker get their dogs. Some they brought from the Arctic, and others they bought from people who did. A lot of the early fanciers of sled dogs knew each other, and the dogs were bought and sold among them. A number of men were part of a U.S. Army sled dog program during World War II. The Army assembled hundreds of sled dogs. Some were Malamutes, and some of these were bought by their drivers at liquidation sales when the war ended. At least two of these dogs ended up with Paul Voelker and became a part of the M'Loot line. A few others also ended up as ancestors of various Malamutes of today.

The important points to be made are that in the mid-1940s, all Malamutes went back only a couple of generations to "Unknown;" that most people who brought dogs out of Alaska, or bought them from people who did, really didn't have much to go on but opinion, and opinions varied widely; that most were more interested in good sled dogs than in scientifically isolating pure Malamute type and in starting a registered Malamute breeding program.

While dozens had been involved in some way, only the Seeleys and Paul Voelker were sticking it out in the late 1940s. At that point, newcomers suddenly became involved. They brought a new level of interest to the Alaskan Malamute breed. My wife, Laura, and I, were two of these people. I became interested when I saw my first Malamute at a U.S. Navy officers' club in Newfoundland in 1941. I began an intensive study of the breed, and we acquired our first Malamutes in 1947 and 1948.

Along with other newcomers to the breed, we added a new dimension. We felt the breed had proved its ability as a working sled dog but deserved more than that. I became dedicated to positioning the Malamute in a new role as a pet and companion to people who wanted a rare and beautiful dog. Type and quality thus became of overriding importance to us.

We immediately encountered the Kotzebue and M'Loot strains and researched them intensively. We also discovered that certain other dogs that were neither M'Loot nor Kotzebue had contributed to the Malamute breed, and their influence cannot be ignored. For want of a better term these dogs are sometimes referred to as the "third strain." This is not an accurate description because these were just individual dogs, not a strain, owned by different people.

Only a handful of these dogs were involved numerically, but some were good enough to be included in early breeding programs that eventually led to AKC registered progeny. At least a couple, in my opinion, materially affected the quality of our breed perhaps for all years to come.

In the mid-1940s, we read everything we could find, journeyed frequently to see dogs all over the country, and corresponded with everyone we could locate whose name had ever been linked with the breed. My wife and I believe that our own major contributions were an all-consuming interest in the Malamute as a purebred dog, intensive effort, and most important, a degree of objectivity.

We may have been the first to see both the strengths and the weaknesses of the two existing strains. This immediately got us into serious difficulties with both camps. In the course of our studies we developed some firm opinions. The Kotzebues were good type, mainly because of good heads and general proportions, but they were smaller than we believed Malamutes should be. The M'Loots had better size, but some were rangy, some considerably lacking in substance. Their fronts were generally better than the Kotzebues, who tended to be somewhat wide in chest and sometimes out at the elbows. The rears of the M'Loots were lacking in angulation, and this led to stilted gait. The M'Loots also tended to long ears and long muzzles.

The Kotzebues were gray dogs with white trim. The M'Loots had a wider range from light gray to black and white. Dispositions differed somewhat. The Kotzebues were less aggressive and easier to control. The M'Loots were often aggressive with other dogs, prone to fighting, and sometimes difficult to handle.

We liked much of what we saw in both strains, but we felt there was more to be done. We got lucky almost right from the start. At Great Barrington, Mass., we found a pair of pups sired by a dog named Alaska (he later became Ch. Spawn's Alaska) that we bought and raised, and took to national championships. This brother and sister pair were Ch. Apache Chief of Husky-Pak and Ch. Arctic Storm of Husky-Pak.

Both became milestones of breed progress. They were three quarters M'Loot and one quarter "other." I never saw Alaska's parents, but his dam, Kiska, was by Gemo out of Sitka. I did see Gemo in the flesh and a number of photographs of Sitka. I am now convinced that, by the standards of the time, these two were outstanding, and from what appeared later on, they deserve much credit for adding good things to our breed.

Gemo was produced by Dave Irwin, the Arctic explorer, from two Malamutes he brought out of the Arctic. Gemo was sold to Lowell Thomas, the famed explorer-newsman, who showed him at least once as a listed dog at the Westminster show at Madison Square Garden. He was probably the breed's first best of breed winner at Westminster.

Lowell Thomas sold or gave Gemo to Dick Hinman of Newbury, Vt. In early pedigrees, this dog is shown as Erwin's Gemo, Irwin's Gemo, or sometimes, Gimo, or even Chimo. Early pedigrees were often made out in handwriting. Misspellings were frequent, and to add to the confusion, there were dozens of Alaskas, Sitkas, Wolfs, etc.

Based on Spawn's Alaska and two of his litter brothers which I saw and studied, Chisholm's Viking and Duke, Gemo and Sitka through Kiska produced progeny which influenced the quality of our breed. Sitka appears in some pedigrees as Hinman's Sitka. She could well have been a better bitch than Gemo was a dog. At any rate, I liked what I saw in her pictures.

Spawn's Alaska was one of the top winners in our breed from his start until Apache Chief and Arctic Storm took over. Included were two bests of breed victories at Westminster, in 1951 and 1953. He won consistently over Ch. Mulphus Brooks Master Otter and Ch. Toro of Bras Coupe, two other top dogs of their time.

Ch. Spawn's Alaska and his offspring Ch. Apache Chief of Husky-Pak and Ch. Arctic Storm of Husky-Pak had that ingredient for which we had been searching. So did their offspring. In the five years from 1953 to 1957, in National specialty competition, Zoller dogs won four bests of breed, five bests of opposite sex, five bests of winners, and every winners dog and winners bitch when Husky-Pak dogs were there to compete.

We found that our strain, compared with the pure M'Loot strain, resulted in dogs of equal size but of heavier bone and more powerful build. In body structure they were not unlike king-size Kotzebues. While their heads, overall, were not as good as the Kotzebues, they had broad skulls and wide-set ears. They had good fronts like the M'Loots, good rears like the Kotzebues, and good overall coats, colors and balance.

To set the type and heavy up the muzzles, we searched for a good quality, not too small Kotzebue and came up with the name of Ch. Toro of Bras Coupe, then owned by Earl and Natalie Norris of Anchorage, Alaska. Toro was a good one. He had been produced at Chinook Kennels, with Eva Seeley listed as his breeder. Toro and all his litter mates, and an entire second litter of the same breeding, were sold en masse to the Bras Coupe winter sports club in Alaska.

Toro was by Ch. Kim of Kotzebue out of Kotzebue Cleopatra. Later, when he was offered for sale, I had first chance at Toro, the best of the two litters. To my eternal unhappiness, I passed him up. At the time, I just couldn't add another dog to my kennel. When we bred Ch. Arctic Storm of Husky-Pak to Toro, she produced a litter of six. Five became champions. The owner of the sixth did not show it.

These dogs made important contributions. Ch. Cliquot of Husky-Pak became the official symbol of the Alaskan Malamute Club of America. Ch. Cherokee of Husky-Pak won the national specialty show three years in a row and was AMCA "Dog-of-the-Year" for three consecutive years.

Mrs. Laura Zoller with Ch. Cherokee of Husky-Pak.

To sum it up, our breed, as it exists today, is the result of a lot of work by a lot of people. It began with the development, distribution, publicizing, and registering of the Kotzebues in New England, and latter in Alaska and California. The same goes for the M'Loots, developed in Michigan, and shown, publicized, and registered in various parts of the country. Our own part came in the development of what we term "the three way cross" as we have told it here.

(Robert Zoller was one of the founders of the Alaskan Malamute Club of America. He has served as its president. For some years he edited and produced the News Letter which has done so much to promote the breed and to acquaint Alaskan Malamute breeders and fanciers with each other across the "lower 48," Alaska, and Canada.—The Authors)

The 1956 and 1957 winners of the National Specialty Show were Ch. Cherokee of Husky-Pak, getting his second and third Bests of Breed, and Ch. Husky-Pak Marclar's Sioux, her second Best of Opposite Sex.

7

Our Alaskan Malamute

An article by Natalie Norris

THE THIRST *for knowledge of the origins of the Alaskan Malamute does not cease with the passing of the years. As recorded elsewhere in this book, Natalie Jubin of Lake Placid drove a dog team and gave passenger rides in order to earn money for her college education. She then went to Alaska, where she met and married Earl Norris. Both won the great Alaskan races.*

Later, as a member of the Alaskan Sled Dog Racing Association, Natalie Norris wrote an article on the Alaskan Malamute. She researched well, both among the Eskimos, and among the white men who had followed the gold rush to Alaska.

One of the authors of this book would like to point out two important facts in the article. Mrs. Norris quotes one of the early Alaskan authorities as saying that he asked again and again whether wolf crosses were made. All said "no." Also quoted is Bill Burke, one of the great mail team drivers, on the size of the dogs used.

One of your authors also asked the wolf-dog cross question of a dozen Eskimo drivers, and got the same answer. He also spent some hours with Bill Burke, and thus can verify the report quoted by Mrs. Norris.

In this article an attempt will be made to clarify data on the Alaskan Malamute, the only dog originating in Alaska recognized by the American Kennel Club.

There were some men of the many that came to the Territory before and around 1900 that were not only observant but recorded their observations. These narratives were written by authors of many vocations: Government employees, journalists, gold seekers, fur traders, church men, and so forth. Although many an account describes the sled dogs of that era, each description varies in detail to some degree. It is important, however, and noteworthy to mention, that a canvassing of available works reveals many points on which all agree. It is these points that I should like to emphasize and show how they fit into the pattern from which the present standard on conformation was taken.

I quote from three books to illustrate the differences and the likenesses of sled dog descriptions of authors from around 1900.

The Klondike Stampede of 1897–1898, by Tappan Adney, published by Harpers and Brothers, Copyright, 1899. This book has a complete chapter on dogs and equipment; it is well illustrated with drawings and pictures and is in excellent detail. The data is authentic and compares favorably with that of other authors of the time. Tappan Adney was a journalist writing for Harper's Weekly. Here are some excerpts:

"The best type of the Yukon dog is the true Eskimo, known by the miners as 'Malamut,' from a tribe of Eskimo of that name at the mouth of the Yukon. It stands about as high as the Scotch collie, which it resembles a little; but with its thick, short neck, sharp muzzle, oblique eyes, short, pointed ears, dense coarse hair, which protects it from the severest cold, it is more wolf-like than any other variety of dog. With its bushy tail carried tightly curled over its back, with head and ears erect, and with its broad chest, it is the expression of energy, vitality, and self-reliance. In color it varies from a dirty white through black and white to jet black; but there is also another sort, a grizzled gray, which suggests an admixture of gray wolf, with which it is known to mate. **Indeed, these wolf-colored dogs so closely resemble a wolf that if the two were placed side by side a little distance off it would be difficult to distinguish them, but at a nearer view the dog lacks somewhat the hard, sinister expression of his wild relative.** The best type of dog is still to be found among the Eskimos, as well as among the Indian tribes of the interior, but these latter, known as 'Siwash' dogs, are frequently inferior in size, though very tough. The purple type has undergone further change by an admixture of 'outside' dog, such as St. Bernard, Newfoundland, and mongrel, that the miners have brought in. The 'inside' dog, as the native dog is called by the miners, endures hunger and cold better than the 'outside,' and is therefore preferred for long journeys over the snow, where speed is desired and food is scarce or hard to carry or procure. For short-distance, heavy freighting, the large St. Bernard or mastiff is unsurpassed, but it eats more . . .

64

"Finest Dog Team On The Klondike" was Tappan Adney's boast about this team photographed in 1897. From the book, *The Klondike Stampede,* Harper & Brothers.

"Jack, the proud one," Malamute in the team of Ely Whitney. From *Wolf, The Storm Leader,* first printed in 1910.   *Dodd, Mead & Co.*

". . . It has been said that the native dog does not manifest affection for its master; but that is not always the case. It depends upon what has been his early training—like master, like dog. As a rule, he is stolid and indifferent, deigning to notice a human only in sharp barks and howls, the most dismal sound in nature, but he hardly ever snaps, and after the first surprise at an act of kindness has worn off he shows himself capable of marked affection . . ."

Ten Thousand Miles with a Dog Sled by Hudson Stuck, published by Charles Scribner's Sons, 1914. Hudson Stuck was an Episcopal bishop whose headquarters were at Nenana, Alaska. Stuck's books, of which there are four, are fertile material for persons interested in sled dogs. I quote:

"There are two breeds of native dogs in Alaska, and a third that is usually spoken of as such. The Malamute is the Esquimau dog; and what for want of a better name is called the Siwash is the Indian dog. Many years ago the Hudson Bay voyageours bred some selected strains of imported dog with the Indian dogs of those parts, or else did no more than carefully select the best individuals of the native species and bred from them exclusively—it is variously stated—and that is the accepted origin of the 'husky.' The malamute and the husky are the two chief sources of the white man's dog teams, though cross-breeding with setters and pointers, hounds of various sorts, mastiffs, Saint Bernards, and Newfoundlands has resulted in a general admixture of breeds, so that the work dogs of Alaska are an heterogeneous lot today. It should also be stated that the terms 'malamute' and "husky" are very generally confused and often used interchangeably.

"The malamute, the Alaskan Esquimau dog, is precisely the same dog as that found amongst the natives of Baffin's Bay and Greenland. Knud Rasmunsen and Amundsen together have established the oneness of the Esquimaux from the east coast of Greenland all round to Saint Michael; they are one people, speaking virtually one language. And the malamute dog is one dog . . .

". . . There was never animal better adapted to environment than the malamute dog. His coat, while it is not fluffy, nor the hair long, is yet so dense and heavy that it affords him a perfect protection against the utmost severity of cold. His feet are tough and clean, and do not readily accumulate snow between the toes and therefore do not easily get sore—which is the great drawback of nearly all 'outside' dogs and their mixed progeny. He is hardy and thrifty and does well on less food than the mixed breeds; and, despite Peary to the contrary, he will eat anything . . . The malamute is affectionate and faithful and, likes to be made a pet of, but he is very jealous and an incorrigible fighter. He has little of the fawning submissiveness of pet dogs 'outside,' but is independent and self-willed and apt to make a troublesome pet. However, pets that give little trouble seldom give much pleasure.

"His comparative shortness of leg makes him somewhat better adapted to the hard, crusted snow of the coast than to the soft snow of the interior, but he is a ceasless and tireless worker who loves to pull. His prick ears, always erect, his bushy tail, carried high unless it curls upon the back as is the case with some, his quick narrow eyes give him an air of keenness and alertness that marks him out amongst dogs. When he is in good condition and his coat is taken care of he is a handsome fellow, and he will weigh from seventy-five to eighty-five or ninety pounds.

"The husky is a long, rangy dog, with more body and longer legs than the malamute and with a shorter coat. The coat is very thick and dense, however, and furnishes a sufficient protection. A good, spirited husky will carry his tail erect like a malamute, but the ears are not permanently pricked up; they are mobile. He is perhaps, the general preference amongst dog drivers in the interior, but he has not the graceful distinction of appearance of the malamute.

"The 'Siwash' dog is the common Indian dog; generally under-sized, uncared for, half starved most of the time, and snappish because not handled save with roughness. In general appearance he resembles somewhat a small malamute, though, indeed, nowadays so mixed have breeds become that he may be any cur or mongrel . . .

"Here it may be worth while to say a few words about the general belief that dogs in Alaska are interbred with wolves. That the dog and the wolf have a common origin there can be no doubt, and that they will inter-breed is equally sure, but diligent inquiry on the part of the writer for a number of years, throughout all interior Alaska, amongst whites and natives, has failed to deduce one authentic instance of intentional interbreeding, has failed to discover one man who knows of his own knowledge that any living dog is the off-spring of such union.

"While, therefore, it is not here stated that such crossbreeding has not taken place, or even that it does not take place, yet the author is satisfied that it is a very rare thing, indeed, and the common stories of dogs that are 'half wolf' are fabulous."

Wolf The Storm Leader by Frank Caldwell, first published by Dodd, Mead and Company in 1910, copyright 1937, illustrates the Alaskan life of Ely Whitney as well as his trek across the States by dog team; he had been sent from Nome to Washington, D.C. by dog team to attract government officials' attention to problems in Alaska. Ely, in the book, describes each of his team dogs to a Washington audience. The following reprinted with permission of the publishers:

"Spot is a gray malamoot. Don't ye think he's a good-lookin' feller? Well, he's jist as good as he looks, always in a good humor an' ready to play or fight, an' never was known to shirk in harness . . . A malamoot is a Bering Sea Eskimo dog . . . he's not a extra big dog, but for work on the mail-trails where ye want a animal what's tough an' has good wind an' speed, ye can't find none what kin quite take the place of the malamoot . . . An' what's more, they're the friendliest an' most affectionate dog I ever see. Now take this here Spot; he likes

Flora, Malamute brood bitch owned by
Lester Corliss of Anchorage, photo-
graphed in 1928 at Nenana by Mr.
Corliss.

Spot, a Malamute in Ely Whitney's
team. Reprinted from *Wolf, The Storm
Leader.* *Dodd, Mead & Co.*

to be petted, an' if I so much as raise my hand as if I was a-goin' to strike him, er if I jist hits him a little tap with my mitten, he'll up an' whine an' cry like a baby an' like he was a-bein' killed. It's his feelin's what's hurt an' not his hide . . . A husky is different. He's a Hudson Bay dog, an' is part English er Scotch hound an' part northern wolf. There's two kinds of huskies, too; the lop-eared, whose ears hang down like a hound's, an' the straight eared, whose ears stand up like a wolf's. Now I'm not a-runnin' down the huskies, fer I've owned an' worked, not one, but many of 'em, an' liked 'em too. They're good workers, but some way I can't like 'em quite as well as I do the malamoots . . ."

A cross-section of works such as the ones I have quoted, as I said, reveal many points on which there is agreement. A clear picture of what the true Malamute was like can be ascertained after digesting the likenesses from a variety of descriptions.

Descriptions by those personally acquainted with the Alaskan dogs at the time early Malamute Breed Club members were gathering all information available in order to draw up a written standard for the Malamute contributed greatly towards perfecting the standard (conformation points).

The following description of an Alaskan Malamute by Lester Corliss, currently of Anchorage, gives us an idea as to what type of information the first members of the Breed Club obtained for contemporaries. Mr. Corliss bred Malamutes during the twenties in Nenana, Alaska, and some of his dogs are behind the foundation stock bred in New Hampshire. In a recent interview Mr. Corliss said:

"A Malamute should be active as a terrier; even a big Malamute should be jaunty, not sluggish or slow-moving. I liked them tapering from front to back, the withers higher than the rump, chest broader than the hips. The tail should be carried high or curled, with the coat standing off, not long or flat. My Malamutes averaged 70 to 75 pounds for males, 55 to 60 pounds for the females. I preferred my dogs to be longer, rather than too shortly coupled; and, I preferred the black and white, masked face Malamutes with silver shading above the white under-quarters, comparable to the shading in a silver fox. These, in my estimation, were the most beautiful.

"The mail teams preferred dogs around 80 to 90 pounds, but seldom did they use a dog over 90 pounds because the over-sized dog could not stand the work. Bill Burke, who had the mail run between Nenana and McGrath on the Kuskokwim used dogs of Malamute type and these averaged 85. He had two teams constantly on the move of some 15 to 20 dogs in a team and around 10 dogs constantly in reserve."

There is conflicting information in the accounts used, but again I point out there is much agreement also. The "husky" used throughout this article should not be confused with the Siberian Husky, which has not been included in this discussion and was an importation in Alaska.

In my opinion the references to the oneness of the Malamute and the Eskimo dog can be explained somewhat as follows: To one not actually picking the animals apart limb by limb, comparisons were not noteworthy. The differences as set up in the standards are minute, but very important. The set of the ear, shape of the ear, shape of the foot, length of the coat, shape and size of the muzzle in comparison to skull are all points of difference an observer looking for these differences can readily note. There is more data to be had on the Eskimo dog in the Canadian Arctic and Greenland than any of the other northern breeds, which a visit to a well-stocked library would reveal. In the early part of this century most observers had not trained themselves to differentiate between these characteristics so important to the breeders of today. Hence, their data does not read like a breed standard. I think it can be said, however, that the Malamute, thanks to those who fancied these dogs 30 and 40 years ago, has changed relatively little in the past decades.

The Malamute is too fine and distinguished a breed to be changed into anything but what centuries of adaptability to its environment has produced. Our efforts should be to breed not only beautiful Malamutes, but as good specimens physically as were originally found in Alaska. It isn't a question of breeding a better Malamute but as good a Malamute. If this article has sparked Malamute breeders into digging for more first-hand information, I shall feel well rewarded for my effort.

"Muk," Hudson Stuck's favorite Malamute. From the book, *The Ascent Of Denali*, by Hudson Stuck, Charles Scribners' Sons, 1914.

70

8

The First International Dog Sled Race

THE GORHAM, New Hampshire winter carnival of 1920 brought in a dog team which gave exhibitions. The team was that of Arthur T. Walden of Wonalancet. His dogs were cross-breds, and the leader was the famous dog, Chinook. Walden and his team created so much interest that an international race was planned for the next season. It did not, however, take place until 1922.

It was this race which truly sparked national interest in the sport of driving teams of dogs. Viewed from this distance, it seems unlikely that either Siberian Huskies or Alaskan Malamutes would have come onto the North American scene as purebred breeds had not this and other races been held. For that reason we give an account of the race here.

W.A. Brown of Berlin, New Hampshire, organized the race. Brown was the owner of the Brown Paper Co., and he was famous for his stable of Arabian horses. Brown sponsored two teams. Walden was the driver of one, and Henri Skeen drove the other. Jean Lebel of Quebec drove the third, and Jacques Suzzaine, a Canadian then living at Lake Placid, the other.

The race was 120 miles, split into segments of 40 miles each day for the three days. The course went from Berlin to Colebrook, to Lancaster, and back to Berlin. That race actually was held under the title of the Eastern International Dog Derby. Camera crews from both news and motion

Harold Lancaster mushes through wet snow at a race at Cleveland, Ohio in 1968. *Paul Tepley*

A racing team moves swiftly in Alaska's North American championship race.

picture services attended to film the great event. Walden won. Henry Skeen was second; Jacques Suzzaine was third; and Jean Lebel was fourth.

The race was then moved to Quebec. That first race had created such interest, that it made North America wake up to the fact that dog sledding could be a great sport. The Quebec races brought Early Brydges from La Pas, Manitoba in 1924. He had learned the gang hitch from Walter Goyne who had seen it in Alaska. Brydges was the first to use it in the East.

In 1925, Emil St. Godard, then only 19 years old, came to race from La Pas, as did "Shorty" Russick, the "little Russian" from Flin Flon. Walden also returned for the 1925 race. These three, plus Leonhard Seppala, became immortals of North American sled dog racing.

Emil St. Godard won the 1925 race. He gained an almost two hour lead over the heavier, freighting type Walden-Chinook team. His time for the race was 12 hours, 49 minutes, 45 seconds, as compared to Walden's 14 hours, three minutes, and 20 seconds. St. Godard finished with seven dogs.

Two things ought to be remembered in this connection. The lighter, faster dogs were coming into vogue for racing. And, although cross-breds did well, and made records, it became evident that the purebred northern dogs had greater stamina and endurance under severe conditions in day after day work. Also, men like Emil St. Godard, Shorty Russick, and Roland Lombard trained equally as hard as their dogs. Some of the younger drivers would run all or most of the way, so as to lighten the load drawn by the dogs.

Bob White drives a team of registered Alaskan Malamutes. See his recommendations on training and harness in another chapter. *Leona Hutchings*

Edmund Miner drives a team at Tamworth, N.H. in the 1974–75 Class C for amateurs.

A team which is being taught to pull moves away toward a forest.
Jack Coolidre

Dr. Thomas Munger III of Anchorage, Alaska, drives a team of registered Alaskan Malamutes.

Dr. Roland Lombard, famous racing driver.

9

Lombard's Big Day

IN THE CHAPTER on recognition of the breed, we have told something of Dr. Roland Lombard and his record as the greatest trainer-driver in the history of sled dog racing. What deserves to be mentioned here is his first great victory, for it must go down in the record books as one of the outstanding feats in all sports history. Here, with a few additions, is the story as Eva Seeley remembers it and tells it.

The dates were Feb. 10, 11, and 12, 1930. A lively throng of people had gathered at Laconia, New Hampshire, to watch an innovation in sled dog racing. This was to be a handicap race, in which all sorts of dogs and teams, amateurs and professionals, could run. There would be heats of 30 miles each day.

The first day was marvelous for racing, very cold, but with a firm trail and no ice. Experienced eyes examined the various teams. Someone remarked: "That lead dog looks as though he knew the geography." Another said: "Isn't it great to see so many different kinds of dogs all competing?" And another: "How great that amateurs and novices can compete against the professionals!"

The most curiosity was expressed over what is known as a "scrub team." The driver was an 18 year old boy from Raymond, Maine. He was neatly but gaily dressed, and he had the strong, slender build of one designed for speed. His name was Roland Lombard. He had worked hard at various jobs in order to buy his team, and he had worked even harder to train it. It carried him to and from school each day.

And such a team! The lead dog, called Buck, was half red Cocker Spaniel and half small, farm Collie, closer to Shetland Sheepdog size than to the modern show Collie. One dog, Rinso, was a purebred German Shepherd. Murphy was a cross-breed of unknown ancestry. The two wheel dogs were white Siberian Huskies. They had been imported from Siberia to Alaska, and then had been brought to Maine by Leonhard Seppala. Murphy had come from The Pas, brought by Emil St. Godard.

Someone asked if Buck was the boy's mascot, and was surprised to be told that it was his lead dog. Meanwhile, the boy picked up Buck and seemed to whisper in his ear. Buck responded by struggling out of his arms, apparently getting the message and being ready to race.

But then, the race was ready to begin and a hush fell over the crowd. News services' movie cameras were positioned. The holders of records went first: winners of blue ribbons, cups, and purses of thousands of dollars. There were 30 starting teams.

Roland Lombard and his team started about 15th. The team seemed a little frightened by the commotion and the crowds. The team started and went directly toward the crowd. Without becoming in the least flustered, and with the great calmness which has characterized him since, Roland Lombard took his lead dog and straightened him out. Then the team was really off and shortly out of sight. A great cheer went up from the crowd.

Yet Buck was, of course, the object of both speculation and scorn. How could such a short legged dog keep up with the huskies? How could such a half pint rule a team? But some knew that Buck was a courageous leader. And they knew also that he had a habit of severely "initiating" new dogs to the team. He would stand perfectly still while being harnessed. Then suddenly he would turn and crash into the newcomer with such fury that the dog would be immediately subdued and would thereafter acknowledge his leadership.

On the night of that first 30 mile run, the temperature began to drop. On the second day, people began to imagine that they were in Alaska. Drivers became more and more crimsoned faced; some of the teams began to slow down. Teams bean to pass one another along the way.

A team in front had to draw aside to let a challenging team pass. This was often difficult to do and required considerable maneuvering. Sometimes there were fights between the dogs of the two teams. But on the whole, the dogs were too intent to want to stop to fight. And often the passing team gave the slower team a little more zest for the race.

Buck kept his scrub team humping right along. He and Lombard's grim determination were carrying them at a regular but fast clip which gave cause for alarm to many of the more experienced drivers. It is true that they had a handicap. At the close of the second day, they had covered the 60 miles in five hours, 28 minutes, and 13 seconds. The fastest team

n historic picture from Alaskan Archives: Leonhard Seppala, left; lead dog, huck; Dr. Roland Lombard. *Couch Alaska Archives*

in the snow, St. Godard's, had a total elapsed time of four hours, 41 minutes, and five seconds.

The third morning broke clear but tingling cold. The teams lined up for the final 30 mile dash, but the order of leaving had changed. The fastest and most experienced teams had opened the race. Now the slower teams were given a head start. It meant that the speed teams had to cover more ground if they wished to pass and keep out the teams which had been given the head start. This, combined with the handicap allowances, placed all the teams on a par. And Emil St. Godard had to work as hard as Roland Lombard.

Spectators began to gather at the twenty-mile post. When the first team reached that point, there would be about an hour left before the winning team crossed the finish line. That last ten miles would be the hardest.

The spectators were on a hill, and as they watched a team appeared in the distance, and then another. The first was a team from Quebec, betassled and with bells ringing. The second team was gaining, and was asking to pass. At that moment, a third team appeared. It seemed at first to have only four dogs. Had the others in the team been injured, and were they riding on the sled? Then as the team drew nearer, little Buck appeared out of a depression. He was leading his team resolutely, and his four backers wre loping easily behind him. So was their driver, Roland Lombard.

The team tackled the hill and passed the spectators. Buck glanced neither right nor left but simply kept his stride. Beyond the hill, the trail left the road and entered rough country. The Lombard team caught and passed both of the teams, and it was Buck who led his team first across the finish line. The team dropped in its tracks, with the dogs acting the perfect gentlemen sports they were.

The Lombard team had finished the 90 mile course in eight hours, 10 minutes, and 38 seconds. With its 33 minute handicap, it had won the race. Meanwhile Emil St. Godard had also been making fast time. His team had won on the total elapsed time, barely half an hour behind the Lombard team.

We should add here that Roland Lombard graduated from the Ontario Veterinary College at Guelph. He then set up his veterinary hospital at Auburndale, Mass. He raced only briefly in 1938 and 1939. Then after the war he began the racing career which has made him world famous.

10

Women in Sled Dog Racing

VERY EARLY in the history of sled dog racing, women began to play an important part. While it is true that many of them drove Siberians, and in one case, Eskimos, a few drove mixed teams and some used Alaskan Malamutes. It seems fitting, therefore, to tell about some of these early women drivers and to remind readers that women can get as much fun out of driving teams of Alaskan Malamutes as can their husbands and children.

The New England Sled Dog Club held its first race during the winter carnival at Newport, New Hampshire, in 1924. Two young women had come from Cambridge, Mass. to spend the winter at Wonalancet Farm. There they fell in love with the dogs, and both learned to drive. They decided to enter the race at Newport.

The two were Clara Enubuskie and Carol Peabody. Clara later became the wife of the late Richard Reed, and Carol married Frederick Lovejoy of Concord, Mass. At the last minute, Carol decided not to race. This particular race was of six miles only, and it was designed for novice drivers. Clara Enubuskie started with her team, but the dogs got hopelessly entangled on the course, and she was unable to finish, yet she gained the publicity needed to inspire other women to become drivers.

After Leonhard Seppala had set up his kennels at Poland Springs, Maine, his partner, Mrs. Ted Ricker, now Mrs. Kaare Nansen, learned to drive. She first raced at Lake Placid, and she entered the first point

Eva "Short" Seeley, drives a team which she has trained.   *Dick Smit.*

to point race sponsored by the New England Sled Dog Club. This type of race was called a "long mileage race." Teams came from all over New England, and overnight housing was arranged for all drivers and dogs at the towns along the three day event. Mrs. Ricker's team once got tangled up with a stray dog. But she finished the race, and within the minimum time limit. I, Mrs. Milton Seeley, was at the Laconia Tavern when she arrived there, and she convinced me that I would someday drive also.

When Milton and I arrived at Wonalancet Farm in 1927, I had a son of Arthur Walden's Chinook, called Nook. Walden had trained him for me, and he became my lead dog. Before long, I was driving as many as 11 dogs in the team. My own first race was at North Conway, New Hampshire.

One of the earliest woman racers was Mrs. Florence Clark of Milan, New Hampshire. She drove a team of matched Eskimos. All had white bodies and black ears. But they were addicted to fighting, and also it was most difficult to get them to obey under all circumstances. For these reasons, the team had been barred from some races, but the team did well enough in other events.

At the time of the Olympic trials given by the New England Sled Dog Club, Mrs. Clark drove her team from Woodstock to Wonalancet. She had to climb over the treacherous Sandwich Range that leads into Wonalancet, and because of a mighty storm, she was forced to spend the night in the open. When the team arrived at Wonalancet, neither she nor the dogs were in fit condition to race. They were taken home by truck.

The Lake Placid Club set up an invitational race for sled dogs and both Leonhard Seppala and Mrs. Ricker entered. Seppala finished first, and Mrs. Ricker second. In another point to point race, Mrs. Ricker drove a Seppala team. But a stray dog got tangled with her team and the team escaped. Spectators helped her to catch it. As far as racing time went, she was disqualified, but the incident again helped to spark interest in women as drivers.

Another sled dog club was formed at Laconia, New Hampshire, and this club still holds a race which is billed as the world championship of sled dog racing. Both Mrs. Clark and Short Seeley entered. Mrs. Clark was forced to drop out, but Mrs. Seeley finished the three day event of 20 miles each day.

Mrs. Moseley Taylor (now Mrs. Lorna Demidoff) also entered racing at this time. Both she and Mrs. Seeley won races, and Lorna Demidoff became one of the best known of women drivers. She used a team of matched gray and white Siberian Huskies.

Natalie Jubin of Lake Placid drove a dog team for passenger rides in order to earn money for her college education. She majored in sociology at Syracuse University. When Milton Seeley died in 1945, Natalie and Margaret Dewey of the Lake Placid Club went to Wonalancet to take care of the dogs while Mrs. Seeley underwent surgery. Natalie took the dogs out daily, even in the worst blizzards.

After college, she planned to go to Juneau, Alaska to teach. Mrs. Seeley had given her a letter of introduction to Earl Norris. She arranged with Earl to take four dogs to Alaska, two large dogs from Chinook Kennels and two Siberian Huskies. Natalie met and married Earl Norris, and their partnership in both Alaskan Malamutes and Siberian Huskies has lasted ever since. Natalie Norris was an early winner in women's races in Alaska, the first of which was held at Anchorage in 1953. She won in 1954.

Mrs. Keith (Jean) Bryar went to Alaska with her husband for the races at Fairbanks and Anchorage. She won twice at Fairbanks. Her teams, driven by Richard Moulton, also compete in Canadian and U.S. professional circuit races.

Perhaps the greatest record made by a woman driver is that of Mrs. Kit Macinnes of Anchorage. She won the world championship at Anchorage four times, in 1955, 1959, 1960, and 1961. Barbara Parker and Shirley Gavin have won three times each. Rosie Losonsky, an Eskimo and always a strong competitor, won in 1957.

Sally Heckman drives a three dog team at Tamworth, N.H. in 1975. Her dogs: Rowdy, Teeko (left) and Wolf.

Mrs. Milton Seeley, only woman driver in the 1933 Olympics is shown with (l.–r.) Wendy of Kotzebue, Finn of Yukon, Gripp of Yukon, and Kearsarge of Yukon. *H.I. Orne*

Ch. Timber Trail Wupee, owned by Lorna Jackson, taken when 10 years of age in 1966.

Ch. Eldor's Little Bo, born in 1960, owned by Mr. and Mrs. D.E. Tarr.

Doris Knorr's Ch. Midnight Shadow Of Kuvak.

11

Champions and Their Pedigrees by Months and Years

THE PREVIOUS CHAPTERS discussed the early champions. This chapter lists the champions, and their sires and dams where known, from 1952 through 1974. A word of explanation is necessary, however. Since the Eskimos did not keep a stud book, many of the early dogs were not registered. This is indicated by an N.R. after the dog's name.

In the early days, people wanting Alaskan Malamutes were free to go to Alaska and bring back what they considered to be representative stock. However, opinions differed as to the proper type, and arguments arose. These arguments have tended to continue ever since.

There was a time when unregistered dogs could be exhibited and could win championships, if good enough. The American Kennel Club had a policy as to how the offspring of such dogs could be registered. At one period, a dog had to win a certain number of championship points. Then, if mated to a registered dog, the offspring could be registered. Later this policy was amended and tightened. If such a dog won a championship, it could not be registered, but if it was mated to a registered dog, the offspring could be.

After the American Kennel Club had decided that there was sufficient breeding stock in what was then the United States, the stud book was closed. Then only dogs eligible for registration or those which were registered could be shown.

In going over this list at least a dozen times, we have each time found errors. Though every effort has been made to eliminate them, some may still be found. If so, we apologize. In some cases, a dog became a champion after some of its offspring had won championships, so the dog may not be listed as a champion in a given pedigree. In most such cases, we have tried to correct this, but we have not otherwise altered the official records.

We have also tried to avoid spelling errors. But in some cases, these were made by owners and in other cases by registrations' typists at the American Kennel Club. Arctic, for instance, is often spelled "Artic" and even "Aritic." For the most part we have left the spellings as they have appeared in official records.

Ch. Sittiak Hoochmou of Arctica, owned by Carol & Charles Browne.

90

1952
Husky-Pak's Mitya of Seguin
Alaska N.R.

1953
Prairie Lash N.R.
Smo-Ki N.R.
Toro of Bras Coupe
  By Ch. Kim of Kotzebue
  x Kotzebue Cleopatra
Yukon Timber Grey N.R.
Sierra Blizzard N.R.
Chee Chee N.R.
Ambush of Husky-Pak N.R.
Buccaneer of Husky-Pak N.R.
Black Hawk of Husky-Pak N.R.
Mulphus Brook's The Bear N.R.
Zorro of Silver Sled N.R.
Starrlet N.R.
Baboo N.R.

1954
Commanche of Husky-Pak
  By Ch. Toro of Bras Coupe
  x Ch. Arctic Storm of Husky-Pak
Yukon of Sno-Shu
  By Ch. Sierra Blizzard
  x Notak of Silver Sled
Taku of Silver Sled N.R.
Toklet of Kobuk II N.R.
Cliquot of Husky-Pak
  By Ch. Toro of Bras Coupe
  x Ch. Arctic Storm of Husky-Pak
Keowuk of Kobuk
  By Ch. Toro of Bras Coupe
  x Helen of Bras Coupe
Tundra of Sno-Shu
  By Ch. Sierra Blizzard
  x Notak of Silver Sled
Cheyenne of Husky-Pak
  By Toro of Bras Coupe
  x Ch. Arctic Storm of Husky-Pak

1955
Baloo W-543686
  By Ch. Prairie Lash
  x Shawnee Belle
Koyuk of Silver Sled
  By Ch. Nahnook II
  x Oogerook of Silver Sled
Cherokee of Husky-Pak
  By Ch. Toro of Bras Coupe
  x Ch. Arctic Storm of Husky-Pak

Kuskokwin Gray Fury
  By Ch. Nahnook II
  x Oogerook II of Silver Sled
Alaskan Star of Roy-El
  By Ch. Husky-Pak Black Hawk C.D.
  x Kiana of Roy-El
Dakota of Husky-Pak
  By Ch. Apache Chief of Husky-Pak
  x Ch. Husky-Pak's Mikya of Seguin
Drum of Husky-Pak
  Litter mate of Dakota of Husky-Pak
Chinook Kotzebue Gripp
  By Ch. Kim of Kotzebue
  x Taku's Mascara of Chinook
Faro's Arctic Flash N.R.
Cochise of Husky-Pak
  By Ch. Toro of Bras Coupe
  x Ch. Arctic Storm of Husky-Pak
Silver Sled's Beau
  By Ch. Nahnook II
  x Ch. Zorro of Silver Sled
Karel's Alberta
  By Ch. Drum of Husky-Pak
  x Ch. Alaskan Star of Roy-El
Cochino of North Star N.R.
Karel's Alinaluk
  By Ch. Drum of Husky-Pak
  x Ch. Alaskan Star of Roy-El
Silver Sled's Master Ace
  By Ch. Nahnook II
  x Ch. Zorro of Silver Sled
Kim of Sno-Pak
  By Ch. Toro of Bras Coupe
  x Musher Lane Kila
Stor-Mi King of Journey's End
  By Ch. Nahnook II
  x Ch. Tuyah of Silver Sled
Aabara of Redhorse N.R.
Banshee of Husky-Pak N.R.
Skilak of North Star N.R.
Czar of Val Verda
  By Frosty of Silver Sled
  x La Teeya of Silver Sled
Kilerak of Kobuk
  By Ch. Toro of Bras Coupe
  x Helen of Bras Coupe

1956
Sno-Pak Kavik's Oopik
  By Chinook Kotzebue Gripp
  x Kavik of Sno-Pak
Black Watch of Yukon N.R.

Mister Yukon of Tobuk
   Ch. Drum of Husky-Pak
   x Pontefract Juneau of Roy-El
Timber
   By Ch. Nahnook II
   x Ch. Tuyah of Silver Sled
Durango of Husky-Pak
   By Ch. Apache Chief of Husky-Pak
   x Ch. Husky-Pak's Mikya of Seguin
Husky-Pak Marclar's Sioux
   By Ch. Apache Chief of Husky-Pak
   x Ch. Cheyenne of Husky-Pak
Marclar's Yukon Otter
   By Yukon King of Lunenberg
   x Bamboo of Husky-Pak
Husky-Pak Erok
   By Ch. Apache Chief of Husky-Pak
   x Kilerak of Kobuk
The Challenge of Tigara
   By Keouk of Kobuk
   x Cookie of Bras Coupe
Koonah of Silver Sled
   By Nahnook II
   x Oogerook of Silver Sled
Karel's Ahteetah
   By Ch. Drum of Husky-Pak
   x Ch. Alaskan Star of Roy-El
Tigara's Adventuress
   By Ch. Toro of Bras Coupe
   x Sno-Pak Kavick's Oonalik

1957
Alaskan Kuvak's Nasota
   By Ch. Toro of Bras Coupe
   x Helen of Bras Coupe
Kobuk's Manassas Mischief
   Ch. Prairie Lash
   x Aylyak of Roy-El
Aktis of Polar Cap N.R.
Chinook Missud's Kamchatka
   By Monad of Musher Lane
   x Musher Lane Denali
Timbertrail Cheechako
   By Chinook of Kotzebue Gripp
   x Ch. Tuyah of Silver Sled
Barb Far Marclar's Machook
   By Apache Chief of Husky-Pak
   x Ch. Cheyenne of Husky-Pak
Crusader of Roy-El
   By Ch. Husky-Pak Black Hawk C.D.
   x Kiana of Roy-El

Tigara's Arctic Explorer
   By Ch. Toro of Bras Coupe
   x Sno-Pak Kavik's Oonalik
Parka
   By Ch. Nahnook II
   x Ch. Tuyah of Silver Sled
Beltane of Redhorse N.R.
   By Durango of Husky-Pak
   x Banshee of Husky-Pak

1958
Barb-Far Marclar's Mikiuk
   By Ch. Apache Chief of Husky-Pak
   x Ch. Cheyenne of Husky-Pak
Rogue of Tigara
   By Ch. Sno-Pak Kavik's Oopik
Husky-Pak Fancy Tail C.D.
   By Ch. Cliquot of Husky-Pak C.D.
   x Deeka of Husky-Pak
Husky-Pak Eagle
   By Ch. Apache Chief of Husky-Pak
   x Ch. Kelerak of Kobuk
Husky-Pak's Flaming Flirt, C.D.X.
   By Ch. Cliquot of Husky-Pak
   x Deeka of Husky-Pak
Aylyak of Roy-El
   By Ch. Husky-Pak Black Hawk, C.D.
   x Kiana of Roy-El
Kobuk's Alaskan Kodiak
   By Ch. Mulphus Brook's The Bear
   x Ch. Baloo
Husky-Pak Echako
   By Ch. Apache Chief of Husky-Pak
   x Ch. Kelerak of Kobuk
Misty of North Wind C.D.
   By Wind of Silver Sled
   x Kamah of Silver Sled
Nannuk N.R.
Spawn's Beau Knight N.R.
Kodiak
   By Ch. Cochise of Husky-Pak
   x Kowuk of Sno-Shu
Tongass of Tigara
   By Sno-Pak Kavik's Oopik
   x Calaeno of Tigara
Khaibar N.R.
Snow-Pak Klaya
   By Ch. Kim of Sno-Pak
   x Musher Lane Pandora
Dagan of Redhorse
   By Ch. Durango of Husky-Pak
   x Ch. Timber Trail Cheechako

Roy Smith's Ch. Sno-Pak Kavik's Oopik.

Husky-Pak Gunsmoke
By Ch. Cherokee of Husky-Pak
x Ch. Kelerak of Kobuk
Tamarack of Tigara
By Ch. Sno-Pak Kavik's Oopik
x Calaeno of Tigara

1959
Yukon Wolf of Yakatat N.R.
Barb-Far Lootok
By Daku of Husky-Pak
x Ch. Konnah of Silver Sled
Midnight Shadow of Kuvak
By Alaskan Kakolik of Kuvak
x Alaskan Oowuk of Kuvak
Tigara's Petite Parka
By Ch. Toro of Bras Coupe
x Sno-Pak Kavik's Oonalik
Amarok (Canada)
By Husky-Pak Forecast
x Barb Far Marclar's Marook
Marshall's Silver Streak
By Faro of Silver Sled
x Mason's Silver Streak
Silver King N.R.
Tigara's Dortic Khan
By Ch. Tongass of Tigara
x Sno-Pak Kavik's Oonalik
Est-El-D-R-CO of Silver Sled
By Ch. Nahnook II
x Ch. Ooloo M'Loot
Kalitan's Kayak N.R.
Silver Saga's Sagitta
By Silver Sleet of Sno-Shu
x Kobuk's Awuna
Tigara's Regina Arctica
By Ch. Toro of Bras Coupe
x Ch. Alaskan Kuvak's Nasota

1960
Narsuks Alaskan Diamond Lill
By Silver Sled El Sabur
x Ch. Kuskokwin Gray Fury
Tigara's Empres
By Ch. Toro of Bras Coupe
x Sno-Pak Kavick's Oonalik
Kalitan's Tobuk N.R.
Nome of Northwind
By Lobo of Northwind
x Klondike Kate of Northwind

Thor of Tigara
By Toro of Bras Coupe
x Ch. Tigara's Adventuress
Tigara's Kortic Shag-Luck
By Tongass of Tigara
x Sno-Pak Kavik's Oonalik
Kobuk's Dynamo
By Ch. Mulphus Brook's The Bear
x Kobuk's Dark Beauty
Kluane's Artic Sinu C.D.
By Kluane's Klimmer
x Malamoot of Kuvak
Sena-Lak's Arctic Silver
By Silver Sleet of Sno-Shu
x Kiana of Klondike
Sno-Crest Aurora of Erowah
By Ch. Cochise of Husky-Pak
x Kobuk's Dark Beauty
Sno-Crest's Mukluk
By Cochise of Husky-Pak
x Kobuk's Dark Beauty
Spawn's Kulak
By Barb-Far Lootok
x Ch. Spawn's Chee Chee
Klondike's Ike
By Barb-Far Marclar's Mikiuk
x Vixen of Silver Sled
Sno-Pak Nashoba
By Ch. Kim of Sno-Pak
x Musher Lane Pandora
Sena-Lak's Arctic Flash
By Silver Sleet of Sno-Shu
x Kiama of Klondike
Kalyuh's Attu
By Ch. Sno-Pak Kavik's Oopik
x Ch. Sno-Pak Nashoba
Sena-Lak's Arctic Thunder
By Silver Sleet of Sno-Shu
x Kiana of Klondike
Sno-Crest's Ebony Sue
By Kodiak Teddy
x Ch. Brook's Wons Neeuq Star
Tanyka of Sno-Shu
By Ch. Sierra Blizzard
x Notak of Silver Sled

1961
Husky-Pak Gazelle
By Ch. Husky-Pak Eagle
x Dawn of Husky Pak

Ch. Treleika of Sky Fyre, Kay and Ed Rodewald, Cottage Grove, Ore., as he won Best of Breed at Ogden, Utah.

Ch. Rouge Of Tigara, owned by Dorothy Dillingham, shown by Glenn Hull. *Ludwig*

Ch. Ninilchik, owned by J.L. Moustakis of Anchorage, Alaska has been a team mate of Ch. Kougarok. *Maxine Vehlow*

Ch. Kougarok, owned by J.L. Moustakis of Anchorage, Alaska is part of a working team of freighting dogs.   *Maxine Vehlow*

Kobuk May-Glen's Achlach
By Ch. Mulphus Brook's The Bear
x Arctic Dawn of Husky-Pak
Karel's Bluff
By Ch. Drum of Husky-Pak
x Ch. Alaskan Star of Roy-El
Spawn's Hot Shot
By Ch. Fakir of Roy-El
x Snowmasque White Diamond
Ambara's Aniu
By Ch. Mulphus Brook's The Bear
x Ch. Alaskan Kuvak's Nasota
Tigara's Artica Tanunak
By Ch. Thor of Tigara
x Ch. Alaskan Kuvak's Nasota
Kimbra's King Notak
By Ch. Tongass of Tigara
x Tigara's Dortic Chena
Kodara's Yanki Lad
By Ch. Husky-Pak Erok
x Kobuk's Dark Beauty
Kimbra's Koyuk
By Ch. Tongass of Tigara
x Tigara's Dortic Chena
Sno-Crest's Snow Bear
By Ch. Husky-Pak Erok
x Sno-Crest Icefloe
Fakir of Roy-El
By Erik of Roy-El
x Marclar's Una
Frosty of North Wind
By Mohawk of North Wind
x Ch. Misty of North Wind, C.D.
Kingmik of Kuvak C.D.
By Alaskan Kakolik of Kuvak
x Alaskan Oowuk of Kuvak
Frey of Redhorse N.R.
Kiska of Redhorse N.R.
Manatoba
By Faro of Silver Sled
x Mason's Silver Streak
Roy-El's Fantom Hawk
By Erik of Roy-El
x Marclar's Una

1962
Alaskan Okiluk of Kuvak
By Alaskan Kakolik of Kuvak
x Alaskan Oowuk of Kuvak
Ambara's Kanik
By Ch. Mulphus Brook's The Bear
x Preston's Cheechako

Eldor's Little Beau
By Kobuk's Manassas Ambition
x Ambara's Kanik
Kodara Kodiak of Erowah
By. Ch. Husky-Pak Erok
x Kobuk's Dark Beauty
Dorry's Sitka of North Wind
By Ch. Midnight Shadow of Kuvak
x Nome of North Wind
Tigara's Chisana of Kayuh
By Tigara's Arctic Explorer
x Tigara's Winsome
Eldor's Put
By Kubuk's Manassas Ambition
x Ambara's Kanik
Kodara's Northern Fantasy
By Ch. Husky-Pak Erok
x Kobuk's Dark Beauty
Little Joe of North Wind
By Ch. Midnight Shadow of Kuvak
x Dorry's Sitka of North Wind
Tigara's Dortic Sitka
By Tongass of Tigara
x Sno-Pak Kavik's Oonalik
Kit Fox of North Wind
By Cuffy of North Wind C.D.
x Bonny Blaze of North Wind
Park N Pulls Mister Blue
By Ch. Husky-Pak Erok
x Brook's Wons Neeuq Star
Bakshu C.D.
By Cuffy of North Wind C.D.
x Shuli Brooke of North Wind
Tigara's Rock of Arctica
By Ch. Rogue of Tigara
x Tigara's Kazana
Vivious of Korok
By Kingmik of Kuvak C.D.
x Snow Queen of Erowah
Shuyak Caro of Cold Foot
By Sno-Pak Kaghi's Tugg
x Alaskan Agnishuk of Kuvak
Frosty Miss of Roy-El
By Erik of Roy-El
x Marclar's Una
Night Frost's Crown Jewel
By Au Sable of Night Frost
x Thunder Talla of Erowah
Pak N Pulls Tahzah
By Mister Blue
x Sno-Crest's Kemano

Ch. King Nikki Of North Wind, C.D.X., handled by Nancy Russell for Marchetta Schmitt. Judge: Albert E. Van Court. *Ritter*

Tigara's Torch of Arctica
  By Ch. Tigara's Arctic Explorer
  x Tigara's Winsome Witch
Kiana of Klondike
  By Kobi of Polar's Wilderness
  x Sno-Valley Twilight
Panuck
  By Ch. Tigara's Dortic Shag-Luck
  x Juneau's Brite Star
Sena-Lak's Thor II
  By Sena-Lak's Thor
  x Aurora of Sena-Lak

1963
Kodara's Shawnee
  By Kodara's Yanki Lad
  x Sno-Crest's Snow Bear
Chinook of Wolf Pack N.R.
Quiet Girl of Korok
  By Kingmik of Kuvak
  x Snow Queen of Erowah
Topock's Silky of North Wind
  By Topock
  x Kiska of North Wind
Tigara's Sabre of Mar-Venus
  By Ch. Tigara's Dortic Shag-Luck
  x Ch. Tigara's Arctic Eve
Furstling of Redhorse N.R.
Husky Spawn of the Yukon N.R.
Sena-Lak's Laskana
  By Sena-Lak's Snow-Wolf
  x Kiana of Klondike
Artic Frost of Erowah
  By Ch. Amarok
  x Snow-Crest Aurora of Erowah
Husky-Pak Jingo
  By Ch. Husky-Pak Eagle
  x Ch. Husky-Pak Marclar's Sioux
Kodara El Toro
  By Ch. Husky-Pak Erok
  x Kobuk's Dark Beauty
Kodara's Royal Reward
  By. Ch. Husky-Pak Erok
  x Kobuk's DARK Beauty
Mala-Nor's Sevalak Kesimi (Canada)
  By Lorn-Hall's Nordic
  x Sena-Lak's Malanor Chikinik
Tina of Northern Star N.R.
Tote-Um's Kooteyah
  By Ch. Kodara's El Toro
  x Erowah Mountain Mist

Knik of Ro-Ala-Ken
  By Kodiak of the Arctic
  x Juneau of Sainak Sunai
Apollo
  By Husky-Pak Echako
  x Delilah of Red Horse
Dark Angel
  By Ch. Sno-Crest's Mukluk
  x Kobuk's Dark Beauty
Mohawk II of North Wind
  By Tadpole's Shadow of North Wind
  x Mohawks Silver of North Wind
Husky-Pak Kiowa
  By Ch. Husky-Pak Eagle
  x Ch. Husky Pak Marclar's Sioux
May-Glen's Shaman
  By Ch. Mulphus Brook's The Bear
  x Arctic Dawn of Husky-Pak
Rowdy of North Wind
  By Ch. Midnight Shadow of Kobuk
  x Ch. Misty of North Wind

1964
Ceba's Silver Bow
  By Cold Foot Chilkott
  x Ceba Sue
Da-Cal's Timber N.R.
Erowah Cinnaman
  By Kodara Kodiak of Erowah
  x Ch. Sno-Crest Aurora of Erowah
Hinook Sno-Foot of Cold Foot C.D.
  By Ch. Shuyak Caro of Cold Foot
  x Cold Foot's Chevak
Kodara's Diana The Huntress N.R.
Silver Star of Bull's Eye
  By Narsuks Dewline Skimo
  x Gold Dust of North Wind
Sno Tara Keeana of Sno-Hill Run
  By Chinnuk of Polar's Wilderness
  x Pixie of Polar's Wilderness
Umnak of Polar's Wilderness
  By Ch. Spawn's Kulak
  x Ch. T'Domar's Gypsy
Boot Hill Bandit of North Wind
  By Chief Mohawk of North Wind
  x Ch. Dorry's Sitka of North Wind
T'Domar's Gypsy
  By Barb Far Lootok
  x Husky-Pak Gazelle
Dee-Cal's Taku N.R.

100

Ch. Hinook Sno-Foot of Cold Foot, owned by Gloria Williams, shown by Dorothy Dillingham to Judge Chris Shuttleworth. *Ludwig*

Kodara's Mr. Shadow
  By Kodara's Yanki Lad
  x Sno-Crest's Snow Bear
Eldor's Botek
  By Ch. Eldor's Little Bo
  x Ch. Ambara's Kanik
Eldor's Little Bo
  By Kobuk's Manassas Ambition
  x Ch. Ambara's Kanik
Kit Fox II of North Wind
  By Ch. Midnight Shadow of Kuvak
  x Ch. Dorry's Sitka of North Wind
Sena-Lak's Lady Kokogiak
  By Sena-Lak's Sno-Wolf
  x Kiana of Klondike
T'Domar's Voodoo King
  By Ch. Spawn's Kulak
  x Ch. Husky-Pak Gazelle
Tigara's Tyson of Arctica
  By Ch. Tigara's Arctic Explorer
  x Tigara's Kiji of Artica
Aialik of Night Frost
  By Ch. Barb-Far Marclar's Mikiuk
  x Lady Night Frost
Akularak Kodi of Sheramae
  By Cold Foot's Chilkott
  x Ceba Sue
Kodara's Black Revenge
  By Husky-Pak Erok
  x Kobuk's Dark Beauty
Kodara's Ebony Echo
  By Husky-Pak Erok
  x Kobuk's Dark Beauty
Satan of Korok
  By Kingmik of Kuvak C.D.
  x Snow Queen of Erowah
Silver Streak's Yukon Lobo
  By Ch. Marshall's Silver Streak
  x Husky-Pak Jingo
Spawn's T'Domar's Panda
  By Ch. Spawn's Hot Shot of Roy-El
  x T'Domar's Taboo
T'Domar's Tonka Chief
  By Ch. Spawn's Hot Shot of Roy-El
  x T'Domar's Taboo
Long-Ron King's Ah-Mah-Yuk
  By Midwest Moosecat Jack
  x Shuli Brooke of North Wind
Tigara's Sadko The Tartar
  By Ch. Tigara's Arctic Explorer
  x Brite Star's Tanana

Kodara's Nikki of Tote-Um
  By Kodara El Toro
  x Siska of Erowah
Rippleridge Reflection N.R.
Sena-Lak's Chena
  By Sena-Lak's Thor
  x Ch. Aurora of Sena-Lak
Aurora of Sena-Lak
  By Silver Sleet of Sno-Shu
  x Kiana of Klondike
Tigara's Eskimo Eddy of Kayuh
  By Tigara's Torch of Arctica
  x Tigara's Kazana
Sena-Lak's Son of Thor II
  By Ch. Sena-Lak's Thor II
  x Red Flash's Mischief
Shaktoolik of North Wind
  By Ch. Midnight Shadow of Kuvak
  x Ch. Dorry's Sitka of North Wind
Tigara's Karluk of Roy-El
  By Tigara's Dortic Shag-Luck
  x Tigara's Artica Eve
Cold Foot's Lucky Strike Mine
  By Sue-Ron's Ringo
  x Hoonah of Cold Foot
Tatoosh
  By Silver Sled Cabara
  x Noma Chitina of May-Glen
Tigara's Tyczar of Arctica C.D.
  By Tigara's Torch of Arctica
  x Tigara's Kazana
Tote-Um's Kenai Rowdy
  By Kodara's El Toro
  x Siska of Erowah

1965
Hyak of Cold foot
  By Shuyak Caro of Cold Foot
  x Cold Foot's Chevak
Budloren's Twx
  By King Tut of Salt Creek
  x Narsuks Dewline Twix
Kee Too
  By Ch. Little Joe of North Wind
  x Chilly Buk
Knotty Pine Angel of Korok
  By Arctic Frost of Erowah
  x Satan of Korok
Tigara's Kiji of Arctica
  By Kimbra's King Notak
  x Tigara's Kiana Kenai

102

Noted winner and sire, Ch. Tigara's Arctic Explorer.

Ludwig

Arctic Wolf of Brenmar
  By Tigara's Karluk of Roy-El
  x Ch. Sno-Pak Nashoba
Chilly-Buk's Keno
  By Ch. Little Joe of North Wind
  x Chilly Buk
Sno-Pak Tacoma
  By Sno-Pak Anvik
  x Snowmasque Sirius
Timber-Trail Tuyah Again
  By Mals-Lane Mohawk Chief
  x Timber-Trail Tuyah
Tote-Um's Shawnee Tu
  By Ch. Erowah Cinnaman
  x Siska of Erowah
Beowulf Thor
  By Aventurero De Korok
  x Ch. Snow Foot Mushy
Night Frost's Dark Lady
  By Au Sable of Night Frost
  x Thunder Talla of Erowah
Tigara's Kamoyak of Arctica
  By Ch. Tamarack of Tigara
  x Tigara's Kazana
Kanangnark Nertuark Lobo C.D.
  By Ch. Little Joe of North Wind
  x Ch. Dorry's Sitka of North Wind
Kuluk of Korok
  By Artic Frost of Erowah
  x Satan of Korak
Ripperidge Sun Dance
  By Ch. Mohawk II of North Wind
  x Kornoka Fury of North Wind
Cold Foot's Chevak
  Shuyak Caro of Cold Foot
  x Kiska Queen of Cold Foot
Eldor's Thunder Puff
  By Ch. Eldor's Put
  x Kobuk's Sainuk Maria
I'm Frosty's Mist of Roy-El
  By Erik of Roy-El
  x Frosty Mist of Roy-El
Kanuk's Niki
  By Kodara Adolph
  x Erowah Kiska Tu
Happy Jack of Roy-El
  By Ch. Fakir of Roy-El
  x Snowmasque White Diamond
Pak N Pull's Gitana
  By Pak N Pull's Rontoo
  x Pak N Pull's Silver Star

Night Frost's De Mr. Christian
  By Au Sable of Night Frost
  x Thunder Talla of Erowah
Sena-Lak's Thora
  By Ch. Spawn's Kulak
  x Sena-Lak's Laskana
Kanangnark Kenai Kita C.D.
  By Ch. Little Joe of North Wind
  x Ch. Dorry's Sitka of North Wind
Kodara's Scarlet Panda
  By Kodara's Yanki Lad
  x Sno-Crest's Sno Bear
Silky
  By Tomiac Bear Paw of North Wind
  x Arctic Teri of North Wind
Zardal Cliquot
  By Ch. Spawn's Kulak
  x Zardal Akutan
Glacier Lady of the Arctic
  By Kodiak of North Star
  x Princess Rose of North Star
Je-Re's Nic-A-Nuchoo
  By Tiara's Rebel of Conrad
  x Narsuks Dewline Twix
Sena-Lak's Cheeko of Lakeview
  By Ch. Sena-Lak's Thor II
  x Red Flash's Mischief
Snow Foot Mushy
  By Tokeeu Nulato
  x Casey Lane
Tote-Um's Alaskan Parka
  By Ch. Erowah Cinnaman
  x Siska of Erowah

1966
Randybrook's Kiana
  By Toro of North Wind
  x Maras' Klondike Kate
Sena-Lak's Kimshan
  By Buck II of Polar's Den
  x Sena-Lak's Thora
Williams Gray Dawn
  By Anana Lobo of North Wind
  x Keena of Manitou Farms
Kanangnark's Silver Shadow
  By Kanangnark's Little Sir Echo
  x Kanangnark's Noma
Mara's King Midas
  By Toro of North Wind
  x Mara's Klondike Kate

Ch. Deepwater of Burbon, owned by Wayne Gibb of Martinsville, N.J. *Gilbert*

Randybrook's Regent
  By Randybrook's Chino
  x Randybrook's Snow Flurrie
Sno Tara's Keechi of Polar's Den
  By Ch. Spawn's Hot Shot of Roy-El
  x T'Domar's Gypsy
Amarok Kingmik Tarka
  By Aventurero De Korok
  x Ch. Snow Foot Mushy
Jingo's Silver Trumpet
  By Ch. Ceba's Silver Bow
  x Ch. Husky-Pak Jingo
Bearpaw Elk of Tote-Um (Canada)
  By Ch. Kodara El Toro
  x Siska of Erowah
Erowah Kiska's Rikki
  By Kodara Aldolph
  x Erowah Kiska Tu
Kodara's Chatte Aluridae
  By Ch. Kodara's Nikki of Tote-Um
  x Ch. Kodara's Northern Fantasy
Kodara's Makushine
  By Ch. Kodara's Kodiak of Erowah
  x Kodara's Scarlett Panda
Log-Ron's Tiko
  By Midwest Moosecat Jack
  x Log-Ron's Blackeye
Zeus of Fleur De Lis
  By Togo of North Wind
  x Shadow's Cupid of North Wind
Bearpaw Geena (Canada)
  By Ch. Erowah Cinnaman
  x Siska of Erowah
Chilanko Bandit
  By Mohawk II of North Wind
  x Taw-Ne of Sheramae
Spring's Kiana Kodara
  By Ch. Kodara Kodiak of Erowah
  x Kodara's Scarlett Panda
Tigara's Gypsy of Winter Haven
  By Tigara's Toro Of Arctica
  x Tigara's Cali Regina
Glaciers' Storm Kloud
  By Kadluk of North Wind
  x Glacier Lady of The Arctic
Kotzebue Bering of Chinook
  By Sno-Pak Sigolumala
  x Tigara's Tundra of Arctica
Lady Sitka of Nordic Valley
  By Prince Kodiak of The Tundra
  x Lady Kiska of The Tundra

Lorri Lane Misty of Windy Hill
  By Log-Ron King William
  x Polar Candy Baar
Pullara's Kazan
  By Togo of North Wind
  x Shadow's Cupid of North Wind
Sena-Lak's Tenana of Roy El
  By Ch. Tamarack of Tigara
  x Ch. Sena-Lak's Laskana
Stormy Weather
  By Yukon's Kodiak
  x Lee's Ka-Hoka
Alyeska Su Son
  By Tigara's Kipnuk of Arctica
  x Sena-Lak's Kiska
Tigara's Keonik of Arctica
  By Ch. Thor of Tigara
  x Tigara's Winsome Witch
Cold Foot Khaibar of Sena-Lak
  By Stikeen of Tyee
  x Cold Foot's Chevak
Kodara's Kinik
  By Ch. Sno-Crest's Mukluk
  x Kodara's Brigitt
Sena-Lak's Kian
  By Ch. Tamarack of Tigara
  x Sena-Lak's Laskana
Sena-Lak's Miss Tardy
  By Red Flash's Streak
  x Kiana of Klondike
Sno-Pak Tananna
  By Sno-Pak Anvik
  x Ch. Tigara's Chisana of Kaiyuh
Tana-Bek's M'Lootko of Sena-Lak
  By Ch. Sena-Lak's Thor II
  x Tara's Tanya of Attu
Tigara's Toro of Arctica
  By Ch. Tigara's Arctic Explorer
  x Tigara's Kiji of Arctica
Tote-Um's Tanook
  By Ch. Kodara El Toro
  x Sno-Pak Princess Kyah
Roy-El's Alashi-Yama
  By Ch. Tigara's Karluk of Roy-El
  x Teena of Polar's Wilderness
Ulak Of The Tundra
  By Moneek Von Forsthaus
  x Tahleguah's Princess
Al Klanu Uka
  By Ch. Sno-Crest's Mukluk
  x Kodara's Ebony Echo

First Best in Show Alaskan Malamute team, handled by Nancy C. Russell. L–R, Am. & Can. Ch. Glaciers' Storm Kloud, C.D.; Russell's Yvetj Rose, C.D.; Ch. Timberlane's Pamiijak; and Am. & Can. Ch. Timberlane's Storm Kloud. *Ritter*

Konge Lubin Edward
  By Pak N Pull's Kazan
  x Pak N Pull's Myki
Spawn's Pengara
  By Ch. Tamarack of Tigara
  x T'Domar's Gypsy

1967
Mars-Artic Leesa
  By Nyak of Sno-Plume
  x Lad-Lin Pita
Sno-Pak Kemo
  By Sno-Pak Anvik
  x Arctic Mishka
Tish of Land O-Toka's Dino
  By Land O'Toka's Dino
  x Beki Silver Lady
Zardal Cotati
  By Ch. Spawn's Kulah
  x Zardal Akoran
Eldor's Cleo
  By Ch. Eldor's Little Bo
  x Abbagale of Eldor's
Kodara's Buster of Double E
  By Ch. Sno-Crest's Mukluk
  x Ch. Erowah Roxanne
Erowah Roxanne
  By Kodara Kodiak of Erowah
  x Ch. Sno-Crest Aurora of
  Erowah
Nicky
  By Roy-El's Ringo
  x Roy-El's Navarra
Sena-Lak's Copper Penny
  By Sena-Lak's Mischief Pupeno
  x Sena-Lak's Chene of Lakeview
Sena-Lak's Yukon Buck
  By Ch. Sena-Lak's Cheeko of
  Lakeview
  x Ch. Sena-Lak's Tenana of Roy-El
Sir Kimo Lee
  By Thunder of Alaska
  x Kiyoot of Gold Dust
Eldor's Pretty Miss Penny
  By Ch. Eldor's Little Bo
  x Abbagale of Eldor
Igloo Koyuk of Cold Foot C.D.
  By Shuyak Caro of Cold Foot
  x Skeba
Marauder of Brenmar
  By Tigara's Karluk of Roy-El
  x Ch. Sno-Pak Nashoba

Pak N Pull Snow Angel
  By Kodara Kodiak Teddi
  x Ch. Dark Angel
Silver Coin's Juneau
  By Kodiak Bear of North Wind
  x Silver Wolf of North Wind
Snow Foot Toyon
  By Aventurero de Korok
  x Ch. Snow Foot Mushy
Orseno's Sno-Raider of Franbee
  By Log-Ron King William
  x Polar Candy Baar
Kamik Chiokyrlie of Snow Foot
  By Aventurero de Korok
  x Ch. Snow Foot Mushy
T'Domar's Juneau
  By Ch. T'Domar's Voodoo King
  x T'Domar's Nootka
Malagold's Panda Bear
  By Kanangnark's Miseha Tedi Bear
  x Kanangnark's Stormy
Penbear's Squeetina
  By Ch. Mulphus Brook's The Bear
  x Ch. Silver Saga's Sagitta
Sena-Lak's Copper Knight
  By Sena-Lak's Mischief Pupeno
  x Sena-Lak's Chena of Lakeview
Bow's Aurora Borealis
  By Ch. Ceba's Silver Bow
  x Chilanko's Malaeska Sioux
Markitz Sno-King
  By Zardal Cliquot
  x Randy Brook Jimlo's Meinu
Sconee's Kiska
  By Kobuk's Manassas Ambition
  x Kobuk's Sainuk Mist
Tigara's Jo-Dan of Artica
  By Tigara's Justin Morgan
  x Tigara's Thais of Arctica
Wakon's Nusha
  By Tote-Um's Tanook
  x Tote-Um's Otter of Wakon
Lorn-Hall's Tlingit
  By Timber Trail Wupee
  x Mala-Nor's Toska Ninoo
T'Domar's Genghiz Kim Shadow
  By Ch. T'Domar's Voodoo King
  x Cold Foot's Chevak
Cold Foot Minto C.D.
  By Stickeen of Tyee
  x Cold Foot's Chevak

108

Ch. Tenakee Chief, handled by Corky Vroom. Judge: Glenn Fancy. Owners: Dr. and Mrs. Richard Woods. *Francis*

Glacier's Tisha Lyng
By Glaciers' Storm Kloud C.D.
x Nabesna
Lorri Lanes Ebony Knight
By Log-Ron King William
x Polar Candy Baar
Nikik Du Nordkyn
By Skol Du Nordkyn
x Koller's Sisak Du Nordkyn
Pak N Pull's Hyak of Tote-Um
By Pak N Pull's Kaltag
x Ch. Dark Angel
Sena-Lak's Talisman Caprice
By Sena-Lak's Mischief Pupeno
x Ch. Sena-Lak's Tenana of Roy-El
Tanya Toy
By Sing Toy
x Black Magic of Silver Tip
Chief of Lake Tomahawk
By Ch. Glaciers' Storm Kloud C.D.
x Silver Sled's Em Babee
Land-O-Toba's Tamahine
By Land-O-Toba's Dino
x Toba's Kachina
Little Silver Crest Nootka
By Roy-El's Panda
x Tobuk's Lady Kim
Midwest's Laska II
By Midwest's Moog
x Can Can Kayah
Miller's Royal Schnook
By Andabark's Kiowa
x Snow Bear's Royal Beauty
Sena-Lak's Laskana Caprice
By Tana-Bek's M'Lootko of Sena-Lak
x Ch. Sena-Lak's Laskana
Sno-Dance's Geronimo
By Toro of North Wind
x Kanagnark's Princetta
Wakon's Maverick Queen
By Wakon's Arctic Bear
x Tote-Um's Otter of Wakon
Zardal Baranof
By Mala-Nor's Senalak Kisimi
x Zardal Akutan
Black Knight of Eldor's
By Kobuk's Manassas Buckeye
x Malaboo's Alaskan Muskeg
Imloot of Redhorse
Ch. Durango Husky-Pak
x Husky-Pak Morning Star

Inuit's Wooly Bully
By Ch. Spawn's Hot Shot of Roy-El
x Balch's Ingrid of Brenmar
Kanangnark's Miss Parka
By Kanangnark's Torch
x Kanangnark's Norma
Kodara Kodiak Teddi
By Ch. Kodara Kodiak of Erowah
x Ch. Sno-Crest Amora of Erowah
Kodara's Koona Karoohonta
By Ch. Sno-Crest's Mukluk
x Ambara's Eyara
Orseno's Sno-Pixie of Franbee
By Log-Ron King William
x Polar Candy Baar
Sena-Lak Kiana's Black Witch
By Ch. Sena-Lak's Thor II
x Ch. Kiana of Klondike
Sno-Run's Sno Shoo
By Zardal Cliquot
x Randy Brook Jingo's Meinu
Alaskan Norris Starr of Kuvak
By Alaskan's Kim-mik-Puk of Kuvak
x Alaskan's Nan-Nak-A-Nak of Kuvak
Coldfoot Yukon Kyak
By Boru's Emooshumak
x Ch. Kyack of Coldfoot
Double E's Artic Snow-Mist
By Ch. Sno-Crest's Mukluk
x Ch. Erowah Roxanne
Frosty Konook of Sno-Hawk
By Star-Rok's Kodiak Silver Chief
x Kiska Kiana
Glacier's Arctic Commando
By Ch. Glaciers' Storm Kloud C.D.
x Glacier's Nabesna
Muktuk Tillicum of North Wind
By Cuffy of North Wind C.D.
x Tahlequah of North Wind
Nahnoonah of Redhorse
By Sena-Lak's Dark Victory
x Tigara's Sitka of Redhorse
Naughty Mike of Lorri Lane
By Kanangnark's Mischa Tedi Bear
x Kanangnark Stormi
Sabre's Misti Dawn of Snopaw
By Ch. Tigara's Sabre of Mar-Venus
x Knotty Pines Dark Devil
Sena-Lak's Blitz of Rebanrock
By Buck II of Polar's Den
x Sena-Lak's Thora

110

Ch. Baronof (l), handled by Billie Lou Robison, Best of Breed. Ch. Sabre's Misty Dawn of Sno Paw, handled by Harry Sharpe. Judge: Herman Cox. Owners: Joseph and Celeste Bouffiou, Baronof Kennels. *Bennett Associates*

Sena-Lak's Cheeka Chisana
  By Cold Foot Khaibar of Sena-Lak
  x Sena-Lak Kiama's Black Witch
Taiga Banshee of Denali
  By Tigara's Kipnuk of Arctica
  x Sena-Lak's Kiska

1968
Artic Sukanuk's Tasha
  By Aventurero de Korok
  x Ch. Snow Foot Mushy
Brigadoon's Lash of Tygara
  By Tigara's Johnny Eagle
  x C.J.'s Kimber of Brigadoon
Coldfoot Oonanik
  By Cold Foot's Lucky Strike Mine
  x Cold Foot's Kareok
Roy-El's Snow Hawk
  By Happy Jack of Roy-El
  x Kodara Black Magic of Roy-El
Roy-El's Tara
  By Ch. Roy-El's Fantom Hawk
  x Quareda of Roy-El
Sena-Lak's Purgha
  By Cold Foot Khaibar of Senalak
  x Ch. Sena-Lak's Thora
Sena-Lak's Saber of Dee-Lac
  By Tana-Bek's M'Lootko of Sena-Lak
  x Ch. Sena-Lak's Thora
Sharavin Cheechako of Jubilee
  By Kodara's Tikikluk of Sharavin
  x Sharavin's Sheeniek
Starfire of Alaska
  By Randybrook's Chino
  x Star of Northern Lights
Tigara's Nucah of Arctica
  By Tigara's Sadko the Tartar
  x Tigara's Tsena of Arctica
Balch's Ingrid of Brenmar
  By Tigar's Karluk of Roy-El
  x Ch. Sno-Pak Nashoba
Mar's Artic Dino of T-Domar
  By Ch. T'Domar's Voodoo King
  x T'Domar's Nootka
Misquah Hills Shinook
  By Bardoublee Little Cavuse
  x Bearpaw Ersulik
Pak N. Pull's Kaltag
  By Maloot of Kuvak
  x Pak N Pull's Arna

Vermaes Frosty Cookie
  By Randybrook's Chino
  x Kanook of Bardwood
Voyageur's Elke
  By Ch. Tigara's Torch of Arctica
  x Ch. Jingo's Silver Trumpet
Sena-Lak's Chena of Lakeview
  By Sena-Lak's Thor II
  x Red Flash's Mischief
Amarok Anina
  By Aventurero De Korok
  x Ch. Snow Foot Mushy
Chitina's Husha-Pup
  By Susitka Bear of Silver Tip
  x Norna Chitina of May-Glen
Glacier's Burbon King
  By Ch. Glaciers' Storm Kloud
  x Rippleridge Black Tempest
Juneau Gentleman
  By Kobuk's Chevalier
  x Kutlark of Erowah
Kanangnark's Autumn Serenade
  By Toro of North Wind
  x Kanangnark's Silky
Old Great Ring's Dan McGrew
  By Sno-Pak Sigdlumala
  x Sno-Pak Holly
Sabre's Stormy Knight
  By Ch. Tigara's Sabre of Mar-Venus
  x Knotty Pines Dark Angel
Von's Big Bad Bill
  By Hall's King
  x Von's North Star
Yukon's Stormy Shuyak
  By Jukon's Arctic Storm
  x Kya of the Yukon
Klahowya's Juneau of Tote-Um
  By Ch. Erowah Cinnaman
  x Ch. Tote-Um's Kooteeyah
T'Domar's Bismarck
  By Ch. T'Domar's Voodoo King
  x T'Domar's Nootka
Thor-Mark's Athena
  By Ch. Eldor's Thunder Puff
  x Eldor's Bolindy
Tigara's Rogue of Winter Haven
  By Tigara's Jo Dan of Arctica
  x Tigara's Tomisha of Mar-Venus
Vermar's Velvet Vikki
  By Randybrook's Chino
  x Kanook of Bardwood

112

Ch. Timberlane's The Yankee with Klea V. Stillwell, Marietta, Ga.
Judge: Maxwell Riddle. *Graham*

Boru's Emooshumak C.D.
  By Ch. Shuyak Caro of Cold Foot
  x Silver Saga's Williwa
Kanangnark's Wildcat
  By Kanangnark Panther
  x Ch. Dorry's Sitka of North Wind
Ku Ku's Miss Koyra
  By Kovak's Double Trouble
  x Stewart's Koda
Lorri Lane's Arctic Whisper
  By Ch. Lorri Lane's Ebony Knight
  x Silver Moon of Lorri Lane
Midnight Sun of Aurora
  By Sue-Ron's Ringo
  x White Nikki Chizhoma
M'London of Redhorse
  By Ch. Dagan of Red Horse
  x Ch. Husky-Pak Morning Star
Northern Storm
  By Kelowna
  x Katalia
Pak N Pull's Eskimo
  By Ch. Kodara's Yanki Lad C.D.
  x Pak N Pull's Arlook
Sno Hawk's Kodiak Silver Mist
  By Ch. Star-Rok's Kodiak Silver Chief
  x Double E's Artic Sno-Mist
Yukon Blaze
  By Ch. Silver Streak's Yukon Lobo
  x Erowah's Kiska Tu
Glacier's First Snowell
  By Ch. Glaciers' Storm Kloud C.D.
  x Rippleridge Black Tempest
Kimo of Sno-Bear
  By Ch. Tigara's Tyczar of Arctica
  C.D.
  x Tigara's Susitna Sue
Pak N Pull's Ice-Floe of Tote-Um
  By Kodara's Barking Bear of Kenai
  x Ch. Pak N Pull's Gitana
Quanah of Redhorse
  By Sena-Lak's Dark Victory
  x Husky-Pak Morning Star
Voyageur's Cougar
  By Ch. Tigara's Torch of Arctica
  x Ch. Jingo's Silver Trumpet
Wakon's Arctic Bear Du Nordkyn
  By Arctic Chief of Cottonwood
  x Erowah's Stormy Trail
Karohonta Ta-Lo-Wah
  By Kodara Kodiak Teddi
  x Kodara's Koona Karohonta

Kayok of Sheramae
  By Eldor's Breezy Kybo
  x Cheeko's Breezy Fleeta
Silcon's Chinouk of Snow Plume
  By Ch. Frosty of North Wind
  x Ch. Kuluk of Korok
Silver Success of Lorri Lane
  By Kanangnark's Wildcat
  x Kanangnark's Kiawah Starlite
Sittiak Barrow
  By Cold Foot Wolf of Sittiak
  x Tigara's Nutok of Arctica
Sno-Dance's Tyeen
  By Ch. Erowah Kiska's Rikki C.D.
  x Ch. Kodarah's Northern Fantasy
Todd
  By Anana Lobo of North Wind
  x Topock's Silky of North Wind
Traleika of Tundra
  By Ch. Frosty of North Wind
  x Tikiluk of Williwau
Vallee's Snow Bandit
  By Ch. Kodara's Nikki of Tote-Um
  x Andabark's Tsara of Anartica
King Nikki of North Wind
  By Chief Mohawk of North Wind
  x Ch. Dorry's Sitka of North Wind
Mari-Lee's Glacier Wind
  By Glacier's Storm Kloud
  x Russell's Yveti Rose
Klahowya Bandit of Tote-Um
  By Pak N Pull's Kaltag
  x Ch. Tote-Um's Kooteyah
Klahowya Caganie of Tote-Um
  By Ch. Erowah Cinnaman
  x Ch. Tote-Um's Kooteyah
Nanook of North Wind
  By Kodiak Bear of North Wind
  x Kenai's Queen Kiana II
Camvik Du Nordkyn
  By Skol Du Nordkyn
  x Koller's Sisak Du Nordkyn
Little Bo of Locust Valley
  By Kenai Rigadu
  x Mars-Arctic Pandora
Roy-El's Princess Pegwa
  By Kim-Tuk of Roy-El
  x Kodara Magic of Roy-El
Tigara's Justin Morgan
  Ch. Tigara's Arctic Explorer
  x Brite Star's Tanana

114

h. Beechwood's Takutu, breeder-owner-handled by Peg Muldoon, Black Forest,
olo. Judge: Larry Downey. *Bennett Associates*

Tojo C.D.
  By Sing Toy
  x Black Magic of Silver Tip
Beowulf Thaera C.D.
  By Aventurero De Korok
  x Ch. Snow Foot Mushy
Inuk of Timberlane
  By Ch. Glacier's Storm Kloud
  x Russell's Yveti Rose
Kiana's Silver Khan
  By Kodiak Bear of North Wind
  x Kenai's Queen Kiana II
Kiana of Kobuk
  By Ch. Kee Too
  x Kee-Nah
Mars-Artic Kamishak
  By Ch. T'Domar's Voodoo King
  x Mars-Artic Leesa
Mitka of Timberlane
  By Ch. Glaciers' Storm Kloud C.D.
  x Russell's Yveti Rose
Night Frost's Happy Fawn
  By Boru's Epeetna of Night Frost
  x Night Frost's Dark Lady
Voyageur's Winged Victory
  By Ch. Tigara's Torch of Arctica
  x Ch. Jingo's Silver Trumpet

1969
Kotzebue's Kuyan of Chinook
  By Sno-Pak's Sigdlumala
  x Tigara's Tundra of Artica
Sena-Lak's Samantha of Jo-An
  By Ch. Sena-Lak's Cheeko of Lake-
  view
  x Sena-Lak's Mitzi Madcap
Tam-Mar-Kel's Candy Apple
  By Klahowya Hoonah of Tote-Um
  x Klahowya Red Takoka
Wagner's Scout of Polar Den
  By Ch. Spawn's Hot Shot of Roy-El
  x Spawn's Bit A Honey of Roy-El
Arctic Czar
  By Imloot of Red Horse
  x Kaya Aleut
Double E's Tanu of Kar-Lyn-Da
  By Ch. Kodara's Black Revenge
  x Ch. Erowah Roxanne
Klahowya Ta wia of Tote-Um
  By Erowah Cinnaman
  x Ch. Tote-Um's Kooleelah

Knotty Pine's Dark Devil
  By Ch. Artic Frost of Wooton
  x Kodara's Royal Reward
Lorri Lane's Dark Shadow
  By Ch. Kanangnark's Wildcat
  x Kanangnark Kiawah Starlite
Rippleridge Lemon Twist
  By Ch. Glacier's Storm Kloud, C.D.
  x Rippleridge Black Tempest
Roy-El's Toma-Hawk
  By Ch. Roy-El's Fantam Hawk
  x Quareda of Roy-El
Sena-Lak's Cheeka of Ricvin
  By Ch. Cold Foot Khaibar of Sena-
  Lak
  x Senalak Kiana's Black Witch
Sittiak Durango
  By Ch. Coldfoot Wolf of Sittiak
  x Tigara's Nitok of Artica
Taw-E-Wak's Patsi Aka Tek
  By Nichola Stevonovich
  x Anna Lece
Thor-Mark's Ares
  By Ch. Eldor's Thunder-Puff
  x Eldor's Bolindy
Tigara's Dangerous Dan McGrew
  By Ch. Tigara's Torch of Arctica
  x Tigara's Thais of Arctica
Voyageur's Witch of the Wind
  By Ch. Tigara's Torch of Arctica
  x Ch. Jingo's Silver Trumpet
Pandora of Big Paw
  By Ch. Alyeska Su-Son
  x Chilanko's Tishka Doll
Two Son's Lucky Lobo
  By Handel's Husky Nikki
  x Taninalee of Muskeg
Sena-Lak's Beowulf Tawechi
  By Sena-Lak's Mischief's Pupeno
  x Ch. Sena-Lak's Tenana of Roy-El
Bar-B-R's Artic Kiska
  By Ch. Kanangnark Wildcat
  x Rippleridge Tempest Storm
Kanangnark Silky's Thor
  By Kanangnark Mischa Tedi Bear
  x Kanangnark's Silky
Ro-Ala-Ken's Kana of Double E
  By Kodara's Buster of Double E
  x Ch. Kodara's Ebony Echo
Silver Frost's Ashuya
  Chief Michigamme
  x Ch. Zero

Dorothy Dillingham shows Ch. Tigara's Dangerous Dan McGrew to Judge Eva Seeley.
Ludwig

Sno-Pak Tananna's Knik
  By Old Great Ring's Dan McGrew
  x Ch. Sno Pak Tananna
Andabark's Kiowa Chief
  By Ch. Tigara's Tyson of Arctica
  x Tigara's Talkeetna of Artica
Bear's Kiska of Timberlane
  By Ch. Glaciers' Storm Kloud C.D.
  x Russell's Yveti Rose
Kodara's La Bonita
  By Ch. Sno-Crest's Mukluk
  x Ch. Kodara's Diana The Huntress
N Bar J's Tundra
  By Ch. T Domar's Bismarck
  x Nordkyn Lightning
Ranjan Cupid
  By Kadluk of North Wind
  x Rippleridge Icebound
Sno-Tara's Arapaho
  By Ch. Spawn's Hot Shot of Roy-El
  x Ch. Sno-Tara Keeana of Sno-Hill
  Run
Tigara's Whip of Artica
  By Tigara's Jo-Dan of Artica
  x Tigara's Tomisha of Mar-Venus
Vermar's My Gy
  By Kiana's Silver Khan
  x Vermar's Frosty Kookie
Zero
  By Kanangnark's Torch
  x Kanangnark's Keisa
Bandit's War Chant
  By Vallee's Snow Bandit
  x Chetina
Dondeil of Kodiak
  By Kanangnark Silky's Thor
  x Karolin's Kiahna
Eldor's Smo-Kee Bear
  By Ch. Eldor's Little Bo
  x Eldor's Talkeeta
Glacier's Dr. Doolittle
  By Ch. Glaciers' Storm Kloud C.D.
  x Rippleridge Black Tempest
Inuit's Mehitabel
  By Ch. Spawn's Hot Shot of Roy-El
  x Balch's Ingrid Of Brenmar
Kanangnark Taki
  By Ch. Midnight Shadow of Kuvak
  x Kotzebue Noatok of North Wind
Mialaskan Sam of Pin Oaks
  By Ch. Alyeska Su Son
  x Chilanko's Tishka Doll

Mighty Flash's Silver Ray
  By Eldor's Yogi The Bear
  x Crenshaw's Jolina
Roy-El's Big Timber
  By Ch. Roy-El's Alashi-Yama
  x Ch. Nicky
Sabre's Arctic Sunshine
  By Ch. Tigara's Sabre of Mar-Venus
  x Knotty Pines Dark Devil
Sabre's Arctic Sweetheart
  By Ch. Tigara's Sabre of Mar-Venus
  x Knotty Pines Dark Devil
Sena-Lak's Simka
  By Tana-Bek's M'Lootko of Sena-Lak
  x Ch. Sena-Lak's Thora
Sno-Tara's Cherokee Knikki
  By Ch. Tigara's Karluk of Roy-El
  x Sno-Tara's Keeara of Polar's Den
Alaskana's Queen of Yukon
  By Alaskana's Frosti
  x Tigara's Little Star of Artica
Squankan's Torrid Bow
  By Kodara's Korock
  x Princess Pat of Ro-Ala-Ken
Stutz's Koda
  By Kodara's Kai Pendragon
  x Eldor's Noro
Warrior's Mist Maid of Sky Fyre
  By Aigani Bear of Silver Tip
  x Frostwinds Red Frost
Lorri Lane's Midnight Shadow
  By Kanangnark's Wildcat
  x Kanangnark's Kiawah Starlite
Malesa's Silver Glacier
  By Ch. King Nikki of North Wind
  C.D.X.
  x Ch. Glacier's Tisha Lyug C.D.
Phantom Of The Icefloe
  By Ch. Tigara's Torch of Arctica
  x Ch. Jingo's Silver Trumpet
Princess of Kodiak
  By Kodiak of North Star
  x Polar Princess Landamute
Rippleridge Imp of Lorri Lane
  By Ch. Glaciers' Storm Kloud C.D.
  x Rippleridge Black Tempest
Rippleridge Lemon Drop Kid
  By Ch. Glaciers' Storm Kloud C.D.X.
  x Rippleridge Black Tempest
Sabre's Revenge
  By Ch. Tigara's Sabre of Mar-Venus
  x Knotty Pines Dark Devil

. Inuit's Mehitabel, shown by owner-breeder Sheila Balch with Judge Kenneth ven at New Brunswick, K.C.

Sena-Lak's Darius of Cold Brook
By Ch. Cold Foot Khaibar of Senalak
x Sena-Lak Kiana's Black Witch
Sena-Lak's Kokolik of Sandi-Vu
By Sena-Lak's Arctic Flash
x Sena-Lak's Lady Tokla
Sno-Tara's Cherokee Tepee
By Ch. Tigara's Karluk of Roy-El
x Sno-Tara's Keeara of Polar's Den
Snow Plume's Chilkoot Mohawk
By Ch. Frosty of North Wind
x Ch. Kuluk of Korok
Tarzan of Troy
By Ch. Midnight Shadow of Kuvak
x Kotzebue Noatok of North Wind
Timberlane's Medicine Man
By Ch. Glaciers' Storm Kloud C.D.
x Timberlane's Heidi Jane
Timberlane's Tuktu Of Snocre
By Ch. Glaciers' Storm Kloud C.D.
x Timberlane's Heidi Jane
Double E's Koko of Kar-Lyn-Da
By Double E's Koyoda Sigoo
x Ch. Erowah Roxanne
Lorri Lane's Dark Rhapsody
By Ch. Kanangnark's Wildcat
x Ch. Lorri Lane's Misty of Windy
Hill
Tigara's Jinx of Winterhaven
By Ch. Tigara's Torch of Arctica
x Tigara's Majeska of Arctica
Fleur De Lis Scheherezade
By Ch. Zeus of Fleur de Lis
x Tatoosh of Tundra
Kanangnark's Kissima
By Ch. Kit Fox II of North Wind C.D.
x Kanangnark's Jodee
Raming's Chickasaw
By Ch. Rippleridge Sun Dance
x Raming's Northern Storm
Squankan's Moose
By Squankan's Torrid Bow
x Double E's Keeda Of Squankan
Alyeska's Mobee of The Sno
By Ch. Alyeska Su Son
x Chilanko's Tiska Doll
Duchess of Nyac C.D.
By Ch. Tigara's Tyczar of Arctica C.D.
x Kyane
Kewpi Doll of Jo-An
By Ch. Alyeska Su Son
x Chilanko's Tiska Doll

Nyac Kiana of Sno Hawk
By Ch. Star-Rok's Kodiak Silver Chief
x Double E's Artic Sno-Mist

1970
Hercules of Snow Ridge
By Ch. Silver Streak's Yukon Lobo
x Ch. Lady Sitka of Nordic Valley
Icefloe's North Star
By Phantom of the Icefloe
x Ch. Bow's Aurora Borealis
Korba of Midnight Storm Kloud
By Ch. Glaciers' Storm Kloud C.D.
x Cobra of Nipigon
Rav-El's Kim-Chee
By Roy-El's Panda
x Tobuk's Lady Kim
Sena-Lak's Chisana C.D.
By Coldfoot Khaibar of Sena-Lak
x Sena-Lak Kiana's Black Witch
T-Domar's Chitina
By T-Domar's Bismarck
x T-Domar's Taboo
Tigara's Diamond Jim
By Tigara's Dangerous Dan McGrew
x Sno-Bear's Amber of Artica
Arctic Mist's Ty-On Sabacca
By Ch. Sno-Crest's Mukluk
x Tote-Um's Amber Angel
Coldfoot's Cheko
By Ch. Shuyak Caro of Cold Foot C.D.
x Sittiak Ayak of Burnt Paw
Glacier's Silver Wampum
By Ch. King Nikki of North Wind
C.D.X.
x Ch. Glacier's Tisha Lyng C.D.
Ninilchik
By Ch. Kee-Too
x Kee-Nah
Sena-Lak's Gigante Grande Toro
Ch. Sena-Lak's Thor II
x Red Flach Mischief
Snopaw's Panda of Arctic Mist
By Arctic Mist's Ty-On Sabacca
x Ch. Sabre's Misti-Dawn of Snopaw
Sno-Tara's Dakota Kim
By Roy-El's Skagway
x Sno-Tara's Blackfoot Cimarron
Snow Lass of Far View
Ch. Kit Fox of North Wind
x Chichay of Ojibwa

nuit's Anganook of Etah, bred by Sheila Balch. *Richard La Branche*

T-Domar's Silver Smoke
  By T-Domar's Bismarck
  x T'Domar's Taboo
Tigara's Natasha of Tumleh
  By Tigara's Justin Morgan
  x Tigara's Tsena of Arctica
Tigara's Togiak Chieftain
  By Tigara's Whip of Artica
  x Tigara's Tsena of Arctica
Timberlane's Pamiiyok
  By Ch. Glaciers' Storm Kloud C.D.
  x Russell's Yveti Rose
Valhalla's Bold Venture
  By Ch. Eldor's Put
  x Kanangnark's Keisa
Van Dike's Arctic Tundra
  By Oomalikbuk of Oak
  x Wilinda's Apache Silver Bear
Watisapape's Misty Skye
  By Kenai's Fearless Ferdie
  x Princess Woanna
Zorba of Brigadoon
  By Ch. Tigara's Torch of Arctica
  x Tigara's Tara of Arctica
Rippleridge Sandstorm
  By Rippleridge Sandman
  x Rippleridge Tic-Toc
Sittiak's Chilka of Wolfpack
  By Coldfoot Wolf of Sittiak
  x Ch. Tigara's Keonik of Arctica
Suisan of Redhorse
  By M'London of Redhorse
  x Ch. Nanoonah of Redhorse
Totemtok's Bojuk
  By Alaskana's Frosti
  x Totemtok's Tiana of Alaskana
Tyanik Thunder of Redhorse
  By M'London of Redhorse
  x Husky-Pak Morning Star
Winterhaven's Gypsy of Amorok C.D.
  By Winterhaven's Buck of Chinook
  x Ch. Tigara's Gypsy of Winterhaven
Roy-El's Comanche Renegade
  By Ch. Roy-El's Fantom Hawk
  x Roy-El's Kameo
Sno-Hawk's Arctic Red of Beowulf
  By Beowulf Thytaen of Snow-Hawk
  x Snow Queen of Sitka
Bar-B-R's Wind of Wineska
  By Ch. Kanangnark's Wildcat
  x La Sorbonne de Paris

Burbon's Aristocrat O'Brenmar
  By Ch. Marauder of Brenmar
  x Kaiyuh's Dot
Chucara's Kyak of Big Shanty
  By Juneau Gentleman
  x Gypsy of Nome
Karohonta Conestoga
  By Ch. Kodara Kodiak Teddi
  x Ch. Kodara's Koona Karohonta
Rippleridge Cinnamon Bear
  By Rippleridge Sandman
  x Rippleridge Tic-Tac
Sena-Lak's Eric The Red
  By Sena-Lak'Mischief's Pupeno
  x Ch. Sena-Lak's Tenana of Roy-El
Silver Shadow of Seldovia
  By Ch. Chief of Lake Tomahawk
  x Sascha
Tarbo's Dream Echo
  By Ch. Rippleridge Sun Dance
  x Eldor's Satin Dancer
Timshajim's Arctic Knik
  By Mars-Artic Rowdy
  x Timick of Kodiak Kamotic
Tinut of Fleur de Lis
  By Togo of North Wind
  x Shadow's Cupid of North Wind
Winterhaven's Kotzebue Cajun
  By Winterhaven's Cisco Kid
  x Tigara's Jinx of Winterhaven
Yukon's Panuck Of Kinik
  By Ch. Kodara's Kinik
  x Kenai's Nikkanda
Yukon's Tanushka
  By Ch. Kodara's Kinik
  x Kenai's Nikkanda
Bearpaw Injun of Tote-Um
  By Pak N Pull's Kaltag
  x Bearpaw Eska
Brutus of White Paw
  By Thor of Northern Telstar
  x Wakan of Jo-M
Fende of the Frostland
  By Ch. Kanangnark's Wildcat
  x La Sorbonne De Paris
Redhorse Tutiak of Noatak
  By M'London of Redhorse
  x Husky-Pak Morning Star
Glacier's Million Dollar Baby
  By Ch. King Nikki of North Wind
  C.D.X.
  x Ch. Glaciers Tisha Lyng C.D.

Ch. Tigara's Prince Igor of Tumleh, owner-handler Richard W. Schwalbe.

Kazan's Sitka C.D.
  By Ch. Kodara's Yanki Lad C.D.
  x Pak N Pull's Yukona of Kazan
Klahowya's Keno
  By Klahowya Hoonah of Tote-Um
  x Klahowya Red Takoka
Lil Storm of Whit-Acres
  By Ch. Northern Storm
  x Tahista Mo
Nunavik's Ila Kavanga
  By Tigara's El Cid
  x Tigara's Nesha of Kiganga
Rippleridge Midnight Fury
  By Rippleridge Warlock
  x Ch. Rippleridge Yukon Star
Wyvern's Bi Frost of Kiualook
  By Ch. Coldfoot Khaibar of Senalak
  x Ch. Sena-Lak's Cooper Penny
Alaskaland's Alta
  By Ch. Tigara's Torch of Arctica
  x Ch. Tish Of Land-O-Toba's Dino
Chilkoot's Koala Bear
  By Alaskana's Sultan of Yukon
  x Alaskana's Queen of Yukon
Kiska Queen of Snow Ridge
  Ch. Silver Streak's Yukon Lobo
  x Ch. Lady Sitka of Nordic Valley
Silver Frost's Blitz
  By Chief Michigamme
  x Ch. Zero
Snocre's Sikku
  By Ch. Glacier's Burbon King
  x Ch. Timberlane's Tuktu of Snocre
Timberlane's Glacier Penny
  By Ch. King Nikki of North Wind,
  C.D.X.
  x Ch. Glaciers Tishkla Lyng C.D.
Yuki Of Wilderness Trail
  By Ch. Zeus of Fleur De Lis
  x Fleur De Lis' Heidi Ghost Dance
Apache Smoke C.D.
  By Skookum's Taluk
  x South Wind Tinker
Burbon's Bandit of Fairwaye
  By Ch. Burbon's Aristocrat O' Bren-
  mar
  x Tonya of High Point
Karohonta Voodoo Muskie
  By Ch. T'Domar's Voodoo King
  x Ch. Karohonta Ta-Lo-Wah

Munchken Dolly
  By Ch. Roy-El's Alashi-Yama
  x Ch. Nicky
Sittiak Dorka of Kabloona
  By Ch. Coldfoot Wolf of Sittiak
  x Tigar's Nitok of Artica
Talu Of Noakak
  By Bernie's Mr. Fourpaws
  x Ford's Ming of Ann Alan
Tigara's King of Arctica
  By Ch. Tigara's Torch of Arctica
  x Totemtok's Tiana of Alaskana
Tote-Um's Littlest Hobo
  By Ch. Kodara El Toro
  x Ch. Tote-Um's Alaskan Parka
Winterhaven's Klondike Klyde
  By Ch. Tigara's Eskimo Eddy of
  Kayuh
  x Jinx of Winterhaven
Akeena of Cedar Trails
  By Ch. Wagner's Scout of Polar Den
  x Lika of Redhorse
Beowulf Thytaen of Sno-Hawk C.D.
  By Ch. Kodara's Nikki of Tote-Um
  x Chitna Katishna of Stor-Rok
Kaigani Bear of Silver Tip
  By Susitka Bear of Silver Tip
  x Noma Chitina of May-Glen
Nordkyn's Tuktuwak of Mazama
  By Wakon's Arctic Bear Du Nordkyn
  x Koller's Melik Du Nordkyn
Panda's Big Shot of Polar Den
  By Ch. Spawn's Hot Shot of Roy-El
  x Ch. Spawn's T'Domar's Panda
T'Domar's Kulak
  By Ch. T'Domar's Voodoo King
  x T'Domar's Taboo
Wind Chime's Velvet Shadow
  By Ch. T'Domar's Genghis Kim
  Shadow
  x Nome's First Frost
Yukon's Silver Hawk
  By Alaskimo of Pine Creek
  x Yukon's Silver Dawn
Glacier's Santa Man
  By Ch. Glaciers' Storm Kloud C.D.
  x Ch. Glacier's Lady of the Arctic
Hombre De La Mancha
  By Ch. Tigara's Torch of Arctica
  x Tigara's Ketchikan Nugget

Ch. Tigara's Whip of Artica, owned by Dorothy Dillingham; Judge
is Robert Salomon.   *Ludwig*

Kamika
By Ch. Pak N Pull's Hyak of Tote-Um
x Wakon's Princess Pat
Roy-El's Black Magic
By Ch. Happy Jack of Roy-El
x Kodara Black Magic of Roy-El
Sno-Tara's Shantar Fox
By Roy-El's Skagway
x Sno-Tara's Blackfoot Arrow
Timberlane's Storm Kloud
By Ch. Glaciers' Burbon King
x Timberlane's Pamiiyok
Totemtok's Tiana of Alaskana
By Alaskana's Toby of Hercules
x Tigara's Kiana Kenai
Karohonta the Apache
By Kodara Kodiak Teddi
x Kodara's Koona Karohonta
Norskogen Sitka of T'Domar
By Ch. T'Domar's Bismarck
x T'Domar's Taboo
Shirley's Morning Venture
Ch. Malesa's Silver Glacier
x Kanangnark's Anna Karenina
Tanya Tiara
By Beowulf Thytaen of Sno-Hawk C.D.
x Sharnak of Oonanik
Whitepaw Ariyek
By Ch. Tigar's Eskimo Eddy of Kayuh
x Wakan of Jo-M

1971
Kanangnark's Panther II
By Kanangnark Panther
x Kanangnark's Misty
Kotzebue Panuck of Chinook
By Sno-Pak Sigdlumala
x Tigara's Tundra Of Arctica
Littlebotu of Marklynne
By Ch. T'Domar's Bismarck
x Ch. Thor-Mark's Athena
Snocre's Kashi
By Ch. Glaciers Burbon King
x Ch. Timberlane's Tuktu of Snocre
Sno-Dance's Czar
By Ch. Voyageur's Cougar
x Ch. Sno-Dance's Tyeen
Sno-Pak Tananna S Mascara
By Ch. Kotzebue's Kuyan of Chinook
x Ch. Sno-Pak Tananna

Von's Kraf Te Miss Mischief
By Ch. Von's Big Bad Bill
x Von's North Ki-Am
Sno-Tara's Arapaho Kiska
By Ch. Spawn's Hot Shot of Roy-El
x Ch. Sno-Tara Keeana of Sno Hill Run
Tote-Um's Snowmiss of Valsun
By Ch. Pak N Pull's Kaltag
x Bearpaw Egavik of Tote-Um
Chigantuan of Little Bo
By Ch. Eldor's Little Bo
x Ch. Chilanko's Tishka Doll
Ford's Artic Pride of Annalan
By Bernie's Mister Fourpaws
x Ford's Ming of Ann Alan
Kazan's Morning Star Shine
By Ch. Malesa's Silver Glacier
x Kanangnark's Anna Karenina
Knottypine Nuewa of Nannuk
By Knotty Pine Artic Ice Man
x Shevalbob's Koteek
Kougarok
By Ch. Kee-Too
x Kee-Nah
Ro-Ala-Ken's Arctic Makoki
By Ro-Ala-Ken's Shadow of Shaluk
x Frostwind's Sparkling Sherry
Snow Plume's Nayani of Sky Fyre
By Kaigani Bear of Silver Tip
x Sky-Fyre's Naya Of Snow Plume
Snowy Peak's Mau Mau Mauler
By Snowy Peak's Kilbuck The Bear
x Snowy Peak's Miss Kipnuk
Snowy Peak's Yukon Bear Bandit
By Snowy Peak's Kilbuck The Bear
x Silver Belle of Washoe Valley
Sikanuk's Skykomish
By Ch. Sabre's Stormy Knight
x Ch. Artic Sukanuk's Tasha
Tigara's Black Baron of Tumleh
By Ch. Tigara's Torch of Arctica
x Tigara's Mariah of Tumleh
Vermars Titanic Tok
By Kiana's Silver Khan
x Ch. Vermars Frosty Kookie
Beowulf's Lynaska Dolly
By Ch. Ninilchik
x Ch. Sena-Lak's Beowulf Tawechi
Bo Doll of Eldor's
Ch. Eldor's Little Bo
x Chilanko's Tishka Doll

Ch. Tigara's Tokiak Chieftain, owner-handler Kathryn Frick.
Judge: Mrs. Lou Richardson. *Ludwig*

Fleur De Lis Hud
By Ch. Zeus of Fleur De Lis
x Fleur De Lis Scheherezade
Jean's Marcho of Land-O-Toba
By Ch. Tigara's Whip of Artica
x Ch. Voyageur's Winged Victory
Klondike of Wilder West
By Ch. Alyeska Su Son
x Akeena of Cedar Trails
Silver Frost Baranof
By Yukon's Stormy Knight
x Kiana Sheri-Grey Mist
Snocre's Scotch On The Rocks
By Ch. Glaciers Burbon King
x Timberlane's Tuktu of Snocre
Sno-Pak Tuktojok
By Kotzebue Panuck of Chinook
x Ch. Sno-Pak Tananna
Sno Tundra of Tun-Yu-Ko
By Silver Muskwa of Tun-Yu-Ko
x Kodaka's Torrey of Wonnuk
Tahkeena's Sitka Tu
By Ch. T'Domar's Juneau
x Sena-Lak's Miluk Tahkeena
Tigara's War Drum of Apple Hill
By Ch. Tigara's Dangerous Dan
McGrew
x Sno-Bear's Amber of Artica
Wynd Chyme's Ikkuma of Igloo
By Ch. Igloo Koyuk of Coldfoot C.D.
x Wind Chime's Velvet Shadow
Wyvern's Anoka
By Ch. Alyseka Su Son
x Ch. Wyvern's Bi Frost of Kiualook
Bar-B-R's Aleutian Calhoun
By Ch. Klahowya Tawia of Tote-Um
x Bar-B-R's Wind of Wineska
Burbon Kotzebue Su of Chinook
By Kotzebue Knik of Chinook
x Kotzebue Muffin of Chinook
Earnscliff Kobuck of Sno Hawk
By Ch. Zorba Of Brigadoon
x Ch. Sno-Hawk's Kodiak Silver
Mist
Far View's Black Glacier
By Ch. Malesa's Silver Glacier
x Moke Teroro Antala
Klahowya Kasaan of Tote-Um
By Pak N Pull's Kaltag
x Ch. Tote-Um's Kooteeyah

Thormark's Silver King of Beis
By Ch. Eldor's Thunder-Puff
x Eldor's Powder-Puff
Tigara's Sunsinger of Artica
By Tigara's Amarok of Arctica
x Tigara's Tsena of Arctica
Coldfoot Ulu
By Coldfoot Minto
x Coldfoot Bi Arctic
Karohonta Voodoo Flame
By Ch. T'Domar's Voodoo King
x Ch. Karohonta Ta-Lo-Wah
Misquah's Migasowin
By Ch. Misquah Hills Shinook
x Kanangnark's Sischu Sitka
Silver Jack of Timberlane
By Ch. Glaciers' Storm Kloud C.D.
x Russell's Yveti Rose C.D.
Squankan's Rustina C.D.
By Ch. Squankan's Moose
x Squankan's Fancy of Double E
Alaskaland's Liger
By Ch. Voyageur's Cougar
x Ch. Tish of Land-O-Toba's Dino
Bar-B-R's Arctic Manook
By Kanangnark's Wildcat
x Rippleridge Tempest Storm
Sena-Lak's Beowulf Thorjhawk
By Ch. Cold Foot Khaibar of Senalak
x Sena-Lak's Kiana's Black Witch
Sindi of Redhorse
By M'London of Redhorse
x Ch. Nanoonah of Redhorse
Arctic Belle of Silver Frost
By Yukon's Stormy Knight
x Silver Frost's Flaming Arrow
Lady Lor-Ren of The North
By Ch. Timshajim's Arctic Knik
x Smokey of North Wind
Sacajawea of North Star
By Oak's Chippawa of North Star
x Wilinda's Black Satin
Saunsoon's Tabul
By Suisun of Redhorse
x Duchess of Petersburgh
Silver Frost Bold Savage
By Yukon's Stormy Knight
x Silver Frost's Flaming Arrow
Sno Paw's Misty Dawn
By Arctic Mist's Ty-On Sabacca
x Ch. Sabre's Misti Dawn of Snopaw

Ch. Talak of Kotzebue, top Best in Show winner in the "70s," shown winning the Group under Mrs. Nicholas Demidoff at Richmond, CA., 1974.   *Bill Francis*

Baronof
By Arctic Mist's Ty-On Sabacca
x Ch. Sabre's Misti Dawn of Snopaw
Chargi's Kiowa of T'Domar
By T'Domar's Khotana
x Ch. T'Domar's Chitina
Double E's Fresca of Koyoda
By Doublee's Koyoda Sigoo
x Ch. Erowah Roxanne
Glaciers Kunu
By Ch. Glaciers' Storm Kloud C.D.
x Rippleridge Black Tempest
Inukunu's Lone Ranger
By Glaciers Soldier of Fortune
x Ch. Glaciers Kunu
Jo-Mar's Northern Belle
By Kovak of Sue-Rons M'Loot
x Stewart's Koda
Northwood's Lord Kipnuk
By Taaralaste Lord Knik
x Eldor's Lea
Orseno' Sno-Fairie of Franbee
By Ch. Malesa's Silver Glacier
x Ch. Kanangnark's Kissima
Sittiak Hipahgo of Jo-Mar
By Tigara's Wolfram of Arctica
x Ch. Sittiak's Chilka of Wolfpack
Snocre's Arctic Flash
By Glaciers Santa Man
x Tigara's Samantha of Snocre
Wyvern's Arctic Vixen
By Ch. Alyeska Su Son
x Wyvern's Bi Frost of Kiualook
Fleur De Lis El Toro
By Ch. Zeus of Fleur De Lis
x Pullara's Pawnee Princess
Frostland's Shot In The Dark
By Ch. Malesa's Silver Glacier
x Kanangnark's Anna Karenina
Kiowa's Comanche Chief
By Ch. Kodara Kodiak of Erowah
x Snow Bear's Royal Beauty
Ku's Yukon Bandit of Cold Brook
By Ch. Kanangnark's Wildcat
x Ch. Ku Ku's Miss Koyia
Princess Of King of The Yukon
By King of The Yukon
x Schmidt's Kim of North Cloud
Silver Frost Senta Marie
By Kanangnark Mischa Tedi Bear
x Silver Frost's Kimluk

Sno Paw's Coco of Arcticpride
By Ch. Glaciers Burbon King
x Ch. Sabre's Misti Dawn of Snopaw
Timberlane's Thunder Kloud
By Ch. Glaciers' Storm Kloud C.D.
x Timberlane's Heidi Jane
Unalik of Redhorse
By M'London of Redhorse
x Ch. Kyana of Kobuk
Artic Dancer
By Cold Brook's Artic Tasso
x Heidi's Princess Misty
Arctic Sky's Black Fury
By Lorri Lanes Midnight Shadow
x Taka of Gary
Coolick's Chinuk
By Ch. T'Domar's Genghis Kim
Shadow C.D.
x Don's Arctic Konuk
Lady Chisana of Burbon
By Burbon's Aristocrat O'Brenmar
x Tonya of High Point
Malagold's Kazan of the North
Ch. Kanangnark Taki
x Malagold's Sable Sitka
Nikkis Wail'n Nanuk of Far View
By Ch. Malesa's Silver Glacier
x Ch. Kanangnark's Kissima
Penguin's Polar Penny
By Ch. Kanangnark's Wildcat
x Lorri Lane's Bright Starlite
Taratu's Artic Star
By Ch. Inuit's Wooly Bully
x Ch. Roy-El's Tara
Sena-Lak's Nyac of Kipnuk
By Ch. Inuit's Wooly Bully
x Sena-Lak's Tanyka
Sno-Hawk's Kodiak Silver Fizz
By Ch. Zorba of Brigadoon
x Ch. Sno-Hawk's Kodiak Silver Mist
Snowpaw's Snoqualmie
By Ch. Glaciers' Burbon King
x Ch. Sabre's Misti Dawn of Snopaw
Sugar River Jackpine
By Kaertok of Cherry Valley
x Misty of Gold Mine Road
Tana-Bek's Natasha
By Ch. Sena-Lak's Thor II
x Tara's Tanya Of Attu

Ch. Baronof. Celeste & Joseph Bouffiou, owners; Billie Lou Robison, handler. Judge: Roy Kibler.

1972

Coldfoot's Chiminuk
By Ch. Shuyak Caro of Cold Foot
C.D.
x Sittiak Ayak of Burnt Paw
Inuit's Nikolai of Colcord
By Ch. Kotzebue Bering of Chinook
x Ch. Balch's Ingrid of Brenmar
Kazan's Kremlin Kylee
By Ch. Malesa's Silver Glacier
x Kanangnark's Anna Karenina
Oak's Kanook of Sno-Fall
By Oomalikbuk of Oak
x Oak's Tuk-Tuk
Silver Sled's Black Buffalo
By Ch. King Nikki of North Wind
C.D.X.
x Silver Sled's Blizzard
Snopaw's Ty-On Togiak
By Arctic Misty's Ty-On Sabacca
x Ch. Sabre's Misti Dawn of Snopaw
Kimsquit of Kwikpak
By Ch. T'Domar's Juneau
x Mucha's Ralla
Laska's Nicki of Lucky Bear
By Sharif Of North Wind
x Laska's Teddy Bear
Misty's Gay Lady
By Chief Michigamme
x Misty Dawn
Nannuk's Thaedra of Skilak
By Ch. Pak N Pull's Eskimo
x Knotty Pine Nuewa of Nannuk
Ot-Key-Luk
By Tote-Um's Alyashak
x Katja
Tigara's Zorena of Teton
By Zorba of Brigadoon
x Tigara's Serena of Artica
Tumleh's Conqueror of Scotmar
By Ch. Tigara's Torch of Arctica
x Tigara's Mariah of Tumleh
Alaskaland's Friendly Grizzly
By Ch. Tigara's Whip of Artica
x Ch. Voyageur's Winged Victory
Borisoff O'Loot
By Silver Tip's Sierra Blizzard
x Nookie O'Loot
Car-Mal Kodiak Kaniq
By Ch. Kodara Kodiak of Erowah
x Frostwinds Teeka of Car-Mal

Chistochina's Oona Poona
By Inuit's Nikolai of Colcord
x Colcord's Chistochina
Frostwinds Teeka of Carmal
By Ch. Kodara's Makushime
x Pak-N-Pull's Sno-Cub
Inuit's Keemak
By Ch. Tigara's Karluk of Roy-El
x Ch. Inuit's Mehitabel
J-Len's Captain Koriak
By Ch. Mars-Artic Dino of T'Domar
x Juneau's Gay Lady
Nanertak Of Pamiiyok
By Ch. Tigara's Karluk of Roy-El
x Roy-El's Black Fury
Oak's Tulukan of Polar Pak
By Ch. T'Domar's Juneau
x Wilinda's Apache Princess
Riciru's Mistress Mary
By Ch. Klahowya Bandit of Tote-Um
x Ch. Sena-Lak's Cheeka of Riciru
River Bend's Belle Star
By Bandit Chief of Nakoo
x Frostwind's Aleutian Mist
Sena-Lak's Brassy Erika
By Sena-Lak's Eric The Red
x Sena-Lak's Ebony Cleopatra
Sno Fall's Imp of Silver Frost
By Silver Frost's Blitz
x Silver Frost's Kimluk
Stormy Jack
By Yukon's Stormy Knight
x Chenik of Silver Frost
Toro's Artic Dust C.D.
By Ch. Kodara El Toro
x Duchess of Nyac C.D.
Tote-Um's Oo-Malik
By Ch. Nikik Du Nordkyn
x Bearpaw Egavik of Tote-Um
Vermars Arclar-Terrific Turk
By Ch. T'Domar's Juneau
x Ch. Lorri Lane's Dark Rhapsody
Viking of Redhorse
By Ch. Suisun of Redhorse
x Ch. Kyana of Kobuk
Wakon's Panada Bear
By Ch. Wakon's Artic Bear Du
Nordkyn
x Wakon's Klatush
Wyvern's Big Smoke
By Ch. Alyeska Su Son
x Ch. Wyvern's Bi Frost of Kiualook

132

Best Brace in Show, Reno, Nev., 1972. Ch. Sena-Lak's Beowulf Thorjhawk (Am. & Can. C.D.) and Ch. Beowulf Tonka. Judge: Charles Kellogg. *Johnnie McMillan*

Yukon's Voodoo Storm of Koyana
  By Yukon's Timber
  x Mars-Artic Noosha of T'Domar
Fleur De Lis Pueblo Chief
  By Ch. Zeus of Fleur De Lis
  x Pullara's Pawnee Princess
Talak of Kotzebue
  By Tigara's Justitia Rebel
  x Tonkia
Eldor's Lea
  By Eldor's Shemya
  x Abbagale of Eldor's
Icefloe's Kishki of Kinouk
  By Ch. Glaciers' Burbon King
  x Ch. Icefloe's North Star
Sena-Lak's Rock of Denali
  By Sena-Lak's Cheeko Chandalar
  x Ch. Sena-Lak's Cheeka Chisana
Silver Frost Forget Me Not
  By Kanangnark's Mischa Tedi Bear
  x Silver Frost Fantasy
Silver Sled's Knik-Knack
  By Ch. King Nikki of North Wind
  C.D.X.
  x Glaciers Tisha Lyng C.D.
Taka of Gary
  By Big Bear of North Wind
  x Neeki of Manitou Farms
Timberlane's The Yankee
  By Ch. Glaciers' Storm Kloud C.D.
  x Cobra of Nipigon
Glaciers Dendee
  By Ch. Sno-Dance's Geronimo
  x Ch. Glacier's Tisha Lyng C.D.
Inuit's Sweet Lucifer
  By Ch. Inuit's Wooly Bully
  x Ch. Voyageur's Elke
N Bar J's Bismarck
  By N Bar J's Geronimo
  x Nordkyn Lightning
Nico Of Glacier Hills
  By Chief Michigamme
  x Ch. Zero
Orseno's Sno-Fresca of Franbee
  By Ch. Malesa's Silver Glacier
  x Ch. Kanangnark's Kissima
Rebel-Den's Silver Boots
  By South-Wind Mars Artic
  x Southern Lady Mars-Artic
Beowulf Tonka
  By Ch. Ninilchik
  x Ch. Sena-Lak's Beowulf Tawechi

Burly King of Fleetwood
  By Ch. Arctic Czar
  x Princes Juneau's Attu
Inuit's Kotzebue Spy
  By Ch. Inuit's Wooly Bully
  x Kotzebue of Chinook
Kiska Carazon
  By Ch. Tigara's Torch of Arctica
  x Tigara's Endora of Artica
Nannuk's Pancho Villa
  By Ch. Pak N Pull's Eskimo
  x Ch. Knotty Pine Nuewa of Nannuk
Sarge's Candy Brute
  By Kanangnark's Happy Fella
  x Jal of Redhorse
Silver Frost's Kimluk
  By Sittiak's Czar of Silver Frost
  x Silver Frost's Ashuya
Sittiak Dakili Nyac
  By Ch. Coldfoot Wolf of Sittiak
  x Tigara's Nitok of Artica
Alcan Applause
  By Silver Frost's Remember Me
  x Misty Dawn
Atkims Miss Holly
  By Land O'Toba's Cupid of Inuit
  x Taratu's Arctic Star
Burbon's Jym Dan Dee
  By Ch. Roy-El's Big Timber
  x Burbon's Cinder
Chief Cearer Bear of Narsuks
  By Ch. Chief of Lake Tomahawk
  x Long-Run Narsuks
Karok-Kusan
  By Kanangnark's Kaltag Kah-Jik
  x Arctic Andolak
La Belle Du Nord C.D.
  By Bruno of Northwind
  x Shaitan's Teri
N Bar J's Snow Princess
  By T'Domar's Kulak
  x Semik
Pak N Pull's Kodiak Attu
  By Ch. Kodara Kodiak of Erowah
  x Ch. Pak N Pull Ice-Floe of Tote-Um
Silver Sled's Nikkitoo
  By Ch. King Nikki of North Wind
  C.D.X.
  x Ch. Glaciers Tisha Lyng C.D.
Sno-Dance's Cheechakos
  By Ch. Voyageur's Cougar
  x Ch. Sno-Dance's Tyeen

134

Ch. Sena-Lak's Rock of Denali. Mrs. Terri Sprague, owner-handling. Judge: Wilfrid E. Shute. *Gilbert*

Timberlane's Kre Muskego
By Ch. Glaciers' Storm Kloud C.D.
x Timberlane's Heidi Jane
Vermars Arclar Kakooshka
By Ch. T'Domar's Juneau
x Ch. Lorri Lane's Dark Rhapsody
Wyvern's Bit-O-Frosty
By Ch. Alyeska Su Son
x Ch. Wyvern's Bi Frost Of Kiualook
Big Paw's Glacier Snow Bear
By Ch. Glacier's Santa Man
x Ch. Pandora of Big Paw
Chechako Bear
By Randybrook's Sinbad
x Silver Kloud of Timberlane
Morgan Gris Loup of Amarok
By Yukon's Panuck of Kinik
x Ro-Ala-Ken's Poona
N-Bar-J's Conquistador
By Ch. T'Domar's Bismarck
x Nordkyn Lightning
Tascha The Howling Wind
By Ch. Chief of Lake Tomahawk
x Sascha
Nordkyn Sheba
By Nikik Du Nordkyn
x Ch. Night Frost's Dark Lady
Sarge's S. Kimo Dolly
By Timberlane's The Yankee
x Sarge's Dixie Contender
Silver Frost Zero's Nanook
By Chief Michigamme
x Ch. Zero
Vermars Arclar Shady Sadie
By Ch. T'Domar's Juneau
x Ch. Sena-Lak's Cheeka of Riciru
Williwaw's Chena
By Klahowya Kasaan of Tote-Um
x Tote-Um's Ketchikan Kiska
Yukon's Pride of Kwasind
By Yukon's Timber
x Yukon's Koya of Arctic Storm
Pandora
By Ch. Kodara's Black Revenge
x Sitka of Northern Star
Sittiak Hoochinoo
By Tigara's Wolfram of Arctica
x Sittiak's Chilka of Wolfpack
Sittiak Kosak Warrior of Mesa
By Tumleh's Conqueror of Scotmar
x Ch. Sittiak Dorka of Kabloona

Sno-Fall's Thor of Silver Frost
By Silver Frost Bold Savage
x Silver Frost Zero's Nanook
Taiga Kim of Pamli Yok
By Roy-El's Handsome Dan
x Roy-El's Black Fury
Uyak Red Rose
By Ch. Karohonta The Apache
x Karohonta Voodoo Fox
Wenaha's Brave
By Tote-Um's Kodiak
x Tote-Um's Silver Selah
Alcan After Dark
By Ch. Silver Frost Bold Savage
x Silver Frost Zero's Papoose
Bar-B-R's Black Elk
By Ch. T'Domar's Juneau
x Ch. Ch. Bar-B-R's Wind of Wineska
Beowulf Keno
By Beowulf's Arctic Nik
x Ch. Beowulf Thaera C.D.
Deepwater of Burbon
By Winterhaven's Black Bandit
x Burbon's Vixen
Glaciers Phoxy of Windcrest
By Snocre's Kimo
x Phantasia of the Icefloe
Icefloe's Cheshire Cat
Ch. Glaciers Burbon King
x Ch. Icefloe's North Star
Kotzebue's Kunek of Seegoo
By Ch. Inuit's Wooly Bully
x Kotzebue of Chinook
Sarge's Merry Eskimo Chief
By Kanangnark's Happy Fella
x Ch. Sindi Of Redhorse
Silver Frost Chief Chinblitz
By Ch. Silver Frost's Blitz
x Silver Frost's Chinga
Sukanuk Su Sitna
By Ch. Sabre's Stormy Knight
x Ch. Artic Sukanuk's Tasha C.D.
Vermars Arclar Defiant Demon
By Ch. T'Domar's Juneau
x Ch. Lorri Lane's Dark Rhapsody
Yukon's Mahlemut Snow Kloud
By Yukon Forty-Ninth State
x Unser Der Kaare
Zardal Faro King
By Ch. Kodara Kodiak Teddi
x Ch. Zardal Cotati

Ch. Dondea's Agamemnon, owned by Donald and Deana Womack, Marietta, Ga.

1973

Frostland's Big Shot
  By Frostland's Shot in the Dark
  x Ch. Fende of the Frostland
Silver Frost Cuyahoga
  By Ch. Silver Frost's Blitz
  x Silver Frost's Kimluk
Stormy Knight's Winsome Witch
  By Ch. Sabre's Stormy Knight
  x Tigara's Dee Dee of Skag-Loo
Gran Chim of Silver Frost
  By Chief Mighigamme
  x Silver Frost's Kimluk
Icefloe's Scarlet O'Hara
  By Ch. Glaciers Santa Man
  x Ch. Icefloe's North Star
Icefloe's Yukon Jake
  By Ch. Glaciers Burbon King
  x Ch. Icefloe's North Star
Inuit's Sitka Bone of Cordova
  By Ch. Tigara's Karluk of Roy-El
  x Ch. Inuit's Mehitabel
Korkees Nikki C
  By Big Paw's Glacier Snow Bear
  x Snowell's Koko-Lik
Silver Sled's Kyna of Nipigon
  By Ch. Kobra of Midnight Storm
  Cloud
  x Silver Sled's Knik-Knack
Snowell's Kobo-Lik
  By Ch. Glaciers Santa Man
  x Ch. Icefloe's North Star
T'Domar's Tabatha Too
  By Ch. T'Domar's Bismarck
  x T'Domar's Taboo
Bandit's Frosty Fang
  By Ch. Chilanko Bandit
  x Snowy Peaks' Mau Mau Maudler
Beechwood's Arctic Knight
  By Mar-Su's Knight of the Glacier
  x Adak Akutan
Boru's Dikagiaktu
  By Boru's Erkloonook
  x Boru's Pipaluk
Cherry Valley Chino
  By Ch. Squankan's Torrid Bow
  x Alma Tonila
Glaciers Laurel of Big Paw
  By Ch. Glaciers' Storm Kloud C.D.
  x Rippleridge Black Tempest

Icefloe's Knave of Hearts
  By Ch. Glaciers Burbon King
  x Ch. Icefloe's North Star
J-Len's Gallopin' Gimlet
  By Ch. T'Domar's Juneau
  x Juneau's Gay Lady
Kianuk's Mukluks Maru
  By Kaigani Bear of Silver Tip
  x Frostwind Kianuk
Rebel-Den's Chena
  By South-Wind Mars Artic
  x Nordkyn Nukola of Rebel-Den
Silver-Sled's Tawa of Nipigon
  By Ch. Kobra of Midnight Storm
  Cloud
  x Silver Sled's Knik-Knack
Sittiak Grand Duke of Arctic
  By Ch. Sittiak Durango
  x Sittiak's Aniuk
Snocre's Mr. Moose
  By Ch. Glaciers' Storm Kloud C.D.
  x Ch. Snocre's Sikku
Tenakee Chief
  By Ch. Knik of Ro-Ala-Ken
  x Ro-Ala-Ken's Ebony Ice of EE
Beowulf Tamira of Belle River
  By Ch. Beowulf Thytaen of Sno-Hawk
  C.D.
  x Amarok's Nuyak
Big Paw's Gypsy Girl
  By Ch. Glacier's Santa Man
  x Ch. Pandora of Big Paw
Kodiak's Etah of Hy-land
  By Ch. Coldfoot Khaibar of Sena-Lak
  x Sena-Lak's Newcah of To-Jan
Sarge's Somethin' Special
  By Timberlane's The Yankee
  x Sarge's Dixie Contender
T'Domar's Shawnee-Bear
  By T'Domar's Bismarck
  x T'Domar's Taboo
Tigara's Prince Igor of Tumleh
  By Ch. Tigara's Torch of Arctica
  x Tigara's Thais of Arctica
Valley View's Tobruk of Oksoah
  By Sena-Lak's Valley View Sno-Wolf
  x Beowulf's Echo of Valley View
Laska Pisano of Sno-Hawk
  By Toros Artic Dust C.D.
  x Ch. Double E's Artic Sno-Mist

Natasha VII
By Klondike Shadow
x Klondike Princess Debbie
Snocre's Sun-King of Midway
By Ch. Glacier's Santa Man
x Tigara's Samantha of Snocre
Snowmass Nikk
By Kanangnark's Dakota Sioux
x Kanangnark's Pussy
Sunshine's Krystal Fantasy
By Ch. Sabre's Arctic Sunshine
x Ch. Sabre's Arctic Sweetheart
Donovic's Chimney Sweep
By Wakon's Black Jack
x Mitzi of Lombard
Eldor's Dude of Ranjan
By Ch. Eldor's Little Bo
x Thor-Mark's Princess
Glaciers' Burbon King
By Ch. Glaciers' Storm Kloud C.D.
x Rippleridge Black Tempest
Kodi North
By Kodiak Sheramae
x Icefloe Kiska Bell
Star of the North
By Oak's Chippewa of North Star
x Kup Kake of North Star
Noatak's Quiet Fury
By Ch. Redhorse Tutiak of Noatak
x Noatak's Namakto
Princess Motonya
By Ch. Muktuk Tillicum of North
Wind C.D.
x Lady Kina of Timberlane
Chenooga of Glacier Isle
By Wood's Artic Prince
x Tara Kassan
Hamilton's Nik-Kenoyuk
By Kanangnark's Happy Fella
x Ch. Sindi of Redhorse
Icefoot Shanwonnick
By Ch. Coldfoot Oonanik
x Ch. Alaskan Norris Star of Kuvak
Kimba Bear of Kodiak
By Dawson Bear of Timberlane
x Chena's Molly of Mal-Bay
Kodiak's Chirikof of Roy-El
By Barcilla's King Kong Kodiak
x Shag's Silver Yukon
Lucky Bear's Koala Bear
By Sharif of North Wind
x Laska's Teddy Bear

Rippleridge Grand Wizard
By Ch. Rippleridge Warlock
x Ch. Rippleridge Yukon Star
Aristeed's Frost Shadow
By Ch. Glaciers' Storm Kloud C.D.
x Remberg's Tahdi of Dachspa
Frosty Jac Snow Devil
By Ch. Silver Frost Bold Savage
x Lady Koshka of Silver Frost
Malesa's Far View Fleet Wing
By Ch. Malesa's Silver Glacier
x Ch. Kanangnark's Kissima
Maluk Of Northern Star C.D.X.
By Ro-Ala-Ken's Shadow Of Shaluk
Northern Light's Dakota Wolf
By Ch. Tinut of Fleur De Lis
x Northern Light's Artic Bear
Oak's Tarrak of Polar Pak
By Oak's Kingittoo Ameroo
x Oak's Tulakan of Polar Pak
Tote-Um's Sno-Star
By Ch. Voyageur's Cougar
x Tote-Um's Tigar Woman
Tsimshian of the Midnight Sun
By King Tobuk of the Arctic Snows
x Sheba Honey Loki of North Wind
Valsun's Gypsy
By Valsun's Chillukki
x Ranjan Cricket
Vermars Captain Midnight
By Ch. T'Domar's Juneau
x Juneau's Gay Lady
Whittwind's Midnight Sun
By Northwest's Ben Bolt
x Vikik Du Nordkyn
Yukon's Timber
By Yukon's Arctic Storm
x Yukon's Queen Sheba
Eskimo Boom Boom The Bandit
Pak N Pull's Eskimo
x Tigara's Shasta of Skag-Loo
Lobito's Cougar Cub
By Ch. Voyageur's Cougar
x Ch. Beowulf's Lynaska
Malesa's Mischief Maker
By Ch. Malesa's Silver Glacier
x Malesa's Miss Mischief
Sitka of the North Wind
By Shaluk's Teddy Bear
x Noh-Chinook of Shaluk

Storm Kloud's Blazing Volcano
  By Ch. Glaciers Santa Man
  x Ch. Timberlane's Pamiiyok
Wardevil of Midnite Sun
  By Rippleridge Warlock
  x Chatanika of Cherry Valley
Yukon King XV
  By Shalgi's Bo Shah-Paja
  x Nan-Nook of Arlington

1974
Eskimo's Charlie Brown
  By Pak N Pull's Eskimo
  x Tigar's Shasta of Skag-Loo
Uyak Buffalo Bill
  By Ch. T'Domar's Kulak
  x Ch. Karohonta Conestoga
Bar-B-R Kahikili
  By Ch. T'Domar's Juneau
  x Ch. Bar-B-R's Wind of Wineska
Cajun Serjeant
  By Ch. Winterhaven's Kotzebue Cajun
  x Delilan of North Wind
Cordova's Tasha
  By Ch. Inuit's Wooly Bully
  x Inuit's Kelly of Cordova
Koyuk Satanic Ebony
  By Zorba of Brigadoon
  x Niccole
Malesa's Dynasty of Lost Creek
  By Ch. Malesa's Silver Glacier
  x Kanangnark's Anna Karenina
Rippleridge Flaming Star
  By Ch. Rippleridge Midnight Fury
  x Rippleridge Star Dust
Sarge's Candy Man of Big Paw
  By Ch. Glaciers Santa Man
  x Tigara's Samantha of Snocre
Snowy Peaks' Kiska Bear Mauler
  By Sierra Kipp Kodara
  x Snowy Peaks' Silver Miss
Timberlane's Good Karma
  By Ch. Glaciers' Storm Kloud C.D.
  x Russell's Yveti Rose
Timberlane Gray Knight
  By Ch. Glaciers' Storm Kloud C.D.
  x Cobra of Nipigon
Wattsapape's Golden Aurora
  By Double E's Artic Skokie
  x Viking's Victorian Lady

Cherako's St. Nick of Big Paw
  By Glacier's Santa Man
  x Mikya's Li'l Pokey
Lobito's Sacha Doll'In
  By Ch. Voyageur's Cougar
  x Ch. Beowulf's Lynaska Dolly
N Bar J's Snow Prince
  By T'Domar's Kulak
  x Senik
Ramu of The North
  By Tigara's Justitia Rebel
  x Tonkia
Sena-Lak's Napakiak of Kodiak
  By Ch. Tana-Bek's M'Lootko of Sena-
  Lak
  x Ch. Sena-Lak's Thora
Silver Jack's Sam of Land-O-Toba II
  By Ch. Silver Jack of Timberlane
  x Ch. Voyageur's Winged Victory
Tigara's Sabrina of Arctica
  By Ch. Tigara's Torch Of Arctica
  x Tigara's Susitna Sue
Sarge's Kippikum of T-Bob
  By Ch. Timberlane's The Yankee
  x Glaciers Phanny Too
Silver Frost Savage's Kingmik
  By Ch. Silver Frost Bold Savage
  x Ch. Silver Frost Zero's Nanook
Timberlane's Kadluk
  By Ch. Mutuk Tillicum of North
  Wind
  x Ch. Bear's Kiska of Timberlane C.D.
Williwaw's Tugidak of Kaiyuh
  By Ch. Snopaw's Snoqualmie
  x Williwaw's Chena
Yumah of Redhorse
  By Ch. Viking of Redhorse
  x Ch. Sindi of Redhorse
Alaskaland Inuit Elke Angel
  By Ch. Inuit's Wooly Bully
  x Ch. Voyageur's Elke
Aleutia's Snowfoot Freak
  By Kiowa's Kodiak King
  x Kiowa's Queen Aleutia
Chief Black Buck of Lost Creek
  By Ch. Silver Shadow of Seldovia
  x Malesa's Miss Mischief
Chilkoot's King Notak of Knik
  By Chilkoot's Black Knight
  x Chilkoot's Tanakee

Lady Luk
By Kiowa's Arcturus of Tikikluk
x Tikikluk's Arctic Sno-Mist
Laska Bandit Queen of Nootka
By Korok's Arctic Kayak
x O'Loot's Neewah of The North
Malesa's Silver Banner
By Ch. Malesa's Silver Glacier
x Malesa's Miss Mischief
Polar-Pak's MS Mitzi
By Oak's Tarrak of Polar-Pak
x Polar-Pak's Hi-Jacked Lady
Sittiak Kayak Of Wynd Chimes
By Tumleh's Conqueror of Scotmar
x Ch. Sittiak Dorka Of Kabloona
Storm Kloud's Dartanya
By Ch. Glaciers' Storm Kloud C.D.
x Ch. Bear's Kiska of Timberlane
Berg Strom's Kuicksilver
By Ch. T'Domar's Juneau
x J-Len's Arctic Pandora
Dondea's Agamemnon
By Timberlane's The Yankee
x Ch. Unalik of Redhorse
Gray Phantom's Northern Star
By Gray Phantom of Inukunu
x Chick A Boom Polar Queen
J-Len's Mighty Morgan McGraw
By Ch. T'Domar's Juneau
x Juneau's Gay Lady
Nightwind's Choya
By Miss Koyia's Bingo Bear
x Nightwind's Tawnya
Sarge's Tsarevich Nikka
By Ch. Timberlane's The Yankee
x Craig's Little Chitina
Silverplume's First Time Out
By Sky Fyre's Mr. Four By Four
x Sky Fyre's Tonya Belle Sno-2
Yukon King's Arctic Prince
By Whispering Pine's Yukon King
x Shinook's Arctic Princess
Chief's Shadow of Snow Star
By Chief Michigamme
x Misty Dawn
Kee Too's Kougarok's Demos
By Ch. Kougarok
x Malesa's Silver Reflection
Lorien's Man O War
By Ch. Glaciers Santa Man
x Glaciers Nikishka of Lorien

Mystery Oaks Witch of Kadluck
By Ch. Valsun's Haida of Amok
x Amok's Anana Belle
Tigara's Centurion of Galaxy
By Tigara's Avenger of Malamor
x Tigara's Athena of Tumleh
Tillicum's Suitisi
By Ch. May-Glen's Shaman
x Chitina's Hush-Pup
Valsun's Haida Of Amok
By Ch. Hercules of Snow Ridge
x Ranjan Cricket
Xeronimo Of Redhorse
By Ch. Suisun of Redhorse
x Ch. Tyanik Thunder of Redhorse
Alcan Bold Venture
By Alcan Avenger
x Ch. Alcan After Dark
Big Paw's Santa Baby
By Ch. Glacier's Santa Man
x Big Paw's Frosty-O
Klondike Miss
By Wakon's Tobuk
x Kaltags Chena
Kotzebue Kanuck of Chinook
By Ch. Kotzebue Panuck of Chinook
x Kotzebue Muffin Chinook
Koyuk's Lady Tania
By Tigara's Far Land Thunder
x Sourdoughs Akie of Tshimsian
N Bar J's Lady Jane of To-Be
By Ch. N-Bar-J's Tundra
x N-Bar-J Sumu Semik
Tascha Tonn of Thunder Kloud
By Ch. Timberlane's Thunder Kloud
x Enok-Echo's Toctoo
Tigara's Areesia Storm
By Ch. Tigara Far Land Thunder
Storm
x Tigara's Noosha of Shadowfax
Tigara's Yuri of Koyuk
By Tigara's Far Land Thunder Gust
x Romany Sous-Pied of Brigadoon
Barik's Niki of Northern Light
By Ch. Timut of Fleur De Lis
x Northern Light's Artic Bear
Boru's Dichoso Tu of T'Jano
By Boru's Erkloonook
x Boru's Pipaluk
H. O. T's Pride of Passover
By Ch. N-Bar-J's Conquistador
x N-Bar-J's Natasha

141

Ch. J'Len's Tribute To Mundy, owned by Joyce Fahlsing; B.J. Orsino, handler; Tom Stevenson, judge; Best of Breed at Chicago, 1975. Multiple Group winner.

Booth

Pem's Shandar of Sitaka
  By Ch. Alaskaland Alta
  x Alaskaland's Pakak of Tundra
Sakima's Taum Sauk
  By Timberland's Kre Muskego
  x Ch. Glaciers' Silver Wampum
Sky Fyre's Hunk of Aniuk
  By Ch. Snow Plume's Nayami of Sky
  Fyre
  x Ch. Warrior's Mist Maid of Sky
  Frye
Sno-Down's Chief Tomahawk
  By Ch. Chief of Lake Tomahawk
  x Orseno's Sno-Down of Franbee
Snokimo's Nakina
  By Ch. Kazan's Kremlin Kylee
  x Aleutia
Timberlane's Tasha
  By Ch. Glaciers' Storm Kloud
  x Timberlane's Heidi Jane
Tote-Um's Kluane of Arkel
  By Tote-Um's Oo-Malik
  x Tote-Um's No-Me
Valley View's Osito
  By Sena-Lak's Valley View Sno-Wolf
  x Beowulf's Echo of Valley View
J'Len's Tribute To Mundy
  By Ch. Vermar's Arclar Terrific Turk
  x Ch. J'Len's Gallopin' Gimlet
Maplewood Storm Kloud
  By Ch. Glaciers' Storm Kloud C.D.
  x Russell's Yveti Rose
Nickie II
  By Shady Rocks Taku
  x Sparkman's Northern Prissy
Tote-Um's Artic Panther
  By Ch. Voyageur's Cougar
  x Tote-Um's Tigar Woman
Alaskaland's American Pie
  By Ch. Inuit's Wooly Bully
  x Ch. Voyageur's Elke
Artic Luv's Tonga Girl
  By Kiowa's Kodiak King
  x Kiowa's Montra
Beechwood's Takutu
  By Mar-Su's Knight of The Glacier
  x Adak Akutan
Cherry's Christmas Knight
  By Ch. Todd
  x Cherry's Black Shadow

Eyak's El-Cid
  By N Bar J's Bismarck
  x N-Bar-J's Goodbye Ruby Tuesday
Frostfield Kemosabe
  By Yukon King's Arctic Prince
  x Chonga's Aleutia
Hokie-Hi's Rusty Bear
  By Ch. Eldor's Smo-Kee Bear
  x Sharavin's Sheeniek
Inuit's Hannah of My-T-Fine
  By Inuit's Sweet Lucifer
  x Inuit's Can-De-Aluet
Kotzebue King Of Chinook
  By Ch. Kotzebue Bering of Chinook
  x Tigara's Tundra of Arctica
Lucky Bear of The Southwind
  By Wakon's Lucky Sea-Bear
  x Laska's Teddy Bear
Malesa's Better Be Best
  By Ch. Malesa's Silver Glacier
  x Kanangnark's Anna Karenina
N Bar J's Ahsatan Coo Coo of Kajo
  By Ch. T'Domar's Kulak
  x T'Domar's Bianca
Piker Flats Evil Roy Slade C.D.
  By Ch. Silver Shadow of Seldovia
  x Malesa's Mischief Maker
Snocre's Kaleb of Sanitas
  By Ch. Glacier's Santa Man
  x Tigara's Samantha of Snocre
Snow Star's Stormy Jack-Son
  By Ch. Stormy Jack
  x Ch. Misty's Gay Lady
Storm Kloud's Fresca of Big Paw
  By Ch. Glaciers' Storm Kloud C.D.
  x Ch. Snow Paw's Coco of Articpride
Tigara Far Land Thunder Storm
  By Ch. Tigara's Whip of Artica
  x Ch. Voyageur's Winged Victory
Tigara's Warfire of Arcola
  By Hombre de la Mancha
  x Tigara's Aurora Borealis
Tolkat of Alcor
  By Tara's Toyan
  x Tiana of The Igloo
Tote-Um's Tongass C.D.X.
  By Ch. Voyageur's Cougar
  x Tote-Um's Tigar Woman

Best Brace in Show, Westminster, 1971; O.C. Harriman, judge. Mrs. Nancy Russell with Ch. Timberlane Storm Kloud (left) and Ch. Glaciers' Storm Kloud, C.D. Show Chairman, Dr. Lyman Fisher is at right. *Shafer*

12

Leading Alaskan Malamute Sires

IN THIS CHAPTER we are listing the twenty greatest sires of the breed together with their champion offspring. Some of those listed are still alive, and the next few years may add both to their luster and to their accomplishments. While these lists adequately attest to the greatness of the dogs and to their influence on the breed one may single out Ch. Toro of Bras Coupe for special mention. He was the first of the great champions and, since he sired 16 champions, it can be said that his influence on the breed has been unparalleled.

Ch. Glaciers' Storm Kloud may also be mentioned. Quite apart from the fact that he has sired twice as many champions as has his nearest competitor, he is also the only one to win an obedience title. An obedience title is not a certain guarantee of character, but it does indicate an all important part of character—trainability.

The list includes only American champions. Some of the sires in this list have produced Canadian champions and some champions in other countries as well. Canadian champions are listed in a separate chapter. Where it may appear in this book, "International Champion" refers to a dog which has won such an official title under the rules of the Federation Cynologique Internationale (F.C.I.), the international governing body of Europe, South America, and Asia.

Four generations of champions at Chicago 1972. Left to right: Ch. Glacier Lady of the Artic; her son, Ch. Glacier's Storm Kloud, C.D.; his son, Ch. Glacier's Burbon King, C.D.; and his son, Am. & Can. Ch. Timberlane's Storm Kloud.

Ch. Tigara's Torch of Arctica, owner-handled by Dorothy Dillingham. Judge is Kenneth Tiffin.   *Ludwig*

Ch. Glaciers' Storm Kloud, C.D.   33

Glacier's Arctic Commando
Chief of Lake Tomahawk
Glacier's Tisha Lyng, C.D.
Glacier's Burbon King
Glacier's First Snowell
Mari-Lee's Glacier Wind
Inuk of Timberlane
Mitka of Timberlane
Rippleridge Timberlane
Rippleridge Lemon Twist
Bear's Kiska of Timberlane
Glacier's Dr. Doolittle
Rippleridge Imp of Lorri Lane
Rippleridge Lemon Drop Kid
Timberlane's Medicine Man
Timberlane's Tuktu of Snocre
Korba of Midnight Storm Kloud

Timberlane's Pamiiyok
Glacier's Santa Man
Silver Jack of Timberlane
Glacier's Kunu
Timberlane's Thunder Kloud
Timberlane's The Yankee
Timberlane's Kre Muskego
Glacier's Laird of Big Paw
Snocre's Mr. Moose
Aristeed's Frost Shadow
Timberlane's Good Karma
Timberlane's Gray Knight
Storm Kloud's Dartanya
Timberlane's Tasha
Maplewood Storm Kloud
Storm Kloud's Fresca of Big Paw

Ch. Toro of Bras Coupe   16

Commanche of Husky-Pak
Cliquot of Husky-Pak
Keowuk of Kobuk
Cheyenne of Husky-Pak
Cherokee of Husky-Pak
Cochise of Husky-Pak
Kim of Sno-Pak
Kelerak of Kobuk

Tigara's Adventuress
Alaskan Kuvak's Nasota
Tigara's Arctic Explorer
Tigara's Arctica Eve
Tigara's Petite Parka
Tigara's Regina Arctica
Tigara's Empress
Thor of Tigara

Ch. Tigara's Torch of Artica   16

Voyageur Cougar
Voyageur's Winged Victory
Tigara's Dangerous Dan McGrew
Voyageur's Witch of the Wind
Phantom of the Icefloe
Tigara's Jinz of Winterhaven
Zorba of Brigadoon
Alaskaland's A Ta

Tigara's King of Arctica
Hombre De La Mancha
Tigara's Black Baron
Tumleh's Conqueror of Scotmar
Kiska Carazon
Tigara's Prince Igor of Tumleh
Tigara's Sabrina of Arctica
Voyageur's Elke

Ch. T'Domar's Juneau   13

Bar-B-R Kahikili
Vermar's Captain Midnight
J-Len's Gallopin Gimlet
Vermar's Arclar Defiant Demon
Bar-B-R's Black Elk
Vermar's Arclar Kakooska
Vermar's Arclar Shady Sadie

Vermar's Arclar Terrific Turk
Oak's Tulukan of Polar Pak
Kimsquit of Kwikpak
Tahkeena's Sitka Tu
Big Storm's Knicksilver
J-Len's Mighty Morgan McGrew

147

Ch. Malesa's Silver Glacier   13

Nikki's Wail'n Nanuk of Far View
Kazan's Kremlin Kylee
Orseno's Sno-Fresca of Franbee
Malesa's Far View Fleet Wing
Malesa's Mischief Maker
Malesa's Dynasty of Lost Creek
Malesa's Silver Banner

Malesa's Better Be Best
Frostland's Shot In The Dark
Orseno's Sno-Fairie of Franbee
Far View's Black Glacier
Kazan's Morning Star Shine
Shirley's Morning Venture

Ch. Glacier's Santa Man   11

Snocre's Kaleb of Sanitas
Lorien's Man O War
Big Paw's Santa Baby
Cherako's St. Nick of Big Paw
Storm Kloud's Blazing Volcano
Snocre's Sun-King of Midway

Big Paw's Gypsy Girl
Snowell's Koko-Lik
Icefloe's Scarlet O'Hara
Big Paw's Glacier Snow Bear
Snocre's Arctic Flash

Ch. Glacier's Burbon King   10

Snocre's Sikku
Timberlane's Storm Kloud
Snocre's Kashi
Snocre's Scotch on the Rocks
Sno Paw's Coco of Arcticpride

Snow Paw's Snoqualmie
Icefloe's Kishki of Kinouk
Icefloe's Cheshire Cat
Icefloe's Yukon Jake
Icefloe's Knave of Hearts

Ch. Kodara Kodiak of Erowah   9

Pak N Pull's Kodiak Attu
Car-Mal Kodiak Kaniq
Kiowa's Commanche Chief
Kodara's Kodiak Teddi
Erowah Roxanne

Pak N Pull Snow Angel
Kodara Makushine
Spring's Kiana Kodara
Erowah Cinnaman

Ch. Apache Chief of Husky-Pak   9

Dakota of Husky-Pak
Drum of Husky-Pak
Durango of Husky-Pak
Husky-Pak Marclar's Sioux
Husky-Pak Erok

Barb-Far Marclar's Machook
Barb-Far Marclar's Mikiuk
Husky-Pak Eagle
Husky-Pak Echako

Husky-Pak Erok   9

Kodara's Yanki Lad
Sno-Crest's Snow Bear
Kodara Kodiak of Erowah
Kodara's Northern Fantasy
Pak N Pull's Mister Blue

Kodara El Toro
Kodara's Royal Reward
Kodara's Black Revenge
Kodara's Ebony Echo

Nahnook II   9

Koyuk of Silver Sled
Kuskokwin Grey Fury
Silver Sled's Beau
Silver Sled's Master Ace
Stormi King of Journey's End

Timber
Koonah of Silver Sled
Parka
Est-El De-Ro-Lo of Silver Sled

Glacier's Burbon King, C.D., Mrs. Lois Almem, owner, Mrs. Denise Kodner, ndler. Winner of two all breed Bests in Show. *Booth*

Ch. Spawn's Hot Shot of Roy-El   8

Inuit's Wooly Bully
Sno-Tara's Keechi of Polar's Den
T'Domar's Tonka Chief
Wagner's Scout of Polar Den

Sno-Tara's Arapaho
Inuit's Mehitabel
Panda's Big Shot of Polar Den
Sno-Tara's Arapaho Kiska
Spawn's T'Domar's Panda

Ch. T'Domar's Bismarck   8

T'Domar's Silver Smoke
Norskogen Sitka of T'Domar
Littlebotu of Marklynne
N-Bar-J's Conquistador

T'Domar's Tabatha Too
T'Domar's Shawnee Bear
T'Domar's Chitina
N-Bar-J's Tundra

Ch. Voyageur's Cougar   8

Tote Um's Tongass C.D.X.
Tote Um's Artic Panther
Lobito's Sacha Doll 'In
Lobito's Cougar Cub

Tote-Um's Sno-Star
Sno-Dance's Cheechako
Alaskaland's Liger
Sno-Dance's Czar

Ch. Eldor's Little Bo   7

Eldor's Botek
Eldor's Cleo
Eldor's Pretty Miss Penny
Eldor's Smo-Kee Bear

Chigantuan of Little Bo
Bo-Doll of Eldor's
Eldor's Dude of Ranjan

Ch. T'Domar's Voodoo King   8

T'Domar's Juneau
T'Domar's Genghiz Kim Shadow
Mars'Artic Dino of T'Domar
T'Domar's Bismarck

Mars-Artic Kamishak
T'Domar's Kulak
Karohonta Voodoo Muskie
Karohonta Voodoo Flame

Ch. Mulphus Brooks The Bear   7

Kobuk's Alaskan Kodiak
Kobuk's Dynamo
Kobuk's May-Glen Achlach
Ambara's Aniu

Ambara's Kanik
May-Glen's Shaman
Penbear's Squeetina

Ch. Kanangnark's Wildcat   7

Fende of Frostland
Bar-B-R's Wind of Wineska
Lorri Lane's Dark Rhapsody
Lorri Lane's Midnight Shadow

Bar-B-R's Artic Kiska
Lorri-Lane's Dark Shadow
Silver Success of Lorri Lane

Ch. Aventurero De Korok   7

Beowulf Thaera
Amorok Anina
Artic Sukanuk's Tasha
Kamik Chiokyrlie of Snow Foot

Snow Foot Toyon
Amarok Kingmik Tarka
Beowulf Thor

Ch. Tigara's Arctic Explorer   6

Tigara's Chisana of Kayuk
Tigara's Torch of Arctica
Tigara's Tyson of Arctica

Tigara's Sadko The Tartar
Tigara's Toro of Arctica
Tigara's Justin Morgan

Ch. Spawn's Hot Shot of Roy-El, owned by Roy &
Elsie Truchon. Judge: Melbourne Downing.

Am. & Can. Ch. Inuit's Wooly Bully. Breeder-owner-handler, Sheila Balch, win
Best of Breed at Trenton in 1971 under judge Mrs. Eva Seeley.   *Gilber*

h. Kiska Carazon, handled by Dorothy Dillingham. Judge is Len Carey. *Missy*

Ch. Malesa's Silver Glacier, owned by Mrs. Brenda (Malesa) Mikel, wins Best ⚹
Breed under Mrs. Helen Wittrig, Mrs. B.J. Orseno, handler. *Robert Holida*

13

Leading Alaskan Malamute Dams

IN THIS CHAPTER we are listing 22 dams, whereas we listed only the top twenty sires. The reason for this is that no less than eight bitches sired four champions, and we felt that we could not fail to give recognition to all of them. As in the case of the sires, some were the dams of Canadian champions, and their names may appear in Canadian lists.

Nine of these great producers were not champions, whereas all of the leading sires were American champions. This is hardly surprising since some become brood matrons as soon as they reach maturity, and do not appear in the show ring. Some may still make higher rankings and others may enter with number four in 1975 or even later. We have omitted the "Ch." before the names of the offspring, since all are champions.

Russell's Yveti Rose   9

(Including one American and Canadian champion, but not including Mexican Ch. Timberlane's Misty Rainbow, CD., PC., and Storm Kloud's Kiss Me Again which finished after a cut off date had been set for the charts.)

Mitka of Timberlane
Mari-Lee's Glacier Wind
Inuk of Timberlane
Timberlane's Pamiiyok
Bear's Kiska of Timberlane

Silver Jack of Timberlane
Can. Ch. Timberlane's Good Karma
Maplewood Storm Kloud
Timberlane's Kamchatka

Kobuk's Dark Beauty   9

Kodara's Yanki Lad
Kodara's Northern Fantasy
Kodara El Toro
Kodara Dark Angel
Kodara's Black Revenge

Kodara's Ebony Echo
Pak N Pull Snow Angel
Sno-Crest's Mukluk
Kodata Kodiak of Erowah

Ch. Dorry's Sitka of North Wind   8

Tigara's Karluk of Roy-El
Boot Hill Bandit of North Wind
Kit Fox II of North Wind
Shatoolik of North Wind

Kanangnark Nertuark Lobo C.D.
Kanangnark Kenai Kita C.D.
Kanangnark Wildcat
King Nikki of North Wind

Ch. Kiana of Klondike   7

Sena-Lak's Arctic Silver
Sena-Lak's Arctic Flash
Sena-Lak's Laskana
Aurora of Sena-Lak

Sena-Lak's Miss Tardy
Sena-Lak's Kiana's Black Witch
Sena-Lak's Lady Kokogiak

Sno-Pak Kavick's Oonalik   7

Tigara's Empress
Tigara's Dortic Shag Luck
Tigara's Arctic Explorer
Tigara's Adventuress

Tigara's Petite Parka
Tigara's Dortic Khan
Tigara's Dortic Sitka

Ch. Glacier's Tisha Lyng C.D.   7

Glacier's Silver Wampum
Malesa's Silver Glacier
Glacier's Million Dollar Baby
Timberlane's Glacier Penny

Silver Sled's Knik-Knack
Glacier's Dendee
Silver Sled's Nikkitoo

Kotzebue Pandora of Chinook II, owned by Kioona Kennels, is a present day contender.   *Gilbert*

Greatest brood bitch of all time is shown with owner Nancy Russell—Ch. Russell's Yveti Rose, C.D.

Ch. Tigara's Artica Eve shown with owner, Dorothy Dillingham.   *Ludwig*

Ch. Snow Foot Mushy   7

Snow Foot Toyon
Kamik Chiokyrlie of Snow Foot
Artic Sukanuk's Tasha
Amarok Anina

Amarok Kingmik Taska
Beowulf Thaera C.D.
Beowulf Thor

Kanangnark's Anna Karenina   6

Frostland's Shot in the Dark
Kazan's Morning Star
Shirley's Morning Venture

Kazan's Kremlin Kylee
Malesa's Dynasty of Lost Creek
Malesa's Better Be Best

Ch. Sno-Pak Nashoba   5

Marauder of Brenmar
Balch's Ingrid of Brenmar
Arctic Wolf of Brenmar

Kalyuh's Attu
Tigara's Artica Eve

Ch. Sena-Lak's Thora   5

Sena-Lak's Napakiak Of Kodiak
Snocre's Arctic Flash
Sena-Lak's Purgha

Sena-Lak's Sabre of Dee-Lac
Sena-Lak's Simka

Rippleridge Black Tempest   5

Glacier's Dr. Doolittle
Rippleridge Imp of Lorri Lane

Rippleridge Lemon Drop Kid
Glacier's First Snowell

Ch. Arctic Storm of Husky-Pak   5

Commanche of Husky-Pak
Cliquot of Husky-Pak
Cheyenne of Husky-Pak

Cherokee of Husky-Pak
Cochise of Husky-Pak

Ch. Erowah Roxanne   5

Double E's Artic Sno-Mist
Double E's Tannu of Ker-Lyn-Da
Kodara's Buster of Double E

Double E's Koko of Kar-Lyn-Da
Double E's Fresca of Koyoda

Timberlane's Heidi Jane 5

Timberlane's Tasha
Timberlane's Kre Muskego
Timberlane's Medicine Man

Timberlane's Thunder Kloud
Timberlane's Tuktu of Snocre

Ch. Tuyah of Silver Sled 4

Timbertrail Cheechako
Parka

Stor-Mi-King of Journey's End
Timber

Chilanko's Tiska Doll 4

Alyeska's Mobee Of The Sno
Kewpi Doll of Jo-An

Chigantuan of Little Bo
Bo Doll of Eldor's

Ch. Voyageur's Winged Victory 4

Tigara Far Land Thunder Storm
Silver Jack's Sam of Land O'Toba

Alaskaland's Friendly Grizzly
Jean's Marcho of Land O'Toba

Polar Candy Baar 4

Orseno's Sno-Raider of Franbee
Lorri Lane's Ebony Knight

Orseno's Sno-Pixie of Franbee
Lorri Lane Misty of Windy Hill

Sabre's Misty Dawn of Snopaw 4

Sno Paw's Misty Dawn
Baranof

Snopaw's Snoqualmie
Snopaw's Panda of Arctic Mist

Helen of Bras Coupe 4

Kekolik of Kobuk
Keowik of Kobuk

Kelerak of Kobuk
Alaskan Kuvak's Nasota

Ch. Alaskan Star of Roy-El 4

Karel's Alberta
Karel's Alinaluk

Karel's Ahteetah
Karel's Bluff

Ch. Kanangnark's Kissima 4

Malesa's Far View Fleet Wing
Orseno's Sno-Fresca of Franbee

Orseno's Sno-Fairie of Franbee
Nikki's Wail'n Nanuk of Far View

h. Glacier's Tisha Lyng, C.D., owner-handler, Mrs. Lois Olmem.   *E.H. Frank*

Ch. Tote-Ums Sno Star, owned and handled by Jeri Russell, was top winning bit
for 1974 in Alaskan Malamute Club of America records. *Boo*

Vallee Novarro's Ch. Pak N Pull Snow Angel of Vallee
is shown with judge Vincent Perry. *Bennett*

Can. Ch. Lorn-Hall's Oogorook M'Loot, first Canadian champion, first white Canadian or American champion, shown with an Indian princess at the Honey Harbour Winter Carnival.

14

Alaskan Malamutes in Canada

EARLIER in this book, we have pointed out that the fame of the dogs bred by the Malamute people had spread across Canada. Since the Malamute dogs were large, around 80 pounds, and were famous for their great pulling strength, it came about that any large sled dog might be called a Malamute. Often local names were attached. Thus, in an area along the MacKenzie River there were large freighting dogs which were called MacKenzie River Malamutes, or sometimes MacKenzie River Huskies. In 1925, Freeman Lloyd wrote in the *American Kennel Gazette* that James River Malamutes were being crossed with German Shepherds to give them greater pulling strength. This experiment apparently failed.

The concept of a purebred race of large freighting dogs did not develop until about 1928. Earl and Natalie Norris, Alaskan breed pioneers who are still active, once told one of these writers: "The Alaskan Malamute breed developed 'outside' that is, in the United States."

It was the gathering together of the dogs for the first Byrd Antarctic Expedition at Wonalancet, N.H., in the kennels of Arthur Walden which started it all. There Milton and Eva Seeley first saw Rowdy of Nome. And it was shortly after that they got Yukon Jad from Leonhard Seppala. Walden had a bitch of similar type, Holly, and the Seeleys were on their way.

The world-wide publicity given to the Byrd Expeditions created interest elsewhere, and other people began to collect dogs which they felt to be of Alaskan Malamute type. Capt. Alan Innes-Taylor, in charge of the 157 dogs on the second Byrd expedition, called them "Yukon Malamutes," but the best of them had come from the Seeleys. One area which developed a large concentration of the dogs was Wisconsin.

The real thrust to promote the breed was delayed for a long time. First, many of the best of the Seeley dogs went to the Antarctic, never to return. Some were killed in accidents. Others were deserted as the explorers scrambled to get safely out of the breaking ice. Another Seeley team was lost in training for World War II, and it was that war which truly held back the development of the breed.

Alaskan Malamute history in Canada begins with Lorna Jackson who lived in lower Ontario in the Toronto area. Mrs. Jackson became a professional handler, did a variety of dog training, and has remained to this day a prominent professional.

Gripp of Yukon was the first Alaskan Malamute to be registered in the United States, July 1, 1935, by the Seeleys. Lorna Jackson's first dog was Lorn-Hall Klondyke M'Loot. He was bred in the United States by Paul Voelker, whelped Jan. 1, 1947 and registered in the 1950–1951 stud book. In those days, Cánadian Kennel Club registrations were made through the Canadian National Livestock Records.

The dog was by Mikiuk, a son of Tobuk out of Vixen M'Loot. Mikiuk was a well known stud dog in his own country. Mrs. Jackson also imported Lorn-Hall Oogorook M'Loot, another Voelker-bred dog, whelped July 27, 1945, by Gentleman Jim out of Noma M'Loot.

Mrs. Jackson then imported Lorn-Hill Oogorook M'Loot. He was a son of Gentleman Jim, a son of Dude's Wolf. His dam was Noma M'Loot, a daughter of Silver King. Lorn-Hall Oogorook M'Loot was whelped July 27, 1945. He, too, was registered in the Canadian Kennel Club stud book of 1950–51.

Lorn-Hall Oogorook M'Loot was the first Alaskan Malamute to win a championship in Canada. He was the first white champion, and indeed one of the very few whites ever to win a championship. He weighed 80 pounds and was 24½ inches tall at the shoulder.

The dog made history in another way. He had been police trained, and when Toronto suffered a disastrous hurricane, Lorn-Hall Oogorook M'Loot was used to locate trapped and injured people in the wreckage of homes and buildings. He was also used to locate the bodies of those who did not survive.

His champions under the Lorn-Hall prefix were Lorn-Hall's Nordic and Lorn-Hall's Yu-Kon. The latter sired Ch. Lorn-Hall's Nootka.

The most famous of all Alaskan Malamute Kennels in Canada is that of Dr. T.K.R. Bourns of Lambeth, Ontario. As of Jan. 1, 1975 there were 19 Canadian champions carrying Dr. Bourns' Boru prefix. Ch. Boru's Guy sired five champions, and Boru's Chilcootin Cub, a nonchampion,

Can. Ch. Lorn-Hall's Yukon, owned by Lorna Jackson, Canadian breeder and professional handler.

four. Boru's Elaitutna, leads all Canadian bitches as the dam of five champions. In addition, Dr. Bourns has been a North American leader in the fight to stamp out dwarfism and the Malamute eye syndrome. He is also chairman of the breed standard committee of the Alaskan Malamute Club of America.

We asked Mrs. Mary Ann Breen of Winnipeg, Manitoba, to write a short history of the Alaskan Malamute Club of Canada. What follows is what she has written. In addition, Mrs. Breen was of invaluable aid in compiling the list of Canadian champions and their sires and dams. The names of each dog's sire and dam are indented below its name.

"The Alaskan Malamute Club of Canada was formed in late 1973. At its inception, membership numbered approximately 12 (individuals and families). In just over one year of existence, this club has attracted more than 50 members from all parts of Canada and the U.S.

"The basic aims and purposes of the club are to educate both its members and the general public regarding the breed in general and to encourage the breeding of genetically clear stock. To this end, a bi-monthly Newsletter is published containing news from all parts of the country, as well as articles on harness training, obedience, breeding, ethics, and other matters.

"The officers of the club for 1975 consist of: president: Mrs. Mary Ann Breen, Winnipeg, Manitoba; vice president: Mrs. Joan White, Whitehorse, Yukon Territory; area representatives: Peg Martin, Manuels, Newfoundland (Maritime provinces); Nancy Windover, Gormley, Ont. (Mid-East); Joan Hodgson, Dugald, Man. (Mid-West); Trudy Born, Spruce Grove, Alberta (Rocky Mountain); Marge Wright, Vancouver, B.C. (Pacific); Joan White, Whitehorse, Yukon Territory (Far North).

"The secretary-treasurer had not been selected at the time of writing, but inquiries can be directed to Mrs. Mary Ann Breen, 78 Willow Point Rd., Winnipeg, Manitoba, R2J 2Y3.

"The club is proud to state that it gave its first booster show in May, 1975, and expects that this will evolve into a national specialty in 1976."

In the following list, the Canadian champions are given in alphabetical order. Since all are Canadian champions, we have omitted both Canadian and Champion before their names. However, some dogs are also American champions, and in such cases "A.Ch." appears before their names. "Int. Ch." means that the dog has won an international championship under the rules of the F.C.I.—Federation Cynologique Internationale—which governs shows in most of Europe and in many countries of Latin America.

In addition, obedience titles have been given following the names of the dogs. It is our hope that we have avoided any errors or omissions. But in lists such as this one, errors are almost certain to occur. If so, we apologize in advance. Sires and dams, if Canadian or American champions, have been so listed.

CANADIAN CHAMPIONS

Alcan Carousel of Winnda
  C.Ch. Alcan Avenger
  C.Ch. Alcan After Dark
Alcan After Dark
  A.Ch. Silver Frost Bold Savage
  Silver Frost Zero Papoose
Alcan Avenger
  A.C.Ch. Silver Frost Remember Me
  Misty Dawn
Alcan Remembered In Red
  A.C.Ch. Silver Frost Remember Me
  C.Ch. Silver Frost Forget Me Not
Ambara's Inukpasuk of Boru
  A.Ch. Mulphus Brooks The Bear
  Preston's Chechako
Bearpaw Caribou
  A.C.Ch. Kodara El Toro
  Bearpaw Kiska of Kyoda C.D.
Bearpaw Chico
  A.C.Ch. Kodara El Toro
  Bearpaw Kiska of Kyoda C.D.
A.Ch. Bearpaw Elk Of Tote-Um
  A.C.Ch. Kodara El Toro
  Siska of Erowah
A.Ch. Bearpaw Geena
  C.Ch. Erowah Cinnamon C.D.
  Siska of Erowah
Bearpaw Hinook
  C.Ch. Erowah Cinnamon C.D.
  Bearpaw Eska
Bearpaw Kakumee
  Bearpaw Gaucho
  Kniko's Polar Princess
Bearpaw Lobo Son of Elk
  A.C.Ch. Bearpaw Elk of Tote-Um
  C.Ch. Bearpaw Geena
Beowulf Tassajara Bear
  A.Ch. Ninilchik
  A.Ch. Sena-Lak's Beowulf's Tawechi
Int.Ch. Beowulf Thosca of Snofoot
C.D.X.
  A.Ch. Aventurero de Korok
  A.Ch. Snow Foot Mushy
A.Ch. Bernard
  A.C.Ch. Inuit's Wooly Bully
  Kotzebue of Chinook
A.Ch. Bo Bo Bojangles
  Silver Frost Tarak
  A.Ch. Tanya Tiara

A.Ch. Bo Doll of Eldors
  A.Ch. Eldor's Little Bo
  Chilanko's Tishka Doll
Boru's Debistu of Misquah
  C.Ch. Boru's Erkloonook
  C.Ch. Boru's Pipaluk
Boru's Erkloonook
  A.Ch. Shuyak Caro of Coldfoot C.D.
  Silver Saga's Willawa
Boru's Eevoodloo
  A.Ch. Shuyak Caro of Coldfoot C.D.
  Silver Saga's Willawa
Boru's Famous Lady
  Boru's Chilcootin Cub
  Boru's Elaitutna
Boru's Flambeau
  Boru's Chilcootin Cub
  Boru's Elaitutna
Boru's Fleche
  Boru's Chilcootin Cub
  Boru's Elaitutna
Boru's Flint
  Boru's Chilcootin Cub
  Boru's Elaitutna
Boru's Guy C.D.
  C.Ch. Boru's Erkloonook
  Boru's Eevoodloo
Boru's Imenak
  C.Ch. Boru's Guy C.D.
  Boru's Elft
Boru's Inuk
  C.Ch. Boru's Guy C.D.
  Boru's Elft
Boru's Iyorama
  C.Ch. Boru's Guy C.D.
  Boru's Elft
Boru's Koojakaloo
  C.Ch. Timber Trail Wupee
  Boru's Elaitutna
Boru's Pameeolik O'Stormcrest
  C.Ch. Boru's Guy C.D.
  C.Ch. Boru's Fleche
Boru's Pipaluk
  C.Ch. Boru's Guy C.D.
  C.Ch. Boru's Fleche
Boru's Qayaq
  C.Ch. Boru's Inuk
  Boru's Elft

Can. Ch. Boru's Erkloonook, first Alaskan Malamute to win a Best in Show in Canada (and third in North America). Lorna Jackson, owner-handler. Judge, Pete Smith. *Beaulieu*

an. Ch. Boru's Guy, C.D., Best in Show at St. Catherine's, Ont. April 1968. Owner
r. T.K.R. Bourns, handling; Judge: Peter Smith.

Boru's Quidunc
  C.Ch. Boru's Inuk
  Boru's Elft
Boru's Yonder
  C.Ch. Boru's Erkloonook
  C.Ch. Boru's Koojakaloo
Boru's Xkimo C.D.
  C.Ch. Kelso's Anouk
  C.Ch. Boru's Eevoodloo
Boru's Zirconita
  C.Ch. Kelso's Anouk
  C.Ch. Boru's Pipaluk
Captain Whiskey (shown as C. Midnight)
  Netcha
  Keewatin's Lady Chinook
A.Ch. Chechako Bear
  Randybrook's Sinbad
  Silver Cloud of Timberlane
Chief Black Buck of Lost Creek
  Silver Shadow of Seldovia
  Malessa's Miss Mischief
A.Ch. Chief Caesar Bear of Narsuks
  Chief of Lake Tomahawk
  Log Run Narsuks
A. & Int.Ch. Coldfoot Oonanik U.D.T.
  A.Ch. Coldfoot Lucky Strike Mine
  Coldfoot Kareok
Empers Neeka
  Sascha III
  Keskanow
Eskimbo's Akoda Bear
  Mark's Kiev
  C.Ch. Roesta's Chilakoot Kimba C.D.
Flame of Roy-El
  Erik of Roy-El
  Marclar's Una
A. & Int.Ch. Glaciers Storm Kloud C.D.
  Kadluk of Northwind
  A.Ch. Glacier Lady of the Arctic
Hiebert's Carlo of Dishelda
  Nor-Lan's Loper Fyn
  Nor-Lan's Mite
Heidi of Wobiska
  Arcturus Chief
  Kandic of Camel's Hump
Herb's Trojan
  Arcturus Chief
  Kandic of Camel's Hump
Husky-Pak Forecast by Cliquot C.D.
  A.Ch. Cliquot of Husky-Pak
  Deeka of Husky-Pak

A.Ch. Igloo Koyok of Coldfoot C.D.
  A.Ch. Shuyak Caro of Coldfoot C.D.
  Skeba
A.Ch. Inuit's Wooly Bully
  A.Ch. Spawn's Hot Shot of Roy-El
  Balch's Ingrid of Brenmar
Kanalaskon's Dixie's Toklat
  C.Ch. Kotka's Kainai Chief
  Wilinda's Dixie
Kanoka Mist Princess
  A.Ch. Ro-Ala-Ken's Arctic Makoki
  Tawny Sue
Kelso's Anouk
  C.Ch. Boru's Flint
  Boru's Illkalu
Kiche's Bright Victory
  C.Ch. Alcan Avenger
  Kiche's A-Koobloo
Kiche's Thanks For the Memory
  C.Ch. Silver Frost Remember Me
  Kiche's A-Koobloo
C.Ch. Kiche's Mr. Lucky
  C.Ch. Alcan Avenger
  Kiche's A-Koobloo
Kiche's Past Is Prologue
  C.Ch. Silver Frost Remember Me
  Kiche's A-Koobloo
A.Ch. Kipnuk of Northeast
  Sena-Lak's Nyak of Kipnuk
  Scher's Nicola of Northeast
A. Ch. Klondike Ike
  A.Ch. Barb-Far Marclar's Mikiuk
  Vixen of Silver Sled
Klondike's Tip O'Silver
  A.Ch. Mulphus Brooks The Bear
  A.Ch. Parka
Kniko's Polar Princess
  C.Ch. Bearpaw's Chico
  Kniki of Polar's Wilderness
A.Ch. Kodara El Toro
  A.Ch. Husky-Pak Erok
  Kobuk's Dark Beauty
Kotka's Anastasia
  Egakrik of Clebar
  Highnoon's Blackfoot
Kotka's Kanai Chief
  Egakrik of Clebar
  Highnoon's Blackfoot
Kuni
  Boru's Quinapalus
  Mitielista of Polar Den

h. Yukon's Pride of Kwasind, shown going Best of Breed under Mrs. Jean Fletcher
t St. Catherine's, Ont, owner-handler Robert Dearbaugh *Weston*

A.Ch. La Belle du Nord C.D.
  Bruno of Northwind
  Shaitan Teri
Laska VI
  Lash of the Land of Legend
  Midnight's Arctic Velvet
Lorn Hall's Nootka
  C.Ch. Lorn Hall's Yu-Kon
  Lorn Hall's Tonto M'Loot
Lorn Hall's Nordic
  C.Ch. Lorn Hall Oogorook M'Loot
  Lorn-Hall's Tonto M'Loot
Lorn Hall Oogorook M'Loot
  Gentleman Jim
  Noma M'Loot
Lorn Hall's Yu-Kon
  Lorn Hall Oogorook M'Loot
  Lorn Hall's Tonto M'Loot
Mala-Nor's Nordic Joy
  C.Ch. Lorn-Hall's Nordic
  Kobuk's Manassas Silver
Mark's Kiev
  C.Ch. Wilinda's Apache Chief
  C.Ch. Kotka's Anastasia
Miss Amaryllis
  Kobuk's Manassas Ambition
  C.Ch. Ambara's Kanik
A.Ch. Misquah Hills Migasowin
  A. & C.Ch. Misquah Hills Chinook
  Kanangnark's Sischu Sitka
A.Ch. Misquah Hills Chinook
  Bardoublee Little Cayouse
  Bearpaw Ersulik
Naksla's Kiana
  Egakrik of Clebar
  Destiny Angel
Naksla's Lobo
  Egakrik of Clebar
  Destiny Angel
Naksha's Shangril's Black Monk
  Egakrik of Clebar
  C.Ch. Teaky
A.Ch. N Bar J's Tundra
  A.Ch. T'Domar's Bismarck
  Nordkyn Lightning
Nanook's Satan of Mar-Venus
  A.Ch. Tigara's Torch of Artica
  Thunder Naook of Mar-Venus
Nekanesu's Jai of White Knight
  C.Ch. Wobiska's Teddy of Nekanesu
  Sila Ken Nifka of Nekanesu

Nekanesu's Nalaka
  C.Ch. Wobiska's Teddy of Nekanesu
  Sila Ken Nifka of Nekanesu
A.Ch. Nikik du Nordkyn
  Skol du Nordkyn
  Koller's Sisak du Nordkyn
A.Ch. Northwood's Lord Kipnuk
  Taaralaste Lord Knik
  A.Ch. Eldor's Lea
Nordic Kikki
  Zardal Frostwin Yukon
  Sugarbush Nooka
Oak's Kanuyak Kakka of Wilinda
  Oomalikbuk of Oak
  Oak's Kitchee
Oak's Kudlooktoo
  Oomalikbuk of Oak
  Oak's Tuktuk
Oak's Looshoo of Wilinda C.D.
  Oomalikbuk of Oak
  Wilinda's Apache Silver Bear
Oak's Otonabee of Wilinda
  Oomalikbuk of Oak
  Duchess of Sharlee
Oak's Tarak of Polar Pak
  Oak's Kingitoq Ameroo
  C.Ch. Oak's Tulaken of Polar Pak
Oak's Tulakan of Polar Pak
  A.Ch. T'Domar's Juneau
  Wilinda's Apache Princess
Packdog's Arctic Frost
  Bearpaw Coyote C.D.
  Coru's Je M'Appelle Kanik
A.Ch. Pak N Pull's Eskimo
  A.Ch. Kodara's Yanki Lad
  Pak N Pull's Arlook
Ridgedown's Kluskus
  A. & C.Ch. Rippleridge Sundance
  Rippleridge Black Tempest
A.Ch. Rippleridge Sundance
  A.Ch. Mohawk II of Northwind
  Komoka Fury of Northwind
Roesta's Chilakoot Kimba
  Double E's Keno
  Ekaluk's Dark Beauty
Sena-Lak's Sabre of De Jac
  C.Ch. Tana-Bek's M'Lootko of Sena-Lak
  A.Ch. Sena-Lak's Thora
Shaman
  Tote-Um's Tahkinni
  C.Ch. Bearpaw Kakumee

174

Can. Ch. Oak's Otonabee of Wilinda, owned by Anita Murphy, Wilinda Kennels, Watford, Ont.

Hodges & Associates

Sila's Iliapak
  C.Ch. Timber Trail Wupee
  C.Ch. Boru's Quidunc
A.Ch. Silver Frost Forget Me Not
  Kanangnark's Mischa
  Silver Frost Fantasy
A.Ch. Silver Frost Remember Me
  A.Ch. Silver Frost Blitz
  A.Ch. Silver Frost Kimluk
Silversheen's Chinook
  Arctic Wild's Silver Chief
  C.Ch. Valsun's Frosty Fox
Silversheen's Meno
  Arctic Wild's Silver Chief
  C.Ch. Valsun's Frosty Fox
A.Ch. Sittiak Dorka of Kabloona
  A.Ch. Coldfoot Wolf of Sittiak
  Tigara's Nitok of Arctica
Sittiak Durango
  A.Ch. Coldfoot Wolf of Sittiak
  Tigara's Nitok of Arctica
Skagway's Ebony Baron
  C.Ch. Wobiska's Teddy of Nekanesu
  Kiska of Skagway
Skagway's Natasha of Snow Foot
  Nor-Lan's Swagman
  Kiska of Skagway
Skagway's Snow Beau
  C.Ch. Oak's Kanuyak Kakka of
  Wilinda
  Skagway's Hi Ho Silver
Skagway's Spades Are Trump
  Wobiska's Tika Rudolph
  Arctic Wild's Alaska Star
A.Ch. Sno Fall's Thor of Silver Frost
  A.Ch. Silver Frost Bold Savage
  Silver Frost Zero's Naook
Sno Hawk's Arctic Red of Beowulf
  A.Ch. Beowulf Thytaen of Sno Hawk
  C.D.
  Snow Queen of Sitka
Snow Hawk's Kodiac Silver Mist
  A.Ch. Star Rok's Kodiac Silver Chief
  Double E's Arctic Snow Mist
A.Ch. Stormy Jack
  Yukon Stormy Knight
  Chenik of Silver Frost
Taaralaste Taku Taiga Amajak
  Taaralaste Copper Karu
  Taarlaste Naki Neiu

Tanya Tiara
  A.Ch. Beowulf Thytaen of Sno Hawk
  C.D.
  Queen Sharnal of Oonanik
Tarbo's Bobcat
  C.Ch. Chief of Lake Tomahawk
  Sascha
Teaky
  C.Ch. Wilinda's Apache Chief
  C.Ch. Kotka's Anastasia
Timberlane's Czar of the North
  A. & Int. & C.Ch. Glaciers Storm
  Kloud C.D.
  A.Ch. Timberlane's Glacier Penny
A.Ch. Timberlane's Good Kama
  A. & Int. & C.Ch. Glaciers Storm
  Kloud C.D.
  Russell's Yveti Rose C.D.
A.Ch. Timberlane's Storm Kloud
  A.Ch. Glacier's Burbon King
  A.Ch. Timberlane's Pamiiyok
A.Ch. Timberlane's The Yankee
  A. & Int. & C.Ch. Glaciers Storm
  Kloud C.D.
  Cobra of Nipigon
Timber Trail Wupee
  Timber Trail Kenai
  Musher Lane Sitka
A.Ch. Timshajim's Arctic Knik
  Mars Arctic Rowdy
  Timick of Kodiak Mamotic
Toro By Choice
  C.Ch. Kotka's Kenai Chief
  Wilinda's Dixie
Tote-Um's Kleana Kleene
  A.Ch. Voyageur's Cougar
  Tote-Um's Tigar Woman
A.Ch. Tote-Um's Kluane of Arkel
  A. & C.Ch. Tote-Um's Oo-Malik
  Tote-Um's No Me
A.Ch. Tote-Um's Kooteyah
  A. & C.Ch. Kodara El Toro
  Erowah Mountain Mist
A.Ch. Tote-Ums' Oo-Malik
  A. & C.Ch. Nikik du Nordkyn
  Bearpaw Egavik of Nordkyn
A.Ch. Tote-Um's Shawna Tu
  A.Ch. Erowah Cinnamon C.D.
  Siska of Erowah
Turner Tuk Tuk
  C.Ch. Wilinda's Apache Chief
  C.Ch. Kotka's Anastasia

176

Can. Ch. Skagway's Ebony Baron, owned by Tuglu Kennels, Winnipeg, is also a noted freighter and pleasure team dog. Judge is Irene Bourassa.

Can. Ch. Taaralaste Taku Taiga Amajak, owned by Peggy MacDonald, BIS, Yukon K.C., 1973.

Am. & Can. Ch. Tote-Um's Kluane of Arkel, first bitch to win a U.S. Group first. A team leader owned by Joan & Ken White, Whitehorse, Yukon Territory.

Valsun's Frosty Fox
  Valsun's Chillukki
  A.Ch. Tote-Um's Snowmiss of Valsun
Wakon's Cascadia
  Wakon's Grizzly Bear
  Wakon's Impuchuk
Wakon's Stormy Daye
  Oak's Kootznahoo
  Wakon's Nuvak
Wenaha's Brave
  Tote-Um's Kodiak
  Tote-Um's Silver Selah
White Knight's Andre
  C.Ch. Wobiska's Teddy of Nekanesu
  Stormcrest Cattoo
White Knight's Chela
  C.Ch. Wobiska's Teddy of Nekanesu
  Stormcrest Cattoo
White Knight's Ochre
  C.Ch. Wobiska's Teddy of Nekanesu
  Candy II
Wilinda's Apache Chief
  C.Ch. Tarbo's Bobcat
  C.Ch. Wobiska's Pogey
Wilinda's Apache Storm
  C.Ch. Tarbo's Bobcat
  C.Ch. Wobiska's Pogey
Wilinda's Apache Wolf
  C.Ch. Oak's Kanuyak Kakka of
  Wilinda
  C.Ch. Heidi of Wobiska

Wilinda's Chippewa
  C.Ch. Tarbo's Bobcat
  Enchantress of Wilinda
Wilinda's Jada
  C.Ch. Tarbo's Bobcat
  Enchantress of Wilinda
Wilinda's Tawny of Skagway
  C.Ch. Oak's Kanuyak Kakka of
  Wilinda
  Enchantress of Wilinda
Wobiska's Pogey
  Cheeko's Sonny Boy of Wobiska
  Wobiska's Snow Gleam
Wobiska's Teddy of Nekanesu
  Arcturus Chief
  Tote-Um's Malala of Wobiska   -
Zardal Baranof
  A.Ch. Mala-Nor's Sena-Lak Kiuni
  Zardal Akutan
Zardal Cliquot
  A.Ch. Spawn's Kulak
  Zardal Akutan
Zardal Cotati
  A.Ch. Spawn's Kulak
  Zardal Akutan
Zardal Ernrutak
  C.Ch. Zardal Baranof
  C.Ch. Zardal Kotati

15

The Admiral Byrd Expeditions and World War II

O N THAT OCTOBER DAY in 1939, a thousand people gathered at Wonalancet to pay tribute to the dogs who had given their lives during the two Byrd Antarctic expeditions. A major actor that day was our old Alaskan Malamute, Rowdy of Nome. He was a veteran sledge dog who weighed 85 pounds. Rowdy had been born in Alaska, and he had been a member of the team that made a thousand mile trek at the bottom of the world. Now he wore his Antarctic harness to which was attached the gang line. Rowdy walked slowly toward me, Mrs. Milton Seeley, and in doing so pulled away the hemlock branches which unveiled the bronze memorial plaque.

Rowdy had never asked anything in life except to work for his master and perhaps to lie at his feet. Now he lifted his ears, sighed and settled down, and at that moment, a loud speaker spoke the message sent by Sir Wilfred Grenfell to that other guest of honor, Rear Admiral Richard E. Byrd: "For this recognition of our debt to our dogs, we owe the admiral an additional debt for his presence today. 'Love me, love my dog,' is an old adage, and in the case of our Husky dogs, he would be indeed an ingrate who, having lived and traveled with them, and whose life has depended upon them, if he would not rise to the toast of today, 'To Admiral

Admiral Richard E. Byrd and aides are greeted by
Mrs. Seeley upon their return from Antarctica.

Byrd and his dogs,' coupled with: 'Our dogs, our best of friends.' " The message was signed: Wilfred Grenfell.

It all began when the then Commander Richard Evelyn Byrd was named to head an expedition of exploration on the Antarctic continent. It was necessary to assemble a large number of dogs for the expedition. And, of course, it was necessary to get thoroughly experienced drivers, to get adequate food for the dogs, and sufficient harnesses, sleds, kennels, and other things.

Arthur Treadwell Walden, one of the most famous dog drivers of his team, was selected to assemble the dogs, drivers, and equipment. Walden had won the first international sled dog race. But more important, he was a thoroughly experienced freight driver.

Walden was then living at Wonalancet, New Hampshire, where his wife, Kate, ran the Inn, and his Chinook Kennels were behind the Inn. The Chinook Kennels were named after Walden's lead dog, a mongrel whose name means warm west winds. Walden brought in another famous Alaskan driver, Scotty Allen of Nome. It was these two who interested Mr. Seeley and me in the Arctic dogs, and it was Allen who had got me to purchase Rowdy of Nome. Rowdy joined the team of Edward (later colonel) Goodale.

In the group of dogs assembled, there were a dozen or more large freighting dogs resembling Rowdy. These were the Alaskan Malamutes. Neither they, nor the Siberian Huskies, were at that time recognized by any kennel club as being distinctive breeds. In fact, Capt. Alan Innes-Taylor, who commanded the contingent of drivers and dogs in the second expedition, wrote that there was only one pure Arctic breed at that time, the Eskimo.

During 1927, many dogs were tested and many were discarded. In addition, clothing, tents, sledges and rations for both men and dogs were worked out. Roald Amundsen sent his formula for pemmican for people.

One hundred dogs were taken by ship to Dunediin, New Zealand, and were placed in quarantine on Quarantine Island, seven miles off the coast. The dogs had not fared well on the long trip, and it was decided that they had not received the proper food. During the past year, my husband, a food chemist, had experimented with a food formula.

Expedition leaders cabled for this formula. Dr. John Malcolm, professor of dietetics at Orange University, and others were brought in as consultants. A Mr. Hudson, who operated a chocolate factory, loaned the use of his ovens at night. After two weeks, twenty five tons of pemmican biscuits had been made. Seal and whale meat were also to be fed during the long Antarctic winter night.

At Little America itself dogs were tethered "on top" until tunnels and pathways through the ice could be dug. Their crates were placed in alleyways, and dogs were tied far enough apart so that they could not get into fights. Drivers began testing their dogs again. In this, they were mostly cold-blooded. For their lives depended upon the dogs. But a Norwegian, who had been a mate on the City of New York, the ship which had brought the expedition to the Antarctic, gathered up the cast off dogs. He then trained them in his own fashion, and he made them into one of the most efficient teams. That driver's name was Sverre Stromm, and he was technically a member of the ice party rather than of the dog drivers.

In his book, *Cold,* the noted geologist, Dr. Lawrence Gould, second in command at Base Two, pays tribute to the dogs. He could not, he wrote, have made his geological explorations without the dogs, for all his trips were made by dog sled. For example, he logged 1500 miles in 90 days during severe weather. Admiral Byrd himself, made the exploratory trip by dog sled which led to the final location of the Little America base.

Walden's great lead dog, Chinook, had been badly injured when a number of dogs jumped him at once. Later, he escaped from his quarters. He was never seen again, and it has been assumed that he went off alone to die.

Before leaving for the Antarctic, Walden had sold a half interest in Chinook Kennels to the Seeleys. Upon his return to Wonalancet, he sold his interest to them. Chinook Kennels was moved to a new location. It was there that the Seeleys got the commission to assemble 150 dogs for the second expedition.

Between the two expeditions, both Siberian Huskies and Alaskan Malamutes were being selectively bred. They were pure breeds now ready for recognition by the American Kennel Club. In addition to these dogs, Eskimos were brought from Greenland, and mixed breed dogs from Canada. Among the dogs were seven Alaskan Malamutes, called the Admiral Byrd greys. They had been born in Little America. In addition, there were both Alaskan Malamutes and Siberian Huskies which had been born at Chinook Kennels.

It should be noted here that every Antarctic expedition followed a sad and distasteful rule. They put down by shooting the weakest of their dogs at the conclusion of their long treks. This practice was followed by the Byrd Expeditions.

For the most part, the dogs were free of contagious diseases, and particularly distemper. Between the first and second expeditions, the Laidlaw-Dunkin immunization vaccine had been placed on the market. This first of the live virus vaccines was used on all the dogs which had not had distemper, and it gave them complete protection for the second expedition.

The Laidlaw-Dunkin vaccine was tested at the Chinook Kennels before its use on the expedition dogs. A report issued by Lederle Laboratories gives this account of the vaccine's use at Chinook Kennels:

> "Since the advent of the preventive in June, 1929, four and a half years ago, every dog and all the puppies in these kennels have received

Dogs on shipboard returning through tropics from Antarctica.

Shipboard crates for housing dogs.

Antarctic Ketchimac, born in Little America.

Army dogs in training, 1943, pass Wonalancet Chapel.

the protective injections. To date, more than 600 dogs have been vaccinated, and in not a single instance has there been a case of distemper in a dog so treated. With regard to the safety of the vaccination, only three of the 600 dogs showed reactions after the injections. These consisted only of a rise in temperature, which disappeared in 12 to 24 hours and did not require treatment."

This official report of Chinook Kennels' part in the early testing of live virus distemper vaccines "in the field" also states that before the use of the vaccines, Chinook lost an average of 15 dogs a year from distemper, and it noted that in severe outbreaks, the kennel had lost from 30 to 75 dogs. It had, in fact, lost 20 choicely bred Alaskan Malamute and Siberian Husky puppies who had contracted the disease from one of the Greenland dogs. The puppies were too young to be vaccinated by the vaccine.

Dogs in the Antarctic were lost through injuries and sometimes from disasters. Captain Finn Ronne, son of one of Roald Amundsen's men who first reached the South Pole, lost an entire team. He was attempting passage at a deep ice barrier when his heavily loaded gee pole type sledge slipped, overturned, and dragged the dogs to their deaths.

As the expedition prepared to return home, the ship faced severe weather conditions which threatened to break up the ice prematurely. The men were notified to board ship immediately. The dogs were to be left behind. For the men, this was a staggering blow. They had had long months with their dogs and had depended upon them for their very lives. Some of the men had planned to take their favorite dogs into their own homes when they again reached North America. The rest of the dogs were to be returned to Wonalancet.

The orders of the ship's captain were law, and these men had lived under a rigid discipline in which obeying orders often meant survival. In the captain's judgment, their lives were now in peril. They staked the dogs to the ice and planted time bombs about them. Then they sailed away. No one aboard ship heard the explosions. It should be noted that when the United States returned to Antarctica for the great international geophysical years 1955–57, 60 dogs from Wonalancet accompanied the expedition.

Wonalancet was also a staging area for dogs collected and trained for the U.S. Army in World War II. Chinook supplied many Alaskan Malamutes and collected others. These dogs were later sent to an Army mountain training area. Many never returned after the war.

The Armed Forces conceived the idea of using sled dogs for three purposes. Dogs could go where horses, tractors, and airplanes could not. This had been shown in Antarctica when the dogs had had to rescue a seriously ill man during weather too rough for flying. Dogs had been used in the Arctic as pack animals, thus they might be useful in lugging gun parts, ammunition, and other supplies in mountainous country. St. Bernard dogs had been used in the Alps, basically to discover and warn of snow covered

Mrs. Milton Seeley with (l.-r.) Ch. Gripp of Yukon, Finn of Yukon, and Kearsarge of Yukon. Latter was abandoned in Antarctica.

yrd fliers (l.–r.) Clare Alexander, Ralph Shropshire, Richard Brophy, Harold June. ommander Byrd is kneeling.

189

This team, trained at Chinook Kennels for U.S. Army service, pulled an Army truck loaded with men six miles. There were 53 dogs in the team, and not a single fight took place.

Army pack dogs from Chinook Kennels were trained to carry machine gun par over rugged terrain.

By-Line Featur

U. S. Search & Rescue Teams being loaded for shipment to European war zone.

Men and dogs in an air transport plane headed for France.

Army teams in training in the Colorado Rockies. *Margaret B. Chase*

Duke, a Seeley lead dog sent to Rimini Mountain with an Army unit, and lost with entire team in a training accident.

crevasses into which men might fall. But they had also been used to locate bodies under snow, and to carry provisions to snow trapped travelers.

The Armed Forces, therefore, decided to use the sled dogs. They had excellent noses. In the previous chapter, we told how Lorna Jackson's Ch. Lorn-Hall Oogorook M'Loot had located a body under many feet of rubble following a hurricane. The sled dogs, therefore, could be avalanche dogs. They were smaller, more agile, and swifter than St. Bernards, and they could stand severe cold.

Many of the sled dogs were brought to Wonalancet for early training. Most were then sent to the rugged mountains of Colorado for further and final training. Pack dogs and search and rescue dogs were also trained in the Rockies.

Some of the Alaskan Malamutes were among dogs killed in training accidents. Search and rescue dogs were not returned after the war. Instead, they were sent to Greenland and Baffin Island to serve at U.S. Weather Bureau stations.

These losses, plus those in the Antarctic expeditions, account for the perilously low base of registered stock which faced the Alaskan Malamute breed in 1947. It was at that time that the stud book was reopened to admit new blood from other sources.

Youngest Alaskan Malamute to win a C.D. title is Actondale's Kara, owned by Bill and Jane Hoops. She got the title at six months and 10 days.

Ch. Maluk of Northern Star, C.D.X., P.C.X. (Mexico), number one Malamute in nation, 1972 & 1973, owned by Bobbi and Ian Leslie.

16

Alaskan Malamutes in Obedience

A GREAT FEATURE of Alaskan Malamutes is their usefulness in a wide variety of activities. If you can afford to own five dogs, you can make a team, either for sledging or for pulling a cart on wheels. If you have one dog, you can teach it to pull a sled for the children or a cart. It can carry packs on camping trips. There are weight pulling contests it can enter. It can enter conformation competition at the shows, and, of course, it can enter obedience competition.

Any dog is the better for its training. Therefore, every owner of an Alaskan Malamute should plan to enter it in obedience training classes, even if it is not planned to enter the dog in competition at the shows.

The aim of every Alaskan Malamute owner should be to give it the necessary training to make it a good canine citizen of the neighborhood. It should be taught to sit and stay, to come when called, to walk at heel off and on a leash, to bark when told to do so and also to obey an order to be silent. Also, it should be taught to allow others to handle the dog, as a judge will do at a dog show.

One of the authors once queried every newspaper in Alaska, seeking stories on Alaskan Malamute hero dogs. The reply came back: "The only records we have on this breed are those dogs which bite our mail boys." This is not a record of which one can be proud, but the fault lies with owners who haven't trained their dogs.

195

Let us now slay one of the most widely held misconceptions in dogdom that obedience training makes a dog unfit for conformation competition. This is simply the excuse people give for failure to train their dogs. Let us therefore repeat: obedience training makes a better dog of every dog. Each single thing a dog learns makes it a better canine citizen, a happier pet for a happier owner, and the dog often becomes the pride of the neighborhood.

Elsewhere we have mentioned Dr. Roland Lombard. He was one of the pioneers in Alaskan Malamutes, and he has become a legend during his life as the most successful of all sled dog racers. Dr. Lombard's wife, Louise, was perhaps the first person to enter an Alaskan Malamute in obedience competition. In 1940 she competed with a home trained Malamute called, simply, Jackie. To Jackie and Louise Lombard go the honor of gaining the first title ever won by the breed in obedience competition. Jackie had scores of 85 to 95 in three shows, and was awarded the C.D., or Companion Dog title in December, 1940. In those days, 100 was a perfect score. Jackie, by the way, was un-registered, as were so many of the dogs of that period.

It was exactly ten years later that the American Kennel Club awarded a Companion Dog degree to Ch. Yukon Timber Gray, owned by E.M. Scott. He won his championship title after winning the C.D. degree, and this is an excellent example of the point made earlier that obedience training is helpful in conformation competition. He was not registered.

Taska of Towline came next, in January 1952. He is sometimes listed as having been unregistered, but he was. He was owned by Anne Wehrer and her husband, Joe. The confusion here comes from the fact that he was not registered until after he had won his degree.

Taska of Towline, C.D., was the first Alaskan Malamute to be registered which carried neither Kotzebue nor M'Loot blood. He was 100% Hinman—Dave Irwin stock, being by Hinman's Smokey out of Hinman's Neeka (or Neela, as it was sometimes spelled).

Later in the spring of 1952, Carol Oelke, now Mrs. Carol Maxfield of Mukwonago, Wisconsin, won a C.D. degree with her bitch, Snow, who was the first of her sex to win an obedience title. Shortly, Ch. Yukon Gray Avalanche, a son of Ch. Yukon Timber Gray, C.D., won a C.D. title.

The first of the Husky-Pak dogs to win a C.D. title was Ch. Husky-Pak Blackhawk, C.D., a registered dog owned by Roy and Elsie Truchon. Here again, obedience did not hurt Blackhawk's show career.

The first Alaskan Malamute to win the Companion Dog Excellent (C.D.X.) title was another Husky-Pak dog, and he, too, was a conformation champion. He was Ch. Cliquot of Husky-Pak, C.D.X. He won his C.D. title in three of four shows, but then he learned that a clown always pleases a crowd.

One of these writers remembers him in Open competition. He really

196

Jackie, first Alaskan Malamute to win an obedience title, was owned and trained by Mrs. Louise Lombard in 1940.

Beowulf Thosca of Snow Foot, Am., Can., Bermuda, Mexican, F.C.I. international champion, and Am. C.D.X., and Mexican C.D.; top winning bitch, 1970, owned by Beth Harris.

did please the crowds, and often he was the best "show" at the dog show. Still, he completed his C.D.X. with good scores when he placed at all. Ch. Cliquot of Husky-Pak, C.D.X. sired Ch. Husky-Pak Flaming Flirt, and she, too, won a C.D.X. title. She also teamed up with her sire to win in brace competitions.

In obedience competition, the highest honors which can be won are the Utility Dog (U.D.) and Utility Dog Tracking (U.D.T.). On the average, it is probably fair to say that for every 50 dogs which win C.D. titles only one wins a U.D. award. Even fewer win the tracking title. It is not that it is so difficult for dogs to learn to track. Alaskan Malamutes, because they belong to an aged family called northern forest dogs, have remarkably keen noses. The reason is that tracking training and tests are so seldom held.

This brings us to the story of the dog called Coldfoot Oonanik. He was born on May 20, 1964, and he was sold to "the wrong person." Nikki, or Nik-Nik, as he was called, then became a vicious outcast, and was scheduled to be destroyed. A Michigan man, Andre Anctil, rescued him and began the long process of making a good citizen out of the dog. Love, patience, firmness, and an understanding of dogs worked a miracle. A dog once called "incorrigible and vicious" became gentle and affectionate.

Coldfoot Oonanik became the first Alaskan Malamute in the world to win a U.D. title. This he did in Dec. 1966. There came a couple of months of training for tracking. They were winter months, months of typical northern weather: cold, snow, rain, slush. Then Nikki won his Tracking Dog title. He won his T.D. in the United States and in Canada on successive days. He then went on to win all three degrees in Canada, thus giving him a U.D.T. title in both the United States and Canada.

Coldfoot Oonanik also won conformation championships in both Canada and the United States. Not content with this, Anctil took him to Bermuda where he won a championship and a Bermudian C.D.X. Then he went to Mexico where he won his conformation championship and a Mexican U.D.T. title. In Mexico he competed also in the International Canine Federation championships, F.C.I. as it is officially known. This is a European federation which grants international championships to dogs considered good enough to win championships in any country. To win such a championship, one must win CACIBs, a type of challenge certificate, under four different judges. Two judges can be from the local country, in this case Mexico, one from North America, and one either from South America or Europe. Further, the dog must prove its working ability. Since Nikki passed the tracking dog test, it was proven that he was a worker as well as a beauty.

The net result is that Ch. Coldfoot Oonanik has won more titles both in conformation and in obedience than any other dog in either North or South America. He died in August, 1974.

Ch. Coldfoot Oonanik, Can., Am., and Mexican U.D.T., owned and trained by Andre Anctil, is shown going Best of Breed, handled by George Heitzman; judge, Nelson Groh.

Amarok's Tuktu, Am. and Can. C.D., owned and trained by Andre Anctil. First Alaskan Malamute to go Highest Scoring Dog in Show.

Ch. Coldfoot Minto became the second Malamute to win a U.D.T. He passed his tracking dog test in October, 1968, or a little more than a year after he had won the U.D. title. Minto was owned by Melvin Pokrefky of New Baltimore, Michigan.

The third Malamute to win the U.D. was Ch. Tigara's Nucah of Arctica, owned by Dr. George M. and Mrs. Joan S. Byrne of La Canada, California. She was the first of two bitches to win the title.

Sena-Lak's Cheeno of Brigham, a male, followed in May, 1972. He is owned and was trained by Lloyd D. Mazur of Gates Mills, Ohio. Cheeno earned his C.D. in three straight shows at eight months with an average of 191. At 14 months, he won his C.D.X. title in four straight shows. Then, competing in 11 shows in 1971 and 1972, he had an average score of 195.5. His utility degree came at 24 months with an average of 193.5. Cheeno competed in three shows in Canada but was not registered there. At Skyway Obedience Club he was highest scoring in trial with 199; got 195.5 the next day, and then at the Hamilton show, 196.

The fifth, and last Alaskan Malamute to win a Utility Dog title was Princess Seeko, who won the third leg on her U.D. on June 17, 1973. She is owned by Charles E. Brancato, but she was trained and handled by his father, Jack J. Brancato of Lincroft, N.J.

In this section on obedience, there is perhaps one more record which should be mentioned. For as much as anything else, it demonstrates the ease with which the normal Alaskan Malamute can be trained. Actondale's Kara, owned by William and Jane Hoops of Neshanic Station, N.J., won her C.D. degree in three straight shows at age six months and ten days. Two of her scores were over 190 out of a possible 200, and one was 195.5.

To Amarok's Tuktu goes the honor of being the first Alaskan Malamute to win highest scoring dog in trial. He was bred, trained, and owned by Andre Anctil. The American Kennel Club no longer looks with favor upon perfect obedience scores, that is, 200 out of a possible 200 points, so judges have to resort to some magnificent stratagems to get around this. Tuktu got a score of 199.5++. We suppose a judge might give three pluses, but we have never heard of it being done. So it can be said that Amarok's Tuktu got as nearly perfect a score as possible. He was a son of Coldfoot Princess Ponoka, C.D., the first Alaskan Malamute to go into service as a guide dog for the blind.

In closing this section we would like to stress what may be evident from the records of some of the dogs whose histories we have just given. The rules and procedures for obedience trials in the United States, Canada, Mexico, and Bermuda are so similar that no special training is required for competition in any of the other countries besides your own. Thus, international obedience competition is open to all Alaskan Malamute owners.

Sena-Lak's Cheeno of Bringham, U.D. owned and trained by Lloyd D. Mazur of Gates Mills, Ohio. *Axel Studio*

Ch. Tote-Ums Tongass, C. D. X., owned and trained by Wendy Aronsen, already had a leg on the coveted U.D. title when this book was completed.

Beowulf Tor, C.D., owned by Jeanne Olbrich of Tor-Jo Kennels, Falls Church, Va.

Ch. Sena-Lak's Beowulf Thorjhawk, Am. & Can. C.D., shown with owner-trainer, Beth Harris. Thorjhawk is a winner of Highest Scoring Dog in Show and is lead dog in a sled dog team. *Lawrence Jenkins*

Coldfoot Princess Ponoka C.D., first Alaskan Malamute to become a guide dog for the blind, and dam of one.

Historic picture of Joanne Byrne and Ch. Tigara's Nucah of Artica, U.D., and Andre Anctil with Ch. Coldfoot Oonanik, U.D., most titled obedience dog in the world.

17

Teaching You to Drive
a Dog Team

D RIVING A DOG TEAM can be one of the greatest thrills of your life, no matter how many times you do it. The unexpected comes up on almost every trip. There are two major rules. Learn and obey all the rules for safety, and live with your dogs and observe them closely so that you know each dog intimately. These are the foundation rules for sledding with dogs.

The first thing you need to know are the basic commands by which you make the dogs obey. These are the same commands used for centuries by American farmers in controlling their horses. "Gee" means to turn right, "Haw" means to turn left, and "Whoa" means to stop.

Let us assume that you own a puppy. It should not be put into harness until at least six months old. You can, however, use a leash and teach it the basic commands. You can walk it through woods and in places where there are dogs and cats and where you can teach it that it must obey in spite of such temptations.

There is another and easier way to teach the puppy, although it may not be available to you. If there is a sled dog club near you, you may be able to find a member who has a retired lead dog. You can use such an "instructor" dog to guide your puppy.

Be careful not to be too strict with a puppy. He may get bored, or you may cause him to lose his spirit. You should try to meet with experienced drivers. They can tell you the type of harness to use. And they can show you how to measure your dog for harness.

Be careful of second-hand harness. Stiff webbing, or any elastic material can bruise the shoulders and back of your dog. In measuring your dog, see to it that the harness falls correctly around the neck, between the windpipe and chest, so that your dog will not have his wind cut off.

Novice dogs get very excited and tend to waste their energy before they start. Try to keep your dog quiet. A good rule is to require your dog to be quiet for at least five minutes after being harnessed and before you start. You should require five to ten minutes at the end of the trip before you unharness your dog.

Once your puppy is six months old, you can start teaching it to pull. Some of the sledding families have started their small children with puppies hitched to skis, or to a child's sled or wagon. Sleds and wagons should have brakes, of course. Also, there are one-dog sledding events at many of the racing meets.

You should banish all thought of racing until you have fully learned to drive. You and your dog, or dogs, must learn first that sledding is for pleasure, and only later for racing.

Even thoroughly trained dogs need regular exercise, and this can be given to them the year around. One of these writers once went out with the great Kit Macinnes when she was training for the Anchorage Rendezvous. Although it was late November, there was little snow. Mrs. Macinnes was using a converted ice cream vendor's wagon.

Several advertisers state that three-wheel gigs are safe for summer work or when there is insufficient snow for sleds. Many feel, however, that these three-wheelers are unsafe, and the New England Sled Dog Club recommends against them. Many drivers feel that the four wheel carts are safer, and that they have better balance. In teaching your dog to pull, you should use a type of harness known as "draft." You should ask an experienced driver to show you how to use it. The so-called Siwash type does not fit well unless one uses a high draft arrangement on the sled.

You must never take your eye, or your concentration off the team. The unexpected can happen, and you may find yourself in a snow bank while your team trots merrily on. Also, a team may have a mischievous dog which will await an opportunity to rush off after a cat or other animal and get your entire team in a tangle.

Always carry a kit bag tied to your sled or summer cart. This kit bag is your emergency outfit, your first aid kit for sled, harness, and even dogs. The kit should contain two collars; one length of a hitch; an ice remover such as a paint remover tool; matches in a wet proof container; and a wax candle. The latter is for waxing runners.

Never begin a trip without first checking the gang line and harnesses. Unless you are clever at making loose hand ties, it is better to use sport snaps. However, these sometimes freeze and come undone. Tie a snub line onto the back of your handlebars, but string it through a large ring fastened to the sled.

It does not matter whether you are using one dog or 12, always snub (fasten) the line to a stationary object. It is the same, winter or summer: always snub the line. This will prevent the dogs from bolting. Moreover, using the brake to hold the dogs before starting often makes them very nervous.

We have assumed that you began with a single puppy. Now you have acquired a team. If you have been wise, you will have bought older and experienced dogs as well as youngsters. Some dogs are slow to learn; others too eager. Some are shy and have to learn to go with other dogs. Older dogs will have more patience if a learner travels beside them, so always place a learner with an older dog. Also, young dogs should be placed in the middle of the team. If you have a team of five, use three with experience.

Tangling is a frequent occurrence, and it can be a difficult situation to handle if you are alone. Some drivers use the brake, but it is far better to snub your leader to a tree or to some other immovable object while you are entangling. You may have to overturn your sled if snubbing is not possible. When your dogs get tangled, do not lose your patience, and do not blame the dogs. Just work quietly and swiftly.

Conditioning your dog's feet is a must. Sore feet can result if your dogs' pads are too hard. Your veterinarian can supply you with a product to moisten the pads, and there are toughening products available. The mileage you travel should be governed by the progress of the dogs. Gradually lengthen the distance as the dogs strengthen their muscles. Observe your dogs, and do not make them travel farther than they can go without severe effort.

Practice in turning around should be one of the first lessons. Commands must be understood by your leader, by your two point dogs, and if five, your wheel dogs. Your wheel dogs are those directly in front of the sled, and they control the movements of the sled.

The best drivers of the past have had an important saying, or rule. This is, if you can make five dogs obey you, and go anywhere you ask them too without effort, you have the nucleus of a team. But too many beginners see men driving with up to 15 dogs and double sleds and think this is the way for a beginner to learn.

It took me, Short Seeley, one year of winter learning to drive nine Alaskan Malamutes. Their strength and eagerness could have caused many accidents had they not been taught absolute obedience to commands as a unit. I started with three, then graduated to five but only after a long summer of training with a heavy woods toboggan. The dogs were pulling three times their own weight. Then I was allowed to train five more.

This puppy, shown with Mrs. Milton Seeley, became Ch. Missuds of Kotzebue. Its parents took part in Operation Deep Freeze in Antarctica in 1955.

When the first snow fall came, seven dogs were taken out for a ten mile easy jaunt, then seven more. Two weeks later, I made up a team of 11 dogs and took my husband for a lovely ride. It was from these dogs that I made up the team which I drove in the Lake Placid sled dog demonstration in the 1933 Winter Olympics.

Consider your team as you would any sports squad—one with new and old candidates. Sometimes you will want to try out a sub. Try your dog on a single hitch in between teams. Or if you think he or she may make a good lead dog, harness it just behind the leader. Make sure that you know its gait, and give it plenty of room. This is a better system than using two lead dogs. The one using two leaders must study his dogs very carefully since each dog is an individual. Some are too aggressive; others are shy and may be timid about trying to advance over dogs with more experience.

A nervous dog should be harnessed beside a placid one. If a dog is a fighter, try to find out why. Perhaps it may need treatment for some physical ailment. Examine each dog's feet immediately after a drive. Cuts stay a long time and need to be treated.

Eventually you may have a litter of puppies, and you will hope to make good team dogs out of most or all of them. You should play around in their yard with them. Mingle with them at regular frolic periods and particularly when they are away from their mother. Name them and begin calling them by name. You can make small harnesses for them. Put these on, and they will get used to them. Then later, real harness will not disturb them.

Sled dogs often steal the show at special functions, but these also condition the dogs to special situations. For you, driving a dog team is also an exercise in physical fitness. You should practice the art of pedaling (one foot on the runner, the other helping to push the sled.) You will discover that if you are out of condition your dogs will recognize this almost immediately.

Spring brings out the bears, foxes, skunks, rabbits, and silly squirrels. You must teach your dogs absolute obedience, else they are likely to take off on the scent of a deer. Or they may decide to chase a wandering cat or a fox. It will help if your leader is an "old man dog" who will always obey your commands. A good leader will often show remarkable intelligence under circumstances where this would not be expected.

For example, I, Short Seeley, once sprained my ankle on a trail. I was four miles from home and there were no houses near. I released my leader, Waska, and tied a glove to her collar. I told her to go home. At first, she did not understand, but she finally understood that I was hurt. Waska raced toward home. We had travelled twenty miles that day, and the dogs lay quietly, resting, but every eye was directed toward home. Finally, a truck driven by my husband appeared. Waska was sitting beside him. She rode between us on the way home, and a kennel boy brought the team to the kennels.

Here are some of the terms traditionally used in teaching and in driving sled dogs:

Mush!	Let's get going.
Gee!	Turn right.
Haw!	Turn left.
Whoa!	Stop.
Brake:	a device to slow the sled.
Lead Dog:	the leader of the team.
Wheel dogs:	dogs directly in front of the sled.
Snub line:	line by which the sled is tied to a stationary object.
Snow hook:	hook jammed into the snow to hold the team briefly.

Ch. King Nikki Of North Wind, C.D.X., pulls owner Ralph Schmitt of Silver Sled Kennels in this specially designed cart.

18

Training the Show Dog

by Nancy C. Russell

N ANCY C. RUSSELL *is one of the most successful breeders of Alaskan Malamutes of the present day. She is a distinguished officer in the Alaskan Malamute Club of America and has become one of the nation's finest professional handlers of show dogs. She has combined her knowledge of the breed with a natural rapport with all dogs.*

Whereas the average professional handler will take dogs which are mature and train them for shows, Mrs. Russell understands the process from puppyhood on. There is no one more competent to tell the owner of an Alaskan Malamute puppy how to train the dog. We are proud to present her instructions just as she wrote them for this book.—The Authors

You have just purchased your new puppy and prospective champion. Assuming he has the proper conformation, whether he becomes a champion or a "show ring drop-out" is entirely up to you. So much of a show dog's success depends on his attitude as well as his training. The true "show dog" is the one that walks in the ring with the presence that says, "Here I am, aren't I beautiful?" He ignores the other dogs; gaits on a loose lead with head up and maneuvers corners and turns without breaking his stride; poses alertly for the bait; allows himself to be stacked and appears to enjoy the judge's examination and almost asks for his attention.

Invariably you find that the show dog loves to travel. He thinks his crate is home and is content in it wherever it is parked. He thoroughly enjoys being groomed and fussed over to the point that he forgets that all tables are not to be jumped upon for grooming. This kind of dog is a real pleasure to show and the kind that wins consistently. So how do you develop this attitude? First experiences of all the things associated with dog shows and going to a dog show must be pleasant ones. This is the cardinal rule.

Traveling

For example, do not make your puppy's first ride in the car a trip to the veterinarian for shots. He will then associate a car ride with an unpleasant experience. Instead take him to the Dairy Queen for an ice cream cone, to the country for a romp, and to a friend's house for lots of petting and attention. A few trips like this will establish an association pattern of pleasant experiences of a ride in the car, and you will have a dog eager to travel.

Crate Training

A show dog must consider his crate his home. This way he will be content wherever his crate is placed. Adjusting to new places readily is a natural characteristic of the Malamute since the Eskimo's were nomads and home was wherever the dogs were staked for the night. So now you only need to introduce your pup to his crate in such a way that he feels this is his home. Place comfortable bedding, food and water in the crate leaving the door open so the pup can come and go as he pleases. Praise him for going in it to sleep and eat, and never scold him in the crate. After he is using the crate without reluctance, start shutting the door for short periods, gradually increasing the time he is left in. Choose a word such as "kennel" or "crate" and use it as a command for entering the crate. Always praise him for obeying. Take his crate along when you visit friends, to training classes, on a picnic, etc. Have him spend time both

212

in and out of the crate. Do not use the crate as a form of punishment. His crate must be his security and his home.

Getting Accustomed to Other Dogs

As soon as your puppy has had his vaccinations, begin exposing him to other dogs. Even if he is too young to participate take him to conformation or obedience classes to observe. Alternate between having him in and out of his crate. Encourage people to go over him and pet him. Although it would be unusual for a young pup to be aggressive towards other dogs, discipline him if he shows any signs of aggressiveness such as growling, snapping or excessive barking. Of course, don't forget to give assurance and praise for proper behavior.

Do not be alarmed if your puppy who has always loved the world, one day suddenly growls at the nearest dog. Usually this occurs between eight months and a year of age. This is a sign he is leaving puppyhood and is trying to establish his place in the pack. The pack instinct is very strong in the Malamute and the more dominant dogs will try to establish their superiority over the others. This leads to the aggressive behavior too frequently seen in the show ring and elsewhere. You must teach your dog this is not acceptable behavior. So be ready for that first growl. Make the punishment so quick and so severe it will leave a lifetime impression. If you are strong enough, pick him up by the ruff, shake him and shout, "No!". If not, then hit him under the jaw with your fist, hard, and shout, "No!" at him. Let him know you are really upset by this behavior. If you administer the discipline properly once or twice will be all it takes. From then on a firm "No" will bring his attention back to you, and he soon learns it is much more pleasant to just ignore other dogs.

Think of it as comparable to a small child who runs out in the street. You run out, grab him, scold him and administer physical punishment because you realize that if he continues this action he'll very likely be killed or severely injured by a car. A dog whose aggressive traits are not controlled by his master has about as much chance of surviving in the show ring, on a sled team or as family pet as the small child who plays in the street.

Lead Training

I find that leash training is the most difficult lesson to make enjoyable for the puppy because it does require restraint and discipline. However, if you are generous with praise and treats the pup will soon associate the leash with pleasant experiences at the same time that he learns to respect it and your commands. I start a young pup on a $\frac{3}{16}$ inch flat Resco show lead. Place the lead right where the neck and skull join, with the lead coming up between the ears. First let the pup go wherever he pleases and just hang on to the end of the lead. Continue this until he seems accustomed to having the lead on. Then as you are walking along with him call him, change directions giving a slight tug on the leash; enough to turn his head in the direction you are taking. At the same time start coaxing him to come. If he does, give lots of praise or even a pat if he comes next to you, but keep on going. Repeat this procedure until he has learned that a tug on the leash means he must change directions.

The next step is to teach him to walk beside you on a loose lead. This is similar to teaching a dog to heel in obedience only you command the dog to stand when you stop and you work your dog on the right side as well as the left side. Corrections are always made with a sharp jerk, release and lots of praise for correct response. Talk to your dog in an encouraging, happy voice. Convince him this is fun. Make left and right turns and complete turns at a walk until he responds properly and happily. If you are teaching an older puppy or an adult dog who pulls constantly, use a slip collar and leash until he has learned to walk with you on a loose lead. Although this may sound exactly like obedience training for heeling there are some slight but important differences. First you do not want your dog to gait looking up at you. This will cause him to throw the outside elbow outward or perhaps even cause side-winding. You want him to look straight ahead. Therefore you should make a habit of moving slightly ahead of him. This way he can watch you for changes in direction and pace without turning his head. Also you do not let the lead drop down beside the dog in the typical obedience loop.

A loose lead in conformation means only that there is no tension on the lead which would interfere with the dog's movement. Unfortunately not all dogs in the show ring have been properly trained, and if another dog should run up on your dog from behind or attack him by the time you reel in your extra lead, they would be into a fight. If you have the proper tension on the lead you will be able to feel a growl through the lead, a shift in weight or even a tensing of the muscles in the neck. This gives you time to anticipate your dog's action and intercept it. For instance, if a dog is going to move his left foot he has to shift his weight to the right one.

When gaiting, have only enough lead out of your hand to allow your dog to move in the proper position without interference from you or the lead. The excess lead is folded up in the palm of the hand nearest the dog. Flexion of the wrist should be all that is necessary to tighten the lead. This gives you good control of your dog. He will know you have control and pay attention to your commands.

As soon as you have your dog walking with you in the proper position gradually increase your speed until he is trotting. Practice the turns as before and practice with the dog on both the left and the right side. If your dog drops his head, correct with a sharp jerk upward and at the same time say enthusiastically, "heads up" or "let's go." The leash must be directly behind the skull, not down on the neck, to make an effective correction. Don't be afraid to talk to your dog while gaiting. A happy dog moving out freely is a beautiful sight.

Grooming Table

Grooming should always be an enjoyable time for both puppy and master. It is also an excellent way to accustom the pup to being handled. If you do not have a grooming table then get a rubber mat or other non-slip surface for any table at a comfortable height for you. The first time on the table may be frightening for the pup so play with him, admire and pet him. Don't start grooming until he has lost his fear. Since a full grown Malamute standing on an ordinary grooming table is too high for comfortable grooming, also teach him to lie down on the table.

Never let him jump off the table except on command. And teaching him to step down to another object and then to the ground can eliminate possible injuries from jumping unto slippery floors or uneven surfaces. Also teach him to climb or jump up on the table. A full grown Malamute is no fun to lift on and off the grooming table.

Posing the Dog

Once your pup enjoys the grooming table it is a good place to practice posing him (also known as stacking). At first, just be satisfied with getting the pup accustomed to having his legs moved and getting him to leave them in that position for a few seconds. Gradually increase the time you require him to stay. This is where being on a table helps as he is less inclined to move around. Always give lots of praise for standing as posed. While he is posed go over him as a judge would: checking teeth, picking up the feet, checking testicles, etc..

The Malamute is set up square. Viewed from the front the outside of the front legs should be a perpendicular line from the side of the body to the ground, feet pointing straight ahead. See Figure A. Viewed from the side the foreleg should be perpendicular to the ground. See Figure B. A common mistake is to set the front feet too far forward. Practicing in front of a mirror will help you to see this error immediately.

The rear legs are placed so that the hocks are perpendicular to the ground and the feet point straight ahead. Viewed from the rear the legs are usually placed so that if a line were dropped to the ground from the widest point of the pelvis it would come along the inside of the hocks. See Figure C. Viewed from the side the hocks are perpendicular to the ground and a line extended upward would touch the rear of the pelvis.

215

See Figure B. Understand this is merely a guideline and should be varied according to the individual dog. Set your dog in varying positions in front of a mirror until you find the one best suited to your dog. Don't forget to view from front and side and rear.

To set the front legs, hold the dog's muzzle in your right hand. Reach over the body and grasp the left leg at the elbow to move it into position. At the same time, turn the head slightly to the right. Change hands on the muzzle moving the head slightly to the left and place the right leg as desired by grasping it at the elbow. To set the rear legs, either hold the muzzle in the right hand or hold the leash at the base of the skull. Control of the head is important in order to keep the dog from moving. Reach under the body and grasp the left leg at the stifle joint and lift and place in position. Place the right leg by grasping either the stifle joint or hock joint to move into position. Bring the tail up over the back but do not flatten it down. The tail should be a waving plume.

Using commands such as stand, stay or show when teaching your pup to pose will be most helpful especially if he will be handled by more than one person. And a well trained dog will perform for any handler. Since our standard specifically states that a Malamute is "not a one-man dog" he should readily adjust to a new handler and will do so especially if trained to voice commands.

Baiting

Once you have taught your pup the words stand and stay you can now step out in front of him and entice him with a piece of liver or other treat. This is done to make him look alert. If he moves do not treat him but scold with the word "no", replace the leg he moved, repeat the command "stay" and try again. Reward with praise and the treat when he performs as requested. One obvious rule: Never teach a pup to sit or sit-up for food.

Next try baiting him into a show stance. Gait your dog and as you slow down give the command "stand" or "stay." At the same time turn to face him with a piece of bait in your hand. Discipline him for not stopping on command or jumping for the bait. And of course reward for proper behavior. A dog which walks into a show stance is most impressive.

Conformation Classes

Make every effort to attend conformation training classes. They are designed to simulate show conditions and are, therefore, the ideal place to train your dog. The people there understand the necessity of discipline for a dog. They like dogs; know how to approach a strange dog and examine him as in a show ring. They can teach you the gaiting patterns used

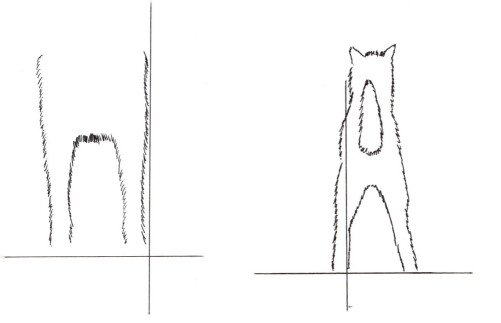

Figure A.

Figure C.

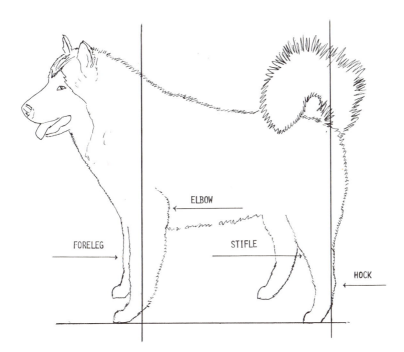

ELBOW

FORELEG

STIFLE

HOCK

Figure B.

Illustrations of Mrs. Russell's instructions in this
chapter on how to pose the Alaskan Malamute
for show.

217

in the show ring and help you to become familiar with some of the judge's hand signals. They can help you discover the best speed at which to gait your dog and the most advantageous way to pose him.

And if you are willing to listen and observe you will gain valuable information about all phases of dog shows. What you learn you can teach your dog. If you love it, so will your dog. And that makes a winning combination!

Ch. Alaskaland's Friendly Grizzly, owned by Denis and Sheila Land, Holladay Utah. Judge: K. M. MacDonald. *Henry*

19

Roger Burggraf's Story of Chinook, Tripod of Cornell

SOME YEARS *ago while on my way to Point Barrow, the northernmost tip of the North American continent, I stopped for an evening with Roger and Malle Burggraf. It was December but we were snug in the Burggraf home. We ate moose meat snacks while Malle cooked, and Roger talked about sledding on the slopes of Mt. McKinley and along the frozen rivers and valleys of interior Alaska.*

It was then that he told me the story of Chinook—"Tripod of Cornell." Later he sent me the written story, as it had appeared in a Cornell University alumni magazine. It is a lovely story, beautifully told, and one that all owners of Alaskan Malamutes will enjoy. For that reason, we reprint it here.

—Maxwell Riddle

On December 20, 1964 at 12:30 P.M. Chinook mushed beyond the great divide after leading a life which was full of many adventures. He was a controversial dog, loved by some and disliked by others.

Chinook, a full blooded Alaskan Malamute, was born at Haines, Alaska in the month of May 1953. He came from proud parentage. His ancestors had served man as companion and helper on the snow covered trails of Alaska for generations. His father and mother were Army sled dogs who had served their country faithfully during World War II.

Chinook entered my life as a thirty-pound silver grey pup who, even in his adolescence, had a majestic head crowned with large, erect ears. He was an awkward pup who was a tremendously strong dog even at three and one half months. Chinook had a mind of his own, and when he wanted to go some where it didn't much matter whether there was some two legged creature on the other end of the leash. When it was time for me to leave for school we tried to find a crate to ship him home in but could find none for a 35 pound pup. A crate was built of scrap lumber and Chinook was shipped by air at the cost of $70.00 to New York State. When Chinook was uncrated at the air terminal he created quite a stir with many curious onlookers. This was just the beginning of the attention he was to receive throughout his life.

At Cornell University, where dogs reigned supreme and had free access to all the educational facilities offered the students, he was immediately welcomed into the fold. He soon became the beloved mascot of my college fraternity, Kappa Delta Rho, and became the unofficial mascot of Cornell.

Tragedy struck on November 27, 1953. While I was visiting friends in Newfield, a small town seven miles from Ithaca, Chinook was playing with another pup and ran into the path of an onrushing car. I heard the screeching of brakes and anguished cries of Chinook. By the time I reached him he lay motionless, barely breathing. We rushed him to the Cornell Veterinary Hospital. There he received all the care that could be mustered by modern science, but it was decided that his left front leg must go if he were to survive. At this time I held the decision for the life or death of Chinook in my hands. This was an extremely difficult decision to make. I hated to see any creature suffer, but I knew that the desire to live is a great one. I consented to the operation.

The veterinarians were impressed with Chinook's rapid recovery, but they felt he would be fortunate to live four or five years due to the additional strain on his heart. It surprised me how quickly Chinook recuperated. His spirit and attitude toward life was remarkable. He adjusted to his new situation quickly and soon was able to approach a fire plug with confidence. His unique ability to balance on a front and hind leg was the topic of more than one student's conversation.

Chinook refused to become an invalid. To most students he became affectionately known as Tripod. He was soon following us to classes and of course wanted to continue with the studies he missed during his illness. In class he never ceased to amaze his professors and fellow students. When the subject being presented was interesting he was alert and attentive, but when it became boring he made no bones about it and set the example for the other students by falling asleep. On one occasion a professor who felt that Tripod was a bad influence on his students ordered one of his assistants to evict him. When the assistant tried to forcibly remove Chinook, he was met by a deep rumbling growl. The assistant beat a hasty retreat. Since the professor did not want to attempt the job himself, he decided that discretion was the better part of valor and let that three legged trouble maker remain a student in the class. During Chinook's tenure at Cornell there were many amusing events that took place in the class rooms which are too numerous to mention.

Life at Cornell was not all work for Tripod. Being the athletic type he attended many football, basketball, baseball and track events. He even became an active participant in many games. He was perhaps best known for the 1954 Syracuse—Cornell football game when he ran through the Syracuse team on the opening kick off. More than once he disrupted the opposition's carefully planned plays when he ran through their lines. Tripod was commonly known as a referee's nightmare. He was more than once expelled from a game, but it was only done so after considerable effort on the part of referees, coaches, assistant coaches, campus patrolmen and players in catching the speedy and maneuverable three legged canine. The fans loved him and he helped to spice things up when the going got rough for our home team.

For five years Chinook reigned supreme as the top canine on campus. He never started a fight but finished many of them when attacked by some over zealous four legged pooch. He loved being the center of attention and during parades, graduations and other big events was always right in the center of things.

On October 12, 1958 a campus patrol car ran over a cat. Tripod, who witnessed the event, intended to put the cat out of its misery, however, the patrolman stopped his car and tried to take the cat from him. Chinook growled at the cop who started all the trouble in the first place and for that was charged with resisting arrest. Shortly thereafter an edict by the Campus Patrol was issued banishing Tripod from Cornell. This was the beginning of the end of a tradition which had been in effect for almost one hundred years allowing dogs to wander on the campus at will. After that, all dogs were declared unwanted on campus.

Chinook did not leave without a battle. In an effort to have his sentence commuted, students, professors and dog lovers came to his rescue. Articles were written in the paper. Public demonstrations were conducted and appeals were made directly to Dean Malott, the President of Cornell University. The president had to support his subordinates even though he was inclined to be sympathetic to the demands of the students at Cornell.

Chinook was rather crestfallen by his exile but took it in his stride. He soon joined Malle (formerly Malle Kapsta, Class of '56) and I at Fort Devens, Massachusetts where I was serving my tour of duty in the Army. He became the mascot of the First Howitzer Battalion 76th Artillery. Chinook really never had it so good. Being an old hand at begging tid bits around Cornell, he was right at home making the rounds to all the mess halls. When on maneuvers he had the back seat of my jeep all to himself and liked the excitement of being at the gun positions when the men were firing or up on the observation posts, observing fire.

Upon completion of my tour of duty at Fort Devens we bade the men of the 76th a fond farewell and headed for Alaska. Chinook sat beside us during the whole trip. At the Canadian border we met the Michigan '59-ers. They were a group of modern day pioneers who were out to settle the wilds of Alaska. We continued the trip with them, helping out wherever we could. Chinook was enjoying his new environment and liked the excitement of all the curious people he met along the way.

After leaving the '59-ers we headed for Fairbanks and the University of Alaska. There Chinook continued his studies. It was said that he was working for his Doctor's degree and that the thesis he chose was "Living in Alaska", with the emphasis on how to grow a heavier coat to keep the —60°F chills away. His studies at Cornell were really "snap courses" compared to the ones at the University of Alaska. While at Cornell he reigned supreme over a few degenerate inbred animals like Boxers, German Shepherds and other, but in Alaska the canine specimens were fresh out of Jack London's epic stories, both in appearance and character. The first time he decided to go courting he met his match, who ruined his classical ears. He soon became resigned to a quiet life with only occasional visits to the University of Alaska. There he created enough gossip and traffic jams to suit his ego and on occasions demanded entrance to lecture halls with his "deep bass" (as the Cornell Campus Patrol and some luckless assistants may still well remember). He no longer chased motor scooters but found more pleasure in trying to attract the attention of big shaggy animals called moose, who frequented his domain.

Chinook settled down and became a family man and sired a string of strong four legged Malamute pups from a grand daughter of Nikki, the star of Walt Disney's production, "Nikki, Wild Dog of the North". He used to enjoy running behind his brood: Ithaca, Ivy, Beebe, Ezra, Cornellia, Cascadilla, Cayuga, Seneca and Taughannock when we were mushing over the snow covered trails of interior Alaska.

Chinook remained healthy and active right until four days before his death. It is believed that he suffered a heart attack, probably when he was following a sled dog team which passed through our property. He had been ill on a few other occasions throughout his life, and we all were hopeful that he would recuperate. We made a bed for him in the cellar. Toward the end, when he let his wishes known I had to carry him outside so he could relieve himself. He would take a deep breath of the minus 50° below zero air and then ask to go inside. At 12:30 p.m. on December 20, 1964 Chinook whimpered a few times and as I got up to carry him outside, I heard a long and mournful howl. How many times before I had listened to his famous call of the north. His sons and daughters heard him and in return gave voice. When I reached Tripod he lay motionless on his side with his mighty front paw stretched outward and his tail curled over his back as if he were in full pursuit of the mysterious phantom of the north.

Chinook met his creator after eleven and one half years of life on this earth. He lived a rich and fully gratifying life. The old boy did not let the loss of his leg hinder him and always adjusted readily to changing situations. He was used to facing and overcoming many hardships. In his dying moments he bade a fond farewell to all he knew.

—Roger C. Burggraf, Class of '55, Cornell U.

Arthur Olmen took this picture of puppies he ha
bred out of American and Canadian Ch. Timbe
lane's Good Karma.

20

Housing, Feeding,
and Grooming
The Alaskan Malamute

MODERN LEASH LAWS make it necessary to confine dogs. Dogs kept in a kennel or in the home need a confinement area, and every responsible Alaskan Malamute owner should provide such an area for the dog. Here are our recommendations, both for single confinement areas and for multiple ones for housing a kennel of dogs.

Long experience indicates that pens should not be too large. Probably the ideal size is a pen six feet wide and twenty feet long. Many companies which specialize in dog run fences make sections to fit these specifications.

Some dogs are diggers, and so it may be necessary to provide a base through which they cannot dig. This can be heavy duty chicken wire fencing laid on the ground, and then covered with the surface material to be used for the runs. Of course if the surface is to be concrete the chicken wire will not be needed, but it may be wise to set the fencing into the concrete.

The surface should have sufficient slope away from the dog house, or gate, so that it drains well. If concrete or asphalt, the surface is easily washed down with a garden hose. Concrete probably comes closest to the ideal surface, though it has its drawbacks, as does asphalt. Neither surface keeps the dog's foot pads in proper condition. Asphalt is a much warmer surface than concrete, thus snow and ice melt from it rather quickly and certainly much faster than on concrete. However, asphalt will be uncomfortably warm in hot climates.

Gravel and No. 6 driveway slag make good surfaces, as far as foot health is concerned. Slag has some deodorant benefits, but both slag and gravel are difficult to disinfect in the control of fleas, ticks and internal parasites.

At Chinook Kennels we feel that an ideal arrangement would be runs in which the first ten feet are concrete, and the second, gravel or slag. Such runs can be kept reasonably clean. And the moisture which is usually present in the gravel helps to keep the dog's pads in condition. Slag also helps to keep pads and nails in good condition.

Let us assume you wish to build an outdoor dog house. This should be about 36 inches tall, although 30 inches will be sufficient in most cases. The roof should have an over-hang at the front, and should have a gentle slope to the rear. The over-hang protects the entrance from rain. The entrance should face east.

The reason for a flat roof is this: first, the house will be easier for the dog to warm with its own body heat; second, the dog can leap onto the roof in good weather. Most dogs greatly enjoy this, and the exercise helps to keep their legs in good shape.

The entrance to the house should be about six inches from the floor. This keeps out drafts and, if it is being used, keeps in bedding. Do not make the entrance too large. A 25 inch tall dog can easily get into a hole 15 inches tall. Few dogs have a chest broader than 12 inches.

An ideal house is one which has been insulated. In cold climates, this protects against frigid weather. In hot climates, it helps protect against heat. If the roof of a flat topped house is placed on hinges, it can be raised slightly for ventilation in hot weather, and it can be fully raised for cleaning the house.

Many an owner who does not wish to build a dog house, or to set up an exercise pen, puts the dog out onto a "trolley." It is possible to teach the dog to go to the far end of the trolley wire to relieve itself. But few dogs ever actually exercise on a trolley. Also, the dog on the trolley feels that it is tied up, as it actually is, and may bark its displeasure.

Of course, dogs in a pen may also bark and disturb neighbors. They may do this out of boredom. One solution is to bring the dog into the house after it has had time to relieve itself and to stretch and exercise. If the dog must be left out for long periods and turns out to be a barker then there are other solutions.

One solution is to arrange a hose so that when the dog begins to bark the hose can be turned on. The dog is squirted, and a stern "no" command is given. One kennel operator made the pen posts of hot house sprinkler pipe. When the dogs barked, the water was turned on and the dogs were driven into the dog house. Another simple arrangement is to hang canvas walls around the pen. This stops the dog from barking at passing dogs or strangers. It also prevents stray dogs from bringing disease to your dog.

If you build a kennel house, entrances should be well above ground so that the dogs have to walk up a ramp to get in. This is particularly necessary for puppies. Walking up and down the ramps gives them sport and exercise, and it helps to strengthen elbow and wrist muscles. It also helps to prevent the tracking in of dirt.

Feeding of dogs is a subject of never ending conversation. No two people will agree on any given procedure. It is a miracle that the dogs survive. We can only give our best advice, based on the feeding of thousands of dogs at Chinook Kennels for nearly 50 years.

Today, the best known commercial dog foods are based on the feeding of thousands of dogs at research kennels. For example, a food maker may have as many as 400 dogs of 15 breeds at its kennels. These dogs are fed not only the company's food, but those of its competitors. The foods are also fed under certain stress conditions, such as pregnancy, lactation, etc..

If anyone studies the labels on dog foods, it will become apparent that no owner could make up such a complex food in the home. It should be added here that almost all of these foods contain more than adequate supplies of vitamins and minerals.

At Chinook Kennels we feed a meal to which we add cod liver oil. Meat supplements and sometimes additional fats can be fed to dogs under stress, such as training for freighting or racing. Cod liver oil is used to prevent rickets. If too much is used, rickets is caused. If you buy cod liver oil in large quantities, re-bottle it into small bottles. Continuous exposure to air in opening and closing a large bottle can cause the oil to become rancid.

Most people feed their dogs at night. They have more free time then. Morning feeding is preferable, however. Dogs relieve themselves after eating. Kennel runs can then be cleaned and are clean for the rest of the day and night. Also, at Chinook Kennels we feel that dogs fare better if they do not have a full, tight stomach at the time of sleep.

When puppies have been weaned, we feed them three meals a day until about four months of age when their permanent teeth have come in. We then cut them to two meals a day until they are a year old or slightly older. After that we cut them to one meal a day.

We do not believe in the plastic chewing articles sold by pet shops and at dog shows. A good knuckle bone is preferred. This will give the dog months of chewing pleasure.

Consult your veterinarian on the problems of immunization. Depending on their experience and the types of vaccines they use, veterinarians' procedures and their times of administering shots will vary. One can now immunize against distemper, leptospirosis and infectious canine hepatitis all at once. In the early days when we were conducting field tests with the newly developed Laidlaw-Dunkin vaccine, one could not immunize puppies until they had their permanent teeth. Now this can be done. Your veterinarian will recommend the proper procedure.

It was once believed that one vaccination with a live virus vaccine would protect the dog for life against distemper. We now know that the immunity level drops unless the dog is regularly "challenged" by exposure. This exposure tends to bring the immunity level back to its highest peak. In earlier days, most dogs ran at large. Exposure was regular, and immunity level was kept at a maximum. Today fewer dogs are allowed to run. Some dogs have a reasonably high immunity level. Many others get no challenge exposure for a year or more while the immunity from the vaccine disappears. For this reason, annual vaccination against distemper is recommended.

There are almost as many ideas about grooming as about feeding. Commercial grooming tools, if used incorrectly, can injure the oil pockets in the skin of Arctic, double-coated dogs. There are several ways to handle the shedding dog. One which we use at Chinook Kennels is to wet a newspaper and massage and rub the coat with it. We use a bristle hand brush dampened in oil of lanolin for daily grooming.

Shedding hair may also be loosened by gently massaging the skin with your fingers then rubbing from head to tail with the palms of the hands. This will get out more dead hair than will combs and brushes. One may then finish grooming with the brush dampened in oil of lanolin. Steel combs are permissible if used in the right way. Guide the comb with your thumb and work in a circular motion. Packs of dead hair are best removed when the coat is in full bloom.

In bathing your dog, use a gentle shampoo and warm water. If you bathe your dog before a show, restore the oil by using a cream rinse, or with a brush dampened in oil of lanolin.

21

Day Blindness
in Alaskan Malamutes

P ROGRESSIVE *retinal atrophy (PRA) and central pro-*
gressive retinal atrophy (CPRA) have appeared in a number of breeds. The
former is first noticed when the dog has trouble seeing as darkness ap-
proaches. It leads to total blindness. CPRA is blindness which appears
in the center part of the retina only so that the dog has peripheral vision,
but cannot see straight ahead. The dog can, however, follow something
which crosses the entire retinal field.

Hemeralopia, or "day blindness", has been discovered in Poodles and
in Alaskan Malamutes. Dr. Kenneth Bourns, Canada's most successful
Malamute breeder, discovered the ailment in his own dogs. Working with
the Ontario Veterinary College at Guelph, and at great personal expense,
Dr. Bourns learned how to eliminate the fault in his own breeding stock.

His courage in making public the problem and his dedication and work
in pioneering a method to eliminate it from breeding stock belong among
the greatest services to dogdom. We here reprint his article which appeared
in Dogs in Canada *in March 1968. Permission has been graciously granted*
for this by Dogs In Canada.

Day Blindness

by Dr. Kenneth Bourns

What should we do when a serious defect crops up in our kennel? Should we ignore it, hoping that it will go away? Should we outcross, hoping to cover it up? Should we neuter or destroy the dogs producing it? What, indeed, should we do? Just this problem faced us at Boru Kennels eight years ago when we discovered that three Malamute puppies in a litter of ten seemed to have difficulty seeing in the daytime, but not at night. What follows is a step by step case history of the discovery of a disease and of the way it was handled, and is presented not only to acquaint the reader with the nature of the condition, but also to show that in some cases at least, undesirable traits can be eliminated without recourse to the actions suggested above. It is also hoped that those who shy away from the word genetics may discover that the elements are not at all difficult to understand—to the contrary, they are amazingly simple.

The condition to be discussed can be detected in pups at seven weeks of age when one notices that under daylight conditions they bump into objects and seem to be unsure of distances. Indoors, in dim outdoor light, or at night, the affected pup's vision is as good as that of a normal dog. Indeed, an affected animal that we know of is an American Champion, having performed well at indoor shows. Since the condition does not worsen with time, a protected dog, having learned the positions and distances of all hazards, may lead a restricted but happy life. In strange surroundings, however, he will undoubtedly come to grief by careening into an unseen wire fence or, perhaps, something worse.

Having become aware of the defect in our puppies, we wrote to a number of breeders with related stock, telling them of our problem and hoping that some light would be shed on the situation. To our surprise, no one had seen anything like it; to our disappointment, most seemed disinterested; to our consternation, some suggested that we had better say nothing about it—"It might hurt the breed".

After our veterinarian and a local ophthalmologist determined that there was nothing structurally wrong with the eyes, we were referred to the Ontario Veterinary College, Guelph, Ont., where Dr. L.H. Lord and his colleagues studied the pups and named the disease "Hemeralopia" (Day Blindness). At this time we didn't know whether or not the defect was caused by something in the environment or whether it was genetically-determined. To answer this question we and Dr. Lord undertook a series of test-matings using the parents and littermates of the affected pups, and soon established that Hemeralopia is an inheritable disease. Shortly after this we learned that a breeder with related stock in the U.S. had encountered Hemeralopia. Also, at this time Dr. Lionel Rubin of the University of Pennsylvania Veterinary School became interested, and with the cooperation of our American colleague, Dr. Rubin and we continued to carry out experimental breedings in order to determine *how* the defect was inherited. We knew, of course, that for most characteristics a genetic message is received by an animal from each of its parents. We assumed that there exists a gene for what we might call bright light vision and that two alternative forms of alleles of this gene exist. One would be, essentially, an "instruction" HAVE NORMAL BRIGHT LIGHT VISION, and the other would be the alternative "instruction" HAVE HEMERALOPIA. We knew, too, that genetic messages can operate in any of three basic ways. The first of these is that one "instruction" may dominate over the other so that the puppy will "obey" one and "ignore" the other even though it received that latter and will pass it on to the next generation. The second involves the reverse of this and is concerned with the "ignored" or recessive "message". If a characteristic is inherited in this way it will be exhibited by the puppy only if the same "instruction" was delivered by both parents (if this were not so, the alternative or dominant "instruction" would have been received and would have been "obeyed"). The third, called blending or incomplete dominance, is seen when a puppy "compromises" and turns out to be about half way between the conflicting "instructions". Perhaps at this point it might be wise to underscore the fact that an allele is not dominant, period, it is dominant *to* something and that something is its alternative allele. Similarly, an allele that is called recessive is recessive *to* its alternative. In the present case, then, we had to determine whether or not the HAVE NORMAL VISION "instruction", or allele, was dominant or recessive or incompletely dominant to the alternative allele HAVE HEMERALOPIA. What one must do here is to determine what would happen in different matings *if* HAVE HEMERALOPIA is the dominant allele, *if* it is the recessive allele, or *if* it shows a blending effect with the alternative "instruction".

The latter possibility was ruled out in our case because there were no detectable grades or in-betweens of vision. Each dog was either normal or Hemeralopic. Further, the fact that our first Hemeralopic pups were produced by parents whose vision was normal implied that Hemeralopia was not dominant to normal vision but was probably recessive to the normal condition. With this in mind we constructed a table to illustrate the results to be expected by a variety of matings *if* a recessive allele was at work (see Table). Then we compared the results actually obtained in the five combinations which had been tested, 110 pups in all, and found that the inheritance of Hemeralopia was turning out to be exactly what would be expected if it were the work of a recessive allele.

Having established the way Hemeralopia is inherited, we then were able to turn to that part of our stock which was involved, with a view to eliminating the offending allele. We had, of course, three types of dog with respect to the anomaly: Group A, being those who received the dominant HAVE NORMAL VISION from both parents, Group B, being those who received one instruction from the sire and the other from the dam, and Group C, being those that received the recessive allele HAVE HEMERALOPIA from both parents. Group A puppies have normal vision and can pass on only the allele for normal vision. They are the ones that we wanted in our breeding program. Group C puppies actually exhibit Hemeralopia, having no dominant shield to hide behind, and are eliminated from breeding. But what of Group B? They have normal vision but they "carry" the allele for Hemeralopia. Not only did they receive it, but also, as can be seen from the Table, they will be expected to pass it on to half of their offspring if bred. How do we distinguish Group A from Group B animals? Again by test-mating. If we mate an animal that *may* be a carrier to an animal that is Hemeralopic, we will get the answer. *If* the animal being tested is indeed a carrier (Group B), the result of the mating will be a litter of which half will be expected to exhibit Hemeralopia. *If,* on the other hand, the test animal is completely free of the defect (Group A), none of the pups will be affected. It must be borne in mind that all such pups, having one Hemeralopic parent, will be carriers and must be dealt with accordingly.

We were fortunate in that one of our foundation bitches was proven by test-mating not to be a carrier. She, bred to a fine American dog of a Hemeralopia-free strain, produced our now well-known "E" litter. Working with our remaining stock, bitter disappointments mounted upon one another as several animals tested proved to be carriers. However, at last we were rewarded when the first one of those who might have been a carrier was proven not to have inherited, and therefore not to be able to pass on, the allele for Hemeralopia. Recently, Irene and Bill Stone of Kelso

(Reg'd) Kennels here in Ontario have similarly test-bred their stock and, like ourselves, are able to certify puppies as being completely free of Hemeralopia. And now, after a long and costly program, punctuated by disappointments and tears, we have the satisfaction of knowing that all of our breeding stock is free of this defect. Our systematic program has enabled us to eliminate an undesirable genetic trait from a fine line of dogs. We believe that to do so was our duty, for surely we are obliged to improve the complete dog—meaning his genetic potential as well as his individual observable characteristics.

Dr. Rubin's research has revealed that Hemeralopia is associated with enzymes which maintain supplies of the chemicals that transform light impinging upon the eye into nervous impulses of electrical energy to be carried along the optic nerve. Although it is not likely that a cure for the condition will be developed, it is probable that our understanding of the very process of seeing will be improved as a result of Dr. Rubin's work.

Finally, we have learned that some sled dogs in the north are called "night dogs", a title which leads us to conclude that they are probably suffering from Hemeralopia. Also, the defect has been reported from another breed, Poodles. Recently we have learned that another kennel in the U.S. and one in England, whose Malamutes are related to our foundation stock, have encountered Hemeralopia. One wonders how many cases have been undetected or ignored and how many carriers are perpetuating this defect. Had our efforts at communication issued years ago been taken seriously and had a frank exchange of information taken place, the numbers would doubtless be much smaller.

Ch. Beowulf Naya of Lancet. Owner-handler,
Donald H. Wald, M.D. Judge: Mrs. Marie Moore.

22

Alaskan Malamute Chondrodysplasia

CANINE CHONDRODYSPLASIA is a genetically caused disease which affects Alaskan Malamutes. It is commonly called dwarfism although this term is neither specific nor entirely correct. The condition results in delayed endochondral bone formation, that is, at the sites of cartilage in all the long bones. Symptoms include lateral bowing of the forelimbs, enlargement of the carpal or wrist joints and lateral deviation of the forepaws. A similar disease known as dyschondroplasia is sometimes seen in human hands.

When genetic or hereditary anomalies appear in dog breeds, the usual reaction is to ignore them or to deny that they exist. The first cases of Alaskan Malamute dwarfism came to the attention of veterinary researchers about 1964, but it was three years later that official notice of the problem was taken.

A breeding colony of purebred Alaskan Malamutes was set up at Washington State University at Pullman, Washington in 1967. Other colonies were set up, notably at the Ontario Veterinary College, University of Guelph, at Guelph, Ontario. The Alaskan Malamute Club of America began a brave attempt to face the problem in June, 1970. The word "brave" is used advisedly. Major battles have been fought in all breed clubs over recognition that hereditary defects occur in their breeds. Thus, the courageous and intelligent work of the Alaskan Malamute Club of America deserves much praise.

Ten people met in a hotel in Denver in June, 1970. Mrs. Alice Jean Lucas has been given credit for almost single handedly getting the parent club to recognize that chondrodysplasia was indeed a major international problem facing Alaskan Malamute breeders. Arguing with her were Dr. Henry W. Dodd Jr., Mrs. Linda Dowdy, and others. After nearly an all-night session, a Master Plan Committee was organized. Mrs. Lucas was named chairman. On the committee, besides Dr. Dodd and Mrs. Dowdy, were Mrs. Dorothy Pearson, and Dr. T. K. R. Bourns.

A sub-committee was then organized with Dr. Dodd and Mrs. Dowdy as co-chairmen. This was called the Probability Committee, with good reason, for both Dr. Dodd and Mrs. Dowdy are systems engineers. Mrs. Dowdy is a full time engineer with UNIVAC at the White Sands Missile Range.

In 1972, Mrs. Lucas stepped down and Dr. Dodd and Mrs. Dowdy continued with Mrs. Dowdy as chairman. Dr. Bourns was made head of a Genetic Research Committee. As such, he has played a major role in interesting universities in the problem and in getting finances for veterinary research projects which the universities have initiated.

Let us first consider the work of the Master Plan Committee. Mrs. Dowdy says little about her own part in the project, but Dr. Dodd says that it could not have been successful without her dedicated efforts. "It was—and is—the efforts of Mrs. Dowdy which have made the project successful," he writes. "For five years now she has spent 30 to 50 hours per week on the project while working full time at UNIVAC. She has never received any remuneration for her work, even though part time help had to be obtained to handle the heavy work load."

Between June of 1970 and the end of that year, Dr. Dodd and Mrs. Dowdy developed the mathematical models upon which pedigrees could be tested. Then the first step was to prove that dwarfism was a simple autosomal recessive. (An autosome is an ordinary chromosome as distinguished from an allosome. An allosome is a term now used as synonymous with sex chromosome but formerly meant any chromosome which differed from an ordinary chromosome in size, shape, or behavior.) This was proved at Guelph by repeated matings of dwarf to dwarf.

Dr. Dodd and Mrs. Dowdy then realized that probability could be applied to a dog's background in order to assess its chances of carrying the gene recessively. In this connection, it should be mentioned that dwarfism has not yet appeared in the Kotzebue strain, but it has in the M'Loot line. Dogs from Hinman Park have also shown dwarfism, but Hinman Park is not actually considered a strain.

If a dog which is normal is mated to a chondrodysplastic, the puppies could all appear to be normal, but all would be carriers of the gene for dwarfism. If two of these clear but carrier dogs were mated, half the puppies might be clear and half might be dwarfs. Since we are dealing with probabilities, there is always the possibility that in a given litter all the puppies might be one or the other. If two dwarfs are mated, all the puppies will be dwarfs. The laws of probability would not work if two normals were mated or two dwarfs were mated.

Mrs. Dowdy has likened this to the flipping of a coin. You should get heads fifty per cent of the time and tails fifty per cent. But you might get a run of ten times all heads or all tails. Similarly, if you were to flip five coins at once, you might get all tails or all heads at some point.

Pedigrees are submitted for analysis. If one shows a probability of being a carrier of 6.25% or less, the dog in question is given a provisional certification. This 6.25% figure corresponds to one carrier as a great-great-great-grandparent. Or, one can say that it corresponds roughly to a 95% confidence level.

Despite this so nearly perfect confidence level, later information has caused the revocation of a provisional breeding certificate. One dog, Kelly of Clover Leas, hit the one hundred percent bottom when her entire litter of six puppies were chondrodysplastic.

In her most recent Master Plan Committee report, Mrs. Dowdy commented on the question of where the guilt lies in establishing chondrodysplasia in the breed. We quote her here.

"The question has once again risen, as it does every so often, as to why the Kotzebue bloodline is considered genetically uninvolved in chondrodysplasia. The answer, to put it simply, is that we have no evidence to the contrary. It has, at various times, been a subject of hot debate as to whether the Kotzebue and M'Loot foundation dogs were actually distinct and unrelated or not.

"It provides an interesting discussion, but actually is irrelevant to our probability analysis. Be they descended from one dog, different dogs, or Rudolph the Reindeer, it makes no difference. In the determination of "a priori" probabilities, to be used as input on pedigree analysis, we are interested only in about four most recent generations on carrier pedigrees.

"Beyond that depth, the mathematical effect becomes so attenuated that little or no information can be gleaned. We know that the gene has come down through pure M'Loot backgrounds. And in carrier pedigrees involving a mixture of Kotzebue and M'Loot these same groups of M'Loot dogs have always appeared in the third and fourth generations.

"In such a case, I know of no statistical weighting procedure that will direct the probable line of genetic descent towards the Kotzebue ancestors rather than the M'Loot ancestors, whose involvement has already been established. In summary then we must conclude that although Kotzebue involvement is certainly possible, it is not probable."

It is time then for Alaskan Malamute owners to stop blaming anyone and to dedicate themselves solely to stamping out the problem. The im-

Front view of a normal Malamut puppy. *Canadian Veterinary Journa*

Front view of a chondrodysplastic puppy. *Canadian Veterinary Journal*

Profile view of a normal Malamute puppy.

Canadian Veterinary Journal

Profile view of a chondrodysplastic puppy.

Canadian Veterinary Journal

mense amount of work done by Dr. Dodd and Mrs. Dowdy with the help of Miss Kim Street shows the following figures, supplied by Dr. Dodd:

"From early 1971 through June, 1975 (4½ years) we have processed approximately 2200 requests involving about 1750 distinct pedigrees (some requests were from owners of litter mates).

"The 2200 requests were received from about 1050 Malamute owners, so the average requester wanted probability ratings on two different Malamutes. Of the 1050 owners, about 450 are Alaskan Malamute Club of America members, and 600 are non-members. So our service certainly has not been restricted to AMCA members.

"From the 1750 different pedigrees, we have issued 864 P-certificates. P-certificates are issued to dogs with 6.25% or less probability of being a carrier of dwarfism. There have also been 29 G-certificates issued to dogs who are considered to be genetically uninvolved.

"Thus, about half the dogs receiving ratings had probabilities in excess of 6.25% and should have been considered candidates for test breeding. We have issued about 300 T-certificates to dogs who have test-bred clear, which leaves about 550 dogs unaccounted for.

"Unfortunately we have no way of finding out which of these dogs were withheld from breeding, which ones were bred by owners who simply disregarded the probability rating, and which were tested and found to be carriers.

"Lack of knowledge about this last category comes about because the universities who read the test litter x-rays treat them as confidential information (rightly so, I believe) and inform only the dog's owner of the results. Naturally, if a dwarf is confirmed in the test litter, the owners of the suspect dog are less anxious to contact us than were those owners whose dogs were found to be clear."

No one who reads the above data can do otherwise than bow to such dedicated people. However, the battle to wipe out chondrodysplasia continues on two other fronts. This work is being done at universities and consists of two parts: blood studies and radiographs.

University Research shows that Alaskan Malamute chondrodysplasia appears to be unrelated to any other form of the disease in animals or man. Yet, as pointed out earlier, dyschondroplasia is sometimes seen in human hands. For that reason, the disease in dogs is of great interest to scientists. Moreover, the causes of the disease in human beings is not known, whereas much is now known about it in dogs.

Researchers working at the Ontario Veterinary College of the University of Guelph discovered that chondrodysplastic Alaskan Malamutes also suffered from a form of anemia. This discovery stirred up great interest among researchers on human diseases, because people also inherit some forms of anemias. This made Dr. Bourns's task to interest colleges in Malamute research easier than it might have been.

Radiographic and blood research is being conducted at a number of universities. We have already mentioned the Ontario Veterinary College and Washington State University. Dr. Kenneth Pierce at Texas A&M University is investigating the effect of parasitic infestation on blood tests. Veterinarians at Michigan State University are reading radiographs for breeders. The University of Saskatchewan, at which Dr. Meg Smart is now connected, is involved, and so is Ohio State University.

When the blood studies were first begun at Guelph, Dr. Smart and Dr. Sheila Fletch were involved. Both are veterinarians. Dr. Smart is the granddaughter of Percy Gudgeon, a Canadian pioneer English Springer Spaniel and Afghan breeder. Dr. Fletch is a Great Dane breeder. Dr. Fletch is now at Sunnybrook Hospital, Toronto, with P.H. Pinkerton, M.D. in the Department of Laboratory Hematology.

These two extremely talented women veterinarians are leaders in the comparative studies now being conducted in all fields of medicine by veterinarians and medical doctors. The two women were among the first to breed dwarfs to dwarfs successfully, proving that chondrodysplasia is inherited by a Mendelian recessive gene. Moreover, work at Sunnybrook has indicated that both the blood and bone defects are manifestations of the same gene.

The Alaskan Malamute anemia shows some resemblance to a group of inherited anemias in man, in that they are due to defects in the outer coat, or membrane, of the red blood cell. This is why research on Alaskan Malamute syndrome has called in the best brains among veterinary medicine, human medicine, and paramedical sciences.

In Alaskan Malamute anemia, the hemoglobin concentration in the blood, that is, the oxygen transport mechanism of the red cell, is reduced in affected dogs because there are fewer red cells. The red cells of the anemic Malamutes are bigger and more fragile than normal, and the life span of the red cell of the anemic dog is shortened.

Immunologic tests show that this shortened red cell life is not due to formation of antibodies in the dog's own cells, which is the common mechanism of hemolytic anemia in dogs. Further, iron and bone marrow (the substance where red cell production occurs) studies indicate that there is no impairment in the ability of the anemic dog to produce red cells.

The cell that is produced, however, is abnormal and contains more water and more sodium than normal. On a blood film, these red cells have a pale central slit-like opening resembling a mouth. Because of this they are termed stomatocytes (stoma-mouth). If viewed in three dimensions, the cells appear like a bowl rather than the normal biconcave disc shape.

Preliminary investigation suggests that in some respects the carrier shows changes intermediate between the full-blown syndrome and normal. The carrier red cell is slightly larger, wetter, and contains more sodium than the normal. However, overlap is considerable, and in order to assess these findings properly further studies are required.

The previous description is taken from a paper delivered by Dr. Fletch, Dr. Pinkerton, and P.J. Brueckner, M.D. at the 57th annual meeting of the Federation of American Societies for Experimental Biology.

There may someday be a simple blood test which will determine which dogs are carriers. If this happens, it will eliminate the need for probability studies of pedigrees, test matings, and even radiographic tests.

Pioneer work in radiographs was done at Guelph, but also at Washington State University. At the latter institution, the work was started as early as 1967, with major radiographic work coming in 1969 when the inheritable nature of the disease became known. The great work there was done by Ronald D. Sande, John E. Alexander, and George A. Padgett, all in the College of Veterinary Medicine.

We have noted the enlargement of the carpal joints, the lateral bowing of the elbows and the lateral deviation or turning outward of the forepaws. There is, of course, skeletal distortion in other parts of the body, including the hind limbs. But the fact that more of the dog's weight must be borne by the front legs makes the distortion greater in the forequarters than in the hind. It is believed, therefore, that no metabolic factor is involved in the differences.

Radiographs may be made as early as three or four days of age in a puppy, but Washington State experience is that the first signs of chondrodysplasia do not appear until seven to ten days. The Washington State researchers believe that the best time for radiographs to be made is when the puppies are three to 12 weeks of age. Negative findings before seven days or after 12 weeks may not be accurate.

23

National Specialty Shows

THE ORIGINAL Alaskan Malamute Club gave a number of specialty shows, but these did not become truly national in scope until the parent club had been expanded into the Alaskan Malamute Club of America. Beginning in 1953, there was one national show each year. These were held with all breed shows.

Later, as the national parent club began to increase its activities, regional specialty shows began to be held. Thus, as many as six regional specialty shows, all held under the parent club, might be held during a year. In the following table, we are listing the Best of Breed and Best of Opposite Sex winners, with their owners, at the national shows, from 1953 through 1974.

Alaskan Malamute Club of America
National Specialty Winners

Best of Breed

Best of Opposite Sex

1953 Ch. Arctic Storm of Husky-Pak
Mr. & Mrs. Robert Zoller

Ch. Apache Chief of Husky-Pak
Mr. & Mrs. Robert Zoller

1954 Ch. Mulphus Brook's the Bear
Mr. & Mrs. James Dawson

Ch. Kelerak of Kobuk
Mr. & Mrs. Robert Zoller

1955 Ch. Cherokee of Husky-Pak
Mr. & Mrs. Robert Zoller

Ch. Kelerak of Kobuk
Mr. & Mrs. Robert Zoller

1956 Ch. Cherokee of Husky-Pak
Mr. & Mrs. Robert Zoller

Ch. Husky-Pak Marclar Sioux
Mr. & Mrs. Robert Zoller

1957 Ch. Cherokee of Husky-Pak
Mr. & Mrs. Robert Zoller

Ch. Husky-Pak Marclar Sioux
Mr. & Mrs. Robert Zoller

1958 Ch. Mister Yukon of Tobuk
Mr. & Mrs. Robert Hall

Ch. Barb-Far Marclar's Machook
Mr. & Mrs. W.R. Gormley

1959 Ch. Aabara of Redhorse
Mr. & Mrs. H.B. Pearson

Ch. Banshee of Husky-Pak
Mr. & Mrs. H.B. Pearson

1960 Ch. Rogue of Tigara
Glenn E. Hull

Ch. Brook's Wons Neeuq Star
Mrs. Martha Guiffre

1961 Ch. Spawn's Hot Shot of Roy-El
Mr. & Mrs. Robert Spawn

Bearden's Arctic Blaze
J.R. Swann

1962 Panuck
Dr. B. Weininger

Erowah Roxanne
Fran & Ouida Epley

1963 Ch. Eldor's Little Bo
Mr. & Mrs. D.E. Tarr

Sno-Tara Keena of Sno-Hill Run
Mr. & Mrs. Paul Reid

1964 Ch. Spawn's T'Domar's Panda
Alice Ann Spawn

Kee-Too
Mr. & Mrs. J. Moustakis

1965 Ch. Sno-Crest's Mukluk
Dr. & Mrs. Leo Rifkind

Ch. Tote-Um's Kooteeyah
Verna S. Dortch & Dianne Ross

1966 Ch.Tigara's Eskimo Eddy of Kayuh
Ralph Boger

Ch. Spawn's T'Domar's Panda
Alice & Bob Spawn

1967 Ch. Kodara Kodiak of Erowah
Mrs. Martha Guiffre

Voyageur's Elke
Sheila Land

Ch. T. Domar's Genghis Kim Shadow, National Specialty Show winner in 1968, shown with owner, Donald Mull. *Cleveland Press*

Ch. Sno-Crest's Mukluk. great Best in Show winner (3) in the '60s for Dr. Leo and Mrs. Belva (handling) Rifkind. Major B. Godsol, judge. *Francis*

Mrs. Nicholas Demidoff gives Best of Breed for his third consecutive year win at the Chicago International to Mrs. Nancy Russell with Ch. Glaciers' Storm Kloud, C.D., Can., Am., Mexican, F.C.I. International champion. *Robert Holiday*

Ch. Inuit's Sweet Lucifer, Best of Breed, National Specialty Show, 1974. Handler, Philip Marsmann; judge, J. Roy Kibler; owner, Sheila Balch. *Gilbert*

Best of Breed	*Best of Opposite Sex*
1968 Ch. T'Domar's Genghis Kim Shadow Donald Mull	Pak 'n Pull's Ice-Floe of Tote-Um Mrs. Martha Guiffre
1969 Ch. Glacier's Burbon King Lois Olmem	Ch. Sabre's Misti Dawn of Snopaw Sally Prince
1970 Ch. Glacier's Storm Kloud C.D. Robert & Nancy Russell	Ch. Sno Tara's Dakota Kim L.C. Ihrig
1971 Ch. Burbon's Aristocrat of Brenmar Frank & Claire Bongarzone	Ch. Sno Tara's Dakota Kim Paul & Helen Reid
1972 Ch. J-Len's Captain Koriak Joyce Fahlsing	Ch. Unalik of Redhorse Donald Womack
1973 Ch. Lobito's Cougar Cub Richard & Dawn Woods	Ch. Sena-Lak's Beowulf Tawechi Beth Harris
1974 Ch. Inuit's Sweet Lucifer Sheila Balch	Ch. Storm Kloud's Dartanya Joan & Wesley Spain

Princess Antoinette de Monaco congratulates Ch. Glaciers' Storm Kloud, C. D. for his Best in Show at Monaco in 1973. Nancy Russell looks on.

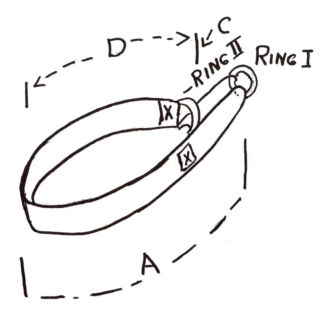

Design for a safety collar by Bob White.

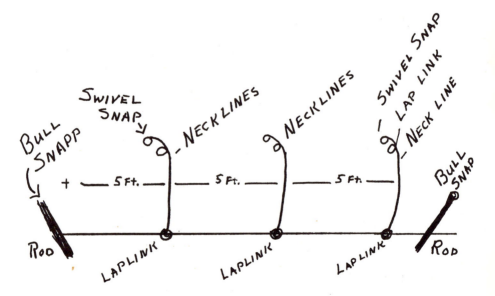

Picket line design by Bob White.

248

24

Harnesses and Sleds

I<small>N</small> THIS CHAPTER, we are using a distillation of experience from many drivers, Mrs. Seeley's own long experience, that of Robert White of Sterling, Michigan, and from the sleds made by the U.S. Army for its search and rescue teams. Some of the drawings were supplied by Jackie Bonafides.

If you are going to drive a dog, you have first to start with a proper collar for it. And if you are going to drive a team, then you must have a proper picket line for the dogs. So we start with these. One drawing illustrates a special type of safety collar which prevents much wearing away of neck fur. It should be made with one inch nylon webbing and with one inch rings. Measure the dog's neck, and stitch B to A. Ring One slides along C. This distance is just sufficient so that the collar opens up to slip over the dog's head. This may be three to four inches. Since the collar will only tighten to the size of the dog's neck, there can be no choking.

To make a picket line, drive iron rods into the ground, much as you would tent stakes. That is, drive them in at an angle away from the picket line, or pointing in opposite directions from each other. The actual picket chain should be of a heavy enough size that the dogs cannot break it. Bull snaps are fastened to each end of the chain, and then slipped over the end rods.

At five foot lengths, neck chains are fastened. These can be 12 to 15 inches long, including the snap, or lap link, which hooks the neck chain to the picket chain. At the other end, swivel snaps are secured. Dogs are then hooked to the neck lines. They are far enough apart so that they cannot fight, and they are securely fastened.

Brass snaps are preferred, since they do not rust, and also will not freeze shut. Nor will they come open as readily as some other types made of other materials. Barrel snaps are preferred to spring snaps because dogs cannot escape from them so easily.

Discipline on the picket line, and indeed at all times, is absolutely necessary. Before they had chain picket lines, the Eskimos used to have to use seal lines. To prevent dogs from chewing through these lines, they hung young dogs up by the neck. Just before choking to death, the dogs had a bowel movement. They were then taken down. Before they became conscious, their big cutting teeth were smashed. This then prevented the dogs from chewing through the lines, but it also minimized the damage they could do to each other in fights.

Since modern sled dogs are allowed to keep all their teeth, discipline is of utmost importance. A favored method of establishing this teaches the dogs that they cannot fight. Get a leather strap and have a snap stitched to one end. This snap will permit you to fasten the strap to your belt or waist.

There are now several things you can do. If you have two dogs who dislike each other, fasten them side by side. If either growls at the other, lash it across the nose with your strap. Give a very strong command "no." Repeat as often as necessary—and it may be necessary to repeat the lesson at least once each time you take out the team.

Next, take a dog on a short lead and parade him back and forth along the line. If any dog shows resentment, lash it across the nose, and command it with a "no." Very shortly, all the dogs will realize that they cannot growl or fight.

Always keep the strap within sight, however. The dogs will watch for it. If you don't have it, a fight may start. One driver has a strap, the upper half of which is chain, that is, the end which fastens to his waist. He sometimes jingles this, and the dogs get the warning.

The equipment required is a gang-line, harnesses, a snub-rope, a hook, and of course, the sled itself. In drawings, we have illustrated the gang hitch and various types of harness.

Also included is a drawing of a typical sled. Drivers have used all sorts of rigs for snow-less periods, and one of these authors once went off in an old ice cream cart. Short Seeley believes that the three wheeled gig is more dangerous than one with four wheels. If you build, or buy such a gig, use great care in its operation.

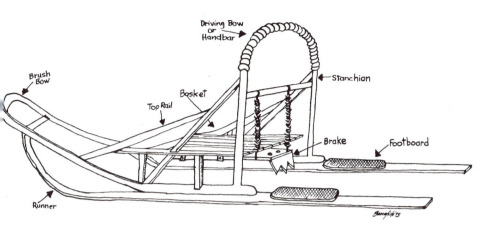

Chinook sled designed by Arthur Walden.   *Jackie Bonafide*

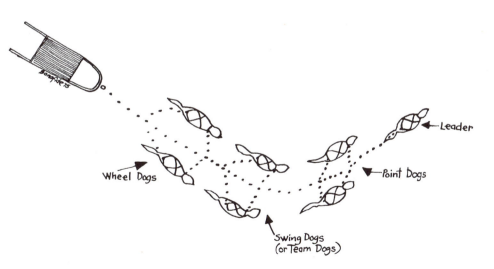

Diagram of a gang hitch and placement of dogs.   *Jackie Bonafide*

Recreation Harness for puppy training.   *Bob White*

Freight harness trains dogs to pull.   *Bob White*

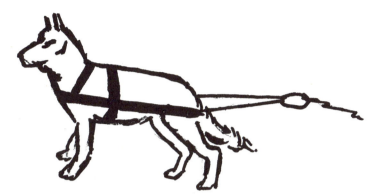

Trail Harness.

Bob White

X-back racing harness.

Bob White

Dogs in action, showing how hitch works.   *Dick Smith*

25

Gait of the
Alaskan Malamute

SINCE the Alaskan Malamute is a freighting dog, it follows that its gait is of great importance. The official breed standard does not have a section on gait. Nor does it mention gait as such. But it does give clues as to what is desired. In its first reference, the standard says: "The Malamute moves with a proud carriage, head erect and eyes alert."

It goes on to say that the feet are of "snowshoe" type, tight and deep, with well cushioned pads; the front legs are straight, with big bone; the hind legs are broad and powerful, moderately bent at stifles, and without cow hocks. The back is straight, gently sloping from shoulders to hips.

"The loin," it says, "should not be so short or tight as to interfere with easy, tireless movement." And in another section, it adds: "The loins should be well muscled and not so short as to interfere with easy, rhythmic movement WITH POWERFUL DRIVE FROM THE HINDQUARTERS. A LONG LOIN WHICH WEAKENS THE BACK IS ALSO A FAULT."

In another section, it adds: "Hind legs must be powerfully muscled through thighs; stifles moderately bent, hock joints broad and strong, moderately bent and well let down. As viewed from behind, the hind legs should not appear bowed in bone, but stand and move true in line with movement of the front legs, and not too close or too wide."

Let us try to interpret all this, as well as to add what the standard does not say. Viewed from the front, the legs should swing forward perpendicular to the ground, and parallel to each other. Or, one should add, nearly so. There is a tendency to move the feet under the centerline of the body if the dog is trotting under pressure, but this is less true with Alaskan Malamutes than with many other breeds.

If the front legs are viewed from the side, the proper angulation of the shoulder and front leg assembly makes it possible for the dog to reach far forward with its front legs. Dogs which do not reach far forward are said to be "stilted." This can come sometimes from lack of exercise and from confinement in too small quarters. It can also come from faulty shoulder angulation.

If we continue to view the dog from the side, there is neither sway nor roach in the back line. If there is sway (a sinking in the middle of the back) the dog will tire easily because there is no straight line of power. Power is therefore lost. A roach often indicates that the hind leg assembly is not correct. And again, power is lost through the roach.

Now that "straight line" of the back applies laterally as well as vertically. If the dog is viewed while moving away, the body should move in a straight line with the direction of movement. One movement fault is called "crabbing" or "side-winding." This means that while the front legs follow the direction of the head, the body moves slightly to the right or left. The hind legs do not move "true in line with movement of the front legs" as required by the standard.

Dogs with long loins may also fail in lateral back movement. When viewed going away, and at a slow gait, there will be a sort of caterpillar action. This may be all right for caterpillars, which aren't going anywhere in particular, but it always means lost motion for a Malamute.

Now the true test of movement comes when dogs are actually pulling, either when pulling a sled, or in weight pulling contests. We are including a number of pictures of teams moving both at a gallop and while trotting. These pictures show that the best dogs do move as the standard says they should. One can notice the great reach of the front legs; that the dogs' front and hind legs do move parallel and in line; and that there is fair width between both the front legs and the hind ones.

In particular, one should notice the truly sound and beautiful movement of the hind legs of these teams. One of the authors, Maxwell Riddle, once traveled 54 miles in a single session, in early December, along the northerly coast of the continent. At the end of that time, the Malamutes were still moving perfectly behind. No finer test of the soundness of movement of the Malamute could be made.

Ch. Beowulf's Danska, bred, owned, and trained by Beth Harris, demonstrates gait. Note ground covering stride and top line.

Lawrence Jenkins

Ch. Tenakee Chief, owned by Dr. Richard and Dawn Woods, Gardena. CA, demonstrates gait. Note great foreleg reach.   *Callea*

Ch. Voyageur's Cougar, at eight years of age, demonstrates marvelous thrust and gait. Note full extensions of forearm and leg to make a perfect line with the shoulder, straight top line, and full drive and extension of hind legs. He is bred and owned by Howard and Virginia Devaney.

Eva Seeley drives a team through heavy snow. Note top lines of struggling dogs.
Dick Smith

Noted dam, Ch. Jingo's Silver Trumpet, here demonstrates the single track, in which the legs move into line under the body but do not cross over beyond that line. Howard and Virginia Devaney are the owners.

A dog team, being trained to pull, shows perfect rear action drive.

Jack Coolidre

Army dogs in training at Wonalancet show excellent front leg action as they pull
a four wheel gig.　　　　　　　　　　　　　　　*International News Photo*

26

Alaskan Malamute Temperament

IT IS perhaps not by accident that the authors of the breed standard made the second heading "TEMPERAMENT." For every Malamute that is kenneled fifty are kept as pets and under modern living conditions, temperature is the most important feature of the dog—of any dog.

"The Alaskan Malamute is an affectionate, friendly dog, not a 'one man' dog. He is a loyal, devoted companion, playful on invitation, but generally impressive by his dignity after maturity." We quote from the standard.

The Alaskan Malamute belongs to an ancient type of dog which is sometimes called the northern forest group. Many of the dogs of this group have been used as servants of man for uncounted centuries. Most of such dogs have not been guard dogs but have generally recognized human beings as their friends. And they have been willing to work until death, and to work to death, for men.

This loyalty, affection, and willingness to work have characterized most of the sled dog group. The Eskimo, at least in recent decades, has been an exception. Their tendency to savagery when allowed to roam caused the Northwest Mounted Police of eastern Canada to discontinue their use.

We mention this here because there is always the danger that, as a breed grows and expands, irresponsible breeders will tend to ignore viciousness. We dare not let this happen with the Alaskan Malamute. But it will unless all breeder-owners are warned and heed this warning.

261

A puppy steps out for the camera of Beth Harris.

In researching for this book, one of the authors wrote to every news-paper in Alaska asking if any had in its files stories of hero feats by Alaskan Malamutes. One replied: "The only records we have are of those Mala-mutes which have bitten our mail boys." No doubt the writer of those words thought he, or she, was being funny. But it is not humorous. It is a problem which must be faced.

The Doberman Pinscher standard, before it was changed and weakened, described viciousness as follows: "Any dog which growls at or attempts to bite the judge, or its handler is vicious, and must be disqualified." It excepted dogs which try to fight with other dogs.

The same standard called for the disqualification of shy dogs. It de-scribed the shy dog as one which shrinks away from the judge when he approaches the dog either from the front or from the rear. The Doberman Pinscher people have also weakened this section.

Now shyness is a curse in any dog breed. And shyness is almost inevita-ble unless breeders eliminate shy dogs from breeding programs. People say of rapidly expanding breeds that dog shows have ruined them, but dog shows haven't. Irresponsible breeders have.

Now when a person buys an Alaskan Malamute puppy, he or she ex-pects to get what the standard calls for—a loyal, affectionate, devoted com-panion. Neither the vicious dog nor the shy dog can qualify. They make unacceptable pets. And the shy dog can become, or often is, a fear biter and therefore dangerous.

The Alaskan Malamute is a large, powerful dog, and one which is highly intelligent and easily trained. This means that it is also easily spoiled. Many a vicious dog is simply one which has been spoiled. The owner excused him for growling—gave him an inch, and he has taken a mile.

In an earlier chapter Bob White tells how he breaks dogs of fighting on the picket line. It sounds cruel, but it is necessary to be stern. And in the end, it pays off. Similarly, the home owner must teach his dog that it cannot growl or bite.

Small Malamute puppies growl at the food dish, that is, when just being weaned, and all are eating from the same dish, or are trying to do so. It is simple to grab such a puppy by the tail, jerk it away and roll it across the floor. It quickly learns that growling caused this.

Every owner should practice taking the food dish away from the eating puppy. If the puppy growls, pick it up by the scruff of the neck, scold it, and slap it lightly upward under the chin. Then return it to the dish. A few such treatments are all that are necessary.

Similarly, one can practice taking bones away from the puppy. If it growls, it is punished. But then, it gets back the bone, and shortly it learns that the master will not tolerate growling.

In play, puppies often get angry and growl and snap. Again they must be punished. But after punishment, the puppy should be encouraged to play again. It then learns that play, even rough play, is okay, but that it can never get angry.

Dog judges hear all sorts of excuses for shy dogs, and also for those who growl or try to bite: "The last judge squeezed his testicles;" "The veterinarian scared him when he took his temperature, and now he doesn't like to have anyone approach his rear end;" "He won't show indoors;" "He won't show on grass;" "This is his first show;" "She got sick coming to the show in the car;" "A dog jumped him just as he was about to come into the ring;" "She doesn't like male judges;" "Women judges in those floppy hats scare him;" etc., etc. But judges can't accept such excuses, and the owner should not have to make them. Get your puppy immunized. Then take it for long walks on a leash. Take it to shopping areas where a lot of people can "oh and ah" over it. Take along a supply of biscuits and ask a stranger to give the puppy a bit of biscuit and a lot of petting.

Take it along streets where traffic is heavy, so that it gets used to a lot of noise. And while you are at it, walk the dog in the street. Every time a car approaches, jerk it severely onto the grass. Shortly, it will always listen for cars, and will get out of the way when one approaches.

A common excuse is that dogs won't walk on lead. Well, let it get hungry. Take it for walks, and then feed it afterward. Shortly it will welcome walking on lead. And shortly, you'll have an experienced, friendly pet.

The standard says: "generally impressive by his dignity after maturity." This is an oblique way of expressing an essential feature of Alaskan Malamute character. Most of them are clowns and show-offs. While they make excellent scores in obedience, they enjoy clowning a bit. They almost always entertain the ringside, and it makes them a joy to own.

So there you have it: a big dog, exceptionally easy to train, possessed of great endurance with a passionate desire to work for its owner and the ability to let down and play when not working. These are the essential character features of the Alaskan Malamute, and they are the reasons they are so desirable to own.

27

Weight Pulling as a Sport

THE JOYS of owning an Alaskan Malamute are great because you can do so many things with them. One of these things is weight pulling. Such events are now being held in various parts of the country. Originally, they were held only in the Far North during times of ice and snow. But they can be held indoors as well.

Of course, other dogs can enter these contests and often do. St. Bernards, if sound, are great weight pullers, and their huge size makes them leaders in the sport. But it can be argued successfully that Alaskan Malamutes are, pound for pound, the greatest of them all.

It is difficult to claim a weight pulling record. There are too many factors involved. Suppose, for instance, that the contests are held outside in the snow. Factors then involved are condition of the snow, temperature, type of sled to be pulled, type of runners, etc. Conditions can be more even, and can be better controlled, at indoor contests. But the type of floor, roughness of the surface, for instance, will have an influence on the results.

One of the great Malamute pullers was Taaralaste Naki Nein, owned by Roger Burggraf of Fairbanks, Alaska. Naki was a bitch weighing 85 pounds. That was also her working weight when in harness with a team. When she made her record, the snow was hard packed and the temperature was between ten and fifteen degrees above zero Fahrenheit. Naki pulled a sled weighing slightly over 150 pounds and loaded with a dead weight of 2200 pounds. The ground was level. Naki began from a dead start and pulled the sled sixty feet.

Ch. Traleika of Tundra strains to the task at Grandby, Colorado.

Three dog weight pulling champions at the North American races, 1970, Fairbanks, Alaska. The dogs pulled 3,700 pounds, over sixty feet, driven from behind, not coaxed, with the temperature at ten degrees. Taaralaste Naki, Tote-Um's Littlest Hobo, and Taaralaste Vosa Villem are from Roger Burggraf's Taaralaste Kennels, Fairbanks.

Little Delta, owned by the Tuglu Kennels of Larry and Mary Ann Breen of Winnipeg, is a noted weight puller.

Ch. Aristeed's Frost Shadow hauls a sled load of children at the Hales Corners Winter Carnival in Wisconsin in 1975.

Under differing conditions, Tuglu Kennels' Little Sheba won the over 1000 pound pull on a heavy sled at Winnipeg, Manitoba. And Ch. Squankan's Moose, a best of breed winner owned by Dr. Richard and Dawn Woods, pulled 1450 pounds. Ch. Aristeed's Frost Shadow has been a consistent winner, or placer, in Midwest events, and placed second at both the 1974 and 1975 International Kennel Club shows at Chicago.

A great Canadian weight puller was Canadian Ch. Bearpaw Lobo Son of Elk. A very big dog, weighing 140 pounds, "Bo" twice won weight pulls of 1370 pounds, once on gravel and once on snow. Tragically, he could not be used for breeding since he was a chondrodysplastic carrier.

The all-time greatest winner, however, has been Sugar River's Tundra Boy, owned and trained by Jerry Winder of Durham, Ill. The dog has been undefeated in more than thirty contests. These include consecutive victories for five years at the Chicago International show. His record includes a pull on snow of 1750 pounds, and a best pull on wheels of a 1963 Chevrolet pick-up truck.

In giving these bare details, two points stand out. Champions rank high as competitors, not only in the show ring, but as weight pullers, as team dogs and as obedience title holders. There can be hardly anything wrong with a breed which can produce such dogs and such records.

First place in the weight pulling contests at the Chicago International K.C. show for the fifth year in a row was Sugar River's Tundra Boy and owner, Jerry Winders Durham, Ill.

Ritte

28

Selected Alaskan Malamute Pedigrees

PEOPLE who buy purebred puppies should get a number of documents which will prove the purity of the dog's breeding. One form is an application to register a puppy from a previously registered litter. If the litter has not been registered, the puppy cannot be registered. The application for registration must be endorsed over to the purchaser and must be signed by the seller.

Sometimes, a puppy will be sold which has already been registered. In that case, the seller merely endorses the registration papers and personally fills in the name of the purchaser. Neither the application to register a puppy from a registered litter, nor a transfer of ownership of a registered dog can be signed, leaving the space for the name of the purchaser blank.

In addition, most breeders will supply a three or four generation pedigree of the puppy, and purchasers should expect this. Such pedigrees are not necessarily accurate, unless certified by the American or Canadian Kennel Club, as the case may be. But usually they are accurate, except possibly for the spelling of certain names.

The purpose of this chapter is to supply people with such additional information as should make it possible to trace their dog's pedigree back to the breed origins. This will not be possible for every dog in the pedigree, perhaps, but the lines of the great dogs will be evident.

In some cases, but not all, the pedigrees will match or go with the dogs pictured. But there have been space limitations. Those dogs not pictured in this section, whose pedigrees appear, may be seen in other chapters of this book.

It is hoped that the pedigrees will help to broaden the knowledge of newcomers to the breed, and to make these newcomers proud of their dogs.

```
                                          Kazan
            Baree, Son of Kazan           Torno
        Silver King                       Happy
            Tosha                         Laska
    Koyak                                 Pucky
            Happy                         Nicki
        Tosha                             Pucky
            Laska                         Nicki

CH. SPAWN'S ALASKA

            Igloo                         Kazan
        Gemo                              Vixen
            Lynx                          Buck
    Kiska                                 Lingo
            Cree                          Bo-Bo
        Sitka                             Miska
            Fox                           Chinook
                                          Lucky Lady
```

```
                    Gray Wolf (gr. grandsire)
                  Gray Cloud (grandsire)
                    Susie (gr. granddam)
            Yukon Jad (sire)

                  Pearl (granddam)


            CH. GRIPP OF YUKON
            ─────────────────────────


                  Bessie (dam)


              (Pedigree otherwise unknown)
```

```
                                        Yukon Jad
                  Ch. Gripp of Yukon     Bessie
                Navarre of Kotzebue      Rowdy of Nome
                  Taku of Kotzebue       Akeela of Kotzebue
          Ch. Kim of Kotzebue            Yukon Jad
                  Ch. Gripp of Yukon     Bessie
                Pandora of Kotzebue      Antarctica Taku's Milt
                  Wray of Antarctica     Taku of Antarctica

      CH. TORO OF BRAS COUPE
      ──────────────────────────────

                  Yukon Jad
              Yukon Blizzard
                  Bessie                (Pedigrees of this
          Kotzebue Cleopatra              generation unknown)
                  Antarctica Taku's Milt
              Antarctica Cleo
                  Taku of Antarctica
```

```
                    Igloo             Kazan
                Dude's Wolf           Vixen M'Loot
                    Lash
            Gentleman Jim             (Other pedigrees
                    Ptargin            of this generation
                Dodge's Lou            of sire unknown)
                    Soo-Loo

      CH. LORN-HALL OOGOROOK M'LOOT
      ────────────────────────────────────

                  Baree, Son of Kazan  Kazan
                Silver King            Torno
                  Tosha                Happy
            Noma M'Loot                Laska (or Lasha)
                  Tarko                Drift
                Silver Girl            Chila
                  Hoonah               Karluk
                                       Kenai
```

271

```
              Oomik
        Tobuk
              Nanook          (Pedigree of this
Mikiuk                        generation of
              Peluk           sire unknown)
        Kapuk
              Oolik
```

CH. MULPUS BROOK'S MASTER OTTER

```
              Baree, Son of Kazan  Kazan
        Silver King               Torno
              Tosha                Happy
Noma                               Laska
              Tarko                Drift
        Silver Girl                Cile
              Hoonah               Karluk
                                   Kenai
```

```
              Tobuk                    Oomik
        Mikiuk                         Nanook
              Kapuk                    Peluk
   Nooka                               Oolik
              Dude's Wolf              Igloo
        Fox                            Lash
              Dodge's Lou              Ptargin
                                       Soo Loo
```

CH. TUYAH OF SILVER SLED

```
           Mikiuk                   Tobuk
        Ch. King M'Loot             Kapuk
           Fox M'Loot               Dude's Wolf
   Oogerook of Silver Sled          Dodge's Lou
           Nahnook I                Mukluk M'Loot
      Ch. Gyana of Silver Sled      Fox M'Loot
           Ch. Ooloo M'Loot         Mikiuk
                                    Noma M'Loot
```

```
                Navarre of Kotzebue   Ch. Gripp of Yukon
        Ch. Kim of Kotzebue          Taku of Kotzebue
                Pandora of Kotzebue   Ch. Gripp of Yukon
    Ch. Toro of Bras Coupe           Wray of Antarctica
            Yukon Blizzard
        Kotzebue Cleopatra            (Balance of this
            Antarctic Cleo I            generation unknown)
```

CH. KELERAK OF KOBUK

```
                Navarre of Kotzebue   Ch. Gripp of Yukon
        Ch. Kim of Kotzebue          Taku of Kotzebue
                Pandora of Kotzebue   Ch. Gripp of Yukon
    Helen of Bras Coupe              Wray of Antarctica
            Yukon Blizzard
        Kotzebue Cleopatra            (Balance of this
            Antarctic Cleo I            generation unknown)
```

	Tobuk	Oomik
Mikiuk		Nanook
	Kapuk	Peluk
Mulpus Brook's Master Otter		Oolik
	Silver King	Baree, Son of Kazan
		Tosha
Noma		Tarko
	Silver Girl	Hoonah

CH. MULPUS BROOK'S THE BEAR

	Koyuk	Silver King
Chisholm's Viking		Tosha
	Kiska	Gemo
Mulpus Brook's Dusty Lane		Sitka
	Schmoos M'Loot	Mikiuk
		Vixen
Chisholm's Northern Star		Gentleman Jim
	Tora M'Loot	Lucky

Navarre of Kotzebue
Ch. Kim of Kotzebue
Pandora of Kotzebue
Ch. Toro of Bras Coupe
Yukon Blizzard
Kotzebue Cleopatra
Antarctica Cleo

Ch. Gripp of Yukon
Taku of Kotzebue
Ch. Gripp of Yukon
Wray of Antarctica
Yukon Jad
Bessie
Antarctica Taku's Milt
Taku of Antarctica

CH. CLIQUOT OF HUSKY PAK, CDX

Koyuk
Ch. Alaska
(later: Spawn's Alaska)
Kiska
Ch. Arctic Storm of Husky Pak
Schmoos M'Loot
Chitina
Tora M'Loot

Silver King
Tosha

Gemo
Sitka
Mikiuk
Vixen
Gentleman Jim
Lucky

276

```
              Mikiuk                          Tobuk
    Ch. Mulpus Brook's Master Otter          Kapuk
              Noma                            Silver King
  Ch. Mulpus Brook's The Bear                Silver Girl
            Chisholms Viking                  Koyuk
      Ch. Mulpus Brook's Dusty Lane          Kiska
            Chisholms Northern Star           Schmoos M'Loot
                                              Tora M'Loot
```

KOBUKS DARK BEAUTY

```
            Ch. Mulpus Brook's Master Otter   Mikiuk
        Ch. Prairie Lash                      Noma
            Tonga                             Gentleman Jim
  Ch. Baloo                                   Tosha
            Ch. Mulpus Brook's Master Otter   Mikiuk
        Shawnee Belle                         Noma
            Tonga                             Gentleman Jim
                                              Tosha
```

```
                                              Navarre of Kotzebue
            Ch. Kim of Kotzebue               Pandora of Kotzebue
      Ch. Chinook Kotzebue Gripp              Chinook Karluk of Kotzebue
         Taku's Mascara of Chinook            Igloo Pak's Neena
   Ch. Sno-Pak Kavik's Oopik                  Ch. Kim of Kotzebue
            Ch. Toro of Bras Coupe            Kotzebue Cleopatra
         Kavik of Sno-Pak                     Igloo Pak's Gripp
            Musher Lane Kila                  Musher Lane Taku of Chinook
```

CH. ROGUE OF TIGARA

```
                                              Ch. Kim of Kotzebue
            Ch. Toro of Bras Coupe            Kotzebue Cleopatra
      Ch. Keowuk of Kobuk                     Ch. Kim of Kotzebue
         Helen of Bras Coupe                  Kotzebue Cleopatra
   Calaeno of Tigara                          Navarre of Kotzebue
            Ch. Kim of Kotzebue               Pandora of Kotzebue
         Cookie of Bras Coupe                 Yukon Blizzard
            Kotzebue Cleopatra                Antarctica Cleo
```

```
                                              Ch. Keowuk of Kobuk
            Alaskan Kakolik of Kuvak          Helen of Bras Coupe
      Ch. Midnight Shadow of Kuvak            Sno-Pak Kaghi's Tugg
         Alaskan Ooowuk of Kuvak              Kiana of Kuvak
   Kadluk of North Wind                       North Wind of Silver Sled
         Lobo of North Wind                   Kamah of Silver Sled
      Ch. Nome of North Wind                  North Wind of Silver Sled
         Klondike Kate of North Wind          Dorrie's Dolly
```

AM. CAN. MEX. INT'L. CH. GLACIERS' STORM KLOUD, C.D.

```
                                              Moosecat of North Wind
            Midwest's Moosecat Jack           Midwest's Flicka
      Kodiak of North Star                    Great Bear of North Wind
         Shuli Brooke of North Wind           Ch. Misty of North Wind
   Ch. Glacier Lady of the Arctic             Moosecat of North Wind
         Midwest's Moosecat Jack              Midwest's Flicka
      Princess Rose of North Star             Kim Loop
         Princess Keena of North Star         Nome of Hales
```

```
                                                 Silver King
            Koyuk                                Tosha
      Ch. Spawn's Alaska                         Gemo
         Kiska                                   Sitka
   Ch. Apache Chief of Husky-Pak                 Mikiuk
         Schmoo's M'Loot                         Vixen
      Chitina                                    Gentleman Jim
         Tora M'Loot                             Lucky
```

CH. HUSKY-PAK MARCLAR'S SIOUX

```
                                              Navarre of Kotzebue
            Ch. Kim of Kotzebue               Pandora of Kotzebue
      Ch. Toro of Bras Coupe                  Yukon Blizzard
         Kotzebue Cleopatra                   Antarctic Cleo I
   Ch. Cheyenne of Husky-Pak                  Koyuk
         Ch. Spawn's Alaska                   Kiska
      Ch. Arctic Storm of Husky-Pak           Schmoo's M'Loot
         Chitina                              Tora M'Loot
```

```
                          Tobuk
         Mikiuk            Kapuk
Ch. Mulpus Brooks Master Otter  Silver King
         Noma             Silver Girl
Kobi of Polars Wilderness      Ch. Nahnook II
         Polar            Kola
    Ch. Spawn's Chee Chee   Kayak of Brookside
    Arrow of Husky Pak      Ch. Husky Pak Mikya of Seguin

CH. KIANA OF KLONDIKE


                          Nahnook I
      Ch. Nahnook II        Ch. Ooloo M'Loot
    Eski of Silver Sled     Ch. King M'Loot
      Oogerook of Silver Sled  Ch. Gyana
Sno Valley Twilight        Nahnook I
      Ch. Nahnook II        Ch. Ooloo M'Loot
    Coco                   Nooka
      Ch. Tuyah of Silver Sled  Oogerook of Silver Sled
```

279

Ch. Keowuk of Kobuk
Alaskan Kakolik of Kuvak
Helen of Bras Coupe
Ch. Kingmik of Kuvak, C.D.
Sno-Pak Kaghi's Tugg
Alaskan Oowuk of Kuvak
Kiana of Kuvak

Ch. Toro of Bras Coupe
Helen of Bras Coupe
Ch. Kim of Kotzebue
Kotzebue Cleopatra
Kachi of Kobuk
Musher Lane's Kila
Ch. Toro of Bras Coupe
Taku's Mascara of Chinook

ADVENTURERO DE KOROK

Can. Ch. Husky-Pak Forecast
By Cliquot, C.D.
Ch. Amarok
Barb-Far Marclar's Marook
Snow Queen of Erowah
Ch. Apache Chief of Husky-Pak
Barb-Far Marclar's Mikwah
Ch. Cheyenne of Husky-Pak

Ch. Cliquot of Husky-Pak, CDX

Deeka of Husky-Pak
Ch. Apache Chief of Husky-Pak
Ch. Cheyenne of Husky-Pak
Ch. Spawn's Alaska
Chitina
Ch. Toro of Bras Coupe
Ch. Arctic Storm of Husky-Pak

Ch. Husky-Pak Erok
Ch. Kodara Kodiak of Erowah
Kobuk's Dark Beauty
Ch. Kodara Kodiak Teddi
Ch. Cochise of Husky-Pak
Ch. Sno-Crest Aurora of Erowah
Kobuk's Dark Beauty

CH. KARAHONTA THE APACHE

Ch. Cochise of Husky-Pak
Ch. Sno-Crest's Mukluk
Kobuk's Dark Beauty
Ch. Kodara's Koona Karohonta
Pawnee Flash of North Wind
Ambara's Eyara
Preston's Cheechako

280

Ch. Mulpus Brooks The Bear
Sena Laks Sno Wolf
    Ch. Kobuks Manassas Mischief
Sena Laks Thor
    Kobi of Polars Wilderness
Ch. Kiana of Klondike
    Sno Valley Twilight

Ch. Mulpus Brooks Master Otter
Mulpus Brooks Dusty Lane
Ch. Prairie Lash
Ch. Ayiyak of Roy El
Ch. Mulpus Brooks Master Otter
Ch. Spawn's Chee Chee
Eski of Silver Sled
Coco

CH. SENA-LAK'S THOR II

Ch. Sierra Blizzard
Silver Sleet of Sno Shu
    Noatak of Silver Sled
Ch. Aurora of Sena Lak
    Kobi of Polars Wilderness
Ch. Kiana of Klondike
    Sno Valley Twilight

Aipuk M'Loot
Oolik M'Loot
Ch. King M'Loot
Ch. Gyana
Ch. Mulpus Brooks Master Otter
Ch. Spawn's Chee Chee
Eski of Silver Sled
Coco

```
              Ch. Apache Chief of Husky-Pak    Ch. Spawn's Alaska
       Ch. Husky-Pak Erok                      Chitina
              Ch. Kelerak of Kobuk             Ch. Toro of Bras Coupe
Ch. Kodara's Kodiak of Erowah                  Helen of Bras Coupe
              Ch. Mulpus Brook's The Bear      Ch. Mulpus Brook's Master Otter
       Kobuk's Dark Beauty                     Mulpus Brook's Dusty Lane
              Ch. Baloo                        Ch. Prairie Lash
                                               Shawnee Belle

CH. EROWAH ROXANNE

              Ch. Toro of Bras Coupe           Ch. Kim of Kotzebue
       Ch. Cochise of Husky-Pak                Kotzebue Cleopatra
              Ch. Arctic Storm of Husky-Pak    Ch. Spawn's Alaska
Ch. Sno-Crest's Aurora of Erowah               Chitina
              Ch. Mulpus Brook's The Bear      Ch. Mulpus Brook's Master Otter
       Kobuk's Dark Beauty                     Mulpus Brook's Dusty Lane
              Ch. Baloo                        Ch. Prairie Lash
                                               Shawnee Belle
```

282

Ch. Bara-Far Lootok
Ch. Spawn's Kulak
Ch. Spawn's Chee Chee
Ch. T'Domar's Voodoo King
Ch. Husky-Pak Eagle
Ch. Husky-Pak Gazelle
Arctic Dawn of Husky-Pak

Ch. Daku of Husky-Pak
Ch. Koonah of Silver Sled
Polar
Arrow of Husky-Pak
Ch. Apache Chief of Husky-Pak
Ch. Kelerak of Kobuk
Ch. Apache Chief of Husky-Pak
Ch. Husky-Pak Mikya of Sequin

CH. T'DOMAR'S BISMARCK

Ch. Fakir of Roy-El
Ch. Spawn's Hot Shot of Roy-El
Snowmasque White Diamond
T'Domar's Nootka
Ch. Spawn's Kulak
T'Domar's Taboo
Ch. Husky-Pak Gazelle

Erik of Roy-El
Marclar's Una
Musherlane Erebus of Chinook
Musherlane Pandora
Ch. Barb-Far Lootok
Ch. Spawn's Chee Chee
Ch. Husky-Pak Eagle
Arctic Dawn of Husky-Pak

283

```
                Ch. Tigara's Arctic Explorer    Ch. Toro of Bras Coupe
      Ch. Tigara's Torch of Arctica            Sno-Pak Kavik's Oonalik
          Tigara's Winsome Witch                Rebel of Tigara
  Ch. Tigara's Dangerous Dan McGrew             Ch. Tigara's Petite Parka
                Ch. Tigara's Arctic Explorer    Ch. Toro of Bras Coupe
      Tigara's Thais of Arctica                Sno-Pak Kavik's Oonalik
          Ch. Tigara's Kije of Arctica          Ch. Kimbra's King Notak
                                                Tigara's Kiana Kenai

CH. TIGARA'S DIAMOND JIM

                Ch. Tigara's Torch of Arctica   Ch. Tigara's Arctic Explorer
      Ch. Tigara's Tyczar of Arctica           Tigara's Winsome Witch
          Tigara's Kazana                       Ch. Toro of Bras Coupe
  Sno Bear's Amber of Arctica                  Sno-Pak Kavik's Oonalik
                Ch. Tamarack of Tigara          Ch. Sno-Pak Kavik's Oopik
      Tigara's Susitna Sue                     Calaeno of Tigara
          Tigara's Winsome Witch                Rebel of Tigara
                                                Ch. Tigara's Petite Parka
```

Ch. Tigara's Arctic Explorer | Ch. Toro of Bras Coupe
Ch. Tigara's Torch of Arctica | Sno-Pak Kavik's Oonalik
Tigara's Winsome Witch | Rebel of Tigara
Ch. Voyageur's Cougar | Ch. Tigara's Petite Parka
Ch. Ceba's Silver Bow | Coldfoot Chilkott
Ch. Jingo's Silver Trumpet | Ceba-Sue
Ch. Husky-Pak Jingo | Ch. Husky-Pak Eagle
| Ch. Husky-Pak Marclar's Sioux

CH. LOBITO'S COUGAR CUB

Ch. Kee Too | Ch. Little Joe of North Wind
Ch. Ninilchik | Chilly Buk
Kee Nah | Ch. Eldor's Little Bo
Ch. Beowulf's Lynaska Dolly, C.D. | Kobuk's Sainuk Maria
Sena-Lak's Mischief's Pupeno | Ch. Sena-Lak's Arctic Flash
Ch. Sena-Lak's Beowulf Tawechi, C.D. | Ch. Kobuk's Manassas Mischief
Ch. Sena-Lak's Tenana of Roy-El | Ch. Tamarack of Tigara
| Ch. Sena-Lak's Laskana

Ch. Karohonta Kingikuk Koona, owned by Ben Ogburn, was the first female to win a working group in the "lower 48," and the second in breed history.

	Ch. T'Domar's Voodoo King	Ch. Spawn's Kulak
Ch. T'Domar's Kulak		Ch. Husky-Pak Gazelle
T'Domar's Taboo		Ch. Spawn's Kulak
Ch. Uyak Buffalo Bill		Ch. Husky-Pak Gazelle
Ch. Kodara Kodiak Teddi		Ch. Kodara Kodiak of Erowah
Ch. Karohonta Conestoga		Ch. Sno-Crest Aurora of Erowah
Ch. Kodara's Koona Karohonta		Ch. Sno-Crest's Mukluk
		Ambara's Eyara

CH. KAROHONTA KINGIKUK KOONA

	Ch. Spawn's Kulak	Ch. Barb-Far Lootok
Ch. T'Domar's Voodoo King		Ch. Spawn's Chee Chee
Ch. Husky-Pak Gazelle		Ch. Husky-Pak Eagle
Ch. Karohonta Voodoo Flame		Arctic Dawn of Husky-Pak
Ch. Kodara Kodiak Teddi		Ch. Kodara Kodiak of Erowah
Ch. Karohonta Ta-Lo-Wah		Ch. Sno-Crest Aurora of Erowah
Ch. Kodara's Koona Karohonta		Ch. Sno-Crest's Mukluk
		Ambara's Eyara

```
                 Ch. Little Joe of North Wind      Ch. Midnight Shadow of North Wind
         Ch. Kee-Too                                Ch. Dorry's Sitka of North Wind
             Chilly-Buk                             Cold Foot's Chilkoot
    Ch. Kougarok                                    Kay Buk
                 Ch. Eldor's Little Bo              Kobuk's Manassas Ambition
         Kee-Nah                                    Ambara's Kanik
             Kobuk's Sainuk Maria                   Ch. Mulpus Brook's The Bear
                                                    Arctic Dawn of Husky-Pak
CH. KEE-TOO'S KOUGAROKS DEMOS
─────────────────────────────

                 Ch. King Nikki of North Wind      Chief Mohawk of North Wind
         Ch. Malesa's Silver Glacier               Ch. Dorry's Sitka of North Wind
             Ch. Glacier's Tisha Lyng              Ch. Glacier's Storm Kloud
    Malesa's Silver Reflection                     Nabesna
             Ski Dust                              Narsuk's Dewline Skimo
         Malesa's Miss Mischief                    Gold Dust of North Wind
             Midwest's Ringo of Rocky Way          Midwest's Moog
                                                   Twilight of Northern Woods
```

BIBLIOGRAPHY

ALL OWNERS of pure-bred dogs will benefit themselves and their dogs by enriching their knowledge of breeds and of canine care, training, breeding, psychology and other important aspects of dog management. The following list of books covers further reading recommended by judges, veterinarians, breeders, trainers and other authorities. Books may be obtained at the finer book stores and pet shops, or through Howell Book House Inc., publishers, New York.

Breed Books

AFGHAN HOUND, Complete	Miller & Gilbert
AIREDALE, New Complete	Edwards
ALASKAN MALAMUTE, Complete	Riddle & Seeley
BASSET HOUND, Complete	Braun
BEAGLE, Complete	Noted Authorities
BLOODHOUND, Complete	Brey & Reed
BOXER, Complete	Denlinger
BRITTANY SPANIEL, Complete	Riddle
BULLDOG, New Complete	Hanes
BULL TERRIER, New Complete	Eberhard
CAIRN TERRIER, Complete	Marvin
CHESAPEAKE BAY RETRIEVER, Complete	Cherry
CHIHUAHUA, Complete	Noted Authorities
COCKER SPANIEL, New	Kraeuchi
COLLIE, Complete	Official Publication of the Collie Club of America
DACHSHUND, The New	Meistrell
DALMATIAN, The	Treen
DOBERMAN PINSCHER, New	Walker
ENGLISH SETTER, New Complete	Tuck & Howell
ENGLISH SPRINGER SPANIEL, New	Goodall & Gasow
FOX TERRIER, New Complete	Silvernail
GERMAN SHEPHERD DOG, Complete	Bennett
GERMAN SHORTHAIRED POINTER, New	Maxwell
GOLDEN RETRIEVER, Complete	Fischer
GREAT DANE, New Complete	Noted Authorities
GREAT PYRENEES, Complete	Strang & Giffin
IRISH SETTER, New	Thompson
IRISH WOLFHOUND, Complete	Starbuck
KEESHOND, Complete	Peterson
LABRADOR RETRIEVER, Complete	Warwick
LHASA APSO, Complete	Herbel
MINIATURE SCHNAUZER, Complete	Eskrigge
NEWFOUNDLAND, New Complete	Chern
NORWEGIAN ELKHOUND, New Complete	Wallo
OLD ENGLISH SHEEPDOG, Complete	Mandeville
PEKINGESE, Quigley Book of	Quigley
PEMBROKE WELSH CORGI, Complete	Sargent & Harper
POMERANIAN, New Complete	Ricketts
POODLE, New Complete	Hopkins & Irick
POODLE CLIPPING AND GROOMING BOOK, Complete	Kalstone
PUG, Complete	Trullinger
PULI, Complete	Owen
ST. BERNARD, New Complete	Noted Authorities, rev. Raulston
SAMOYED, Complete	Ward
SCHIPPERKE, Official Book of	Root, Martin, Kent
SCOTTISH TERRIER, Complete	Marvin
SHETLAND SHEEPDOG, The New	Riddle
SHIH TZU, The (English)	Dadds
SIBERIAN HUSKY, Complete	Demidoff
TERRIERS, The Book of All	Marvin
WEST HIGHLAND WHITE TERRIER, Complete	Marvin
WHIPPET, Complete	Pegram
YORKSHIRE TERRIER, Complete	Gordon & Bennett

Breeding

ART OF BREEDING BETTER DOGS, New	Onstott
BREEDING YOUR SHOW DOG, Joy of	Seranne
HOW TO BREED DOGS	Whitney
HOW PUPPIES ARE BORN	Prine
INHERITANCE OF COAT COLOR IN DOGS	Little

Care and Training

DOG OBEDIENCE, Complete Book of	Saunders
NOVICE, OPEN AND UTILITY COURSES	Saunders
DOG CARE AND TRAINING FOR BOYS AND GIRLS	Saunders
DOG NUTRITION, Collins Guide to	Collins
DOG TRAINING FOR KIDS	Benjamin
DOG TRAINING, Koehler Method of	Koehler
GO FIND! Training Your Dog to Track	Davis
GUARD DOG TRAINING, Koehler Method of	Koehler
OPEN OBEDIENCE FOR RING, HOME AND FIELD, Koehler Method of	Koehler
SPANIELS FOR SPORT (English)	Radcliffe
SUCCESSFUL DOG TRAINING, The Pearsall Guide to	Pearsall
TOY DOGS, Kalstone Guide to Grooming All	Kalstone
TRAINING THE RETRIEVER	Kersley
TRAINING YOUR DOG TO WIN OBEDIENCE TITLES,	Morsell
TRAIN YOUR OWN GUN DOG, How to	Goodall
UTILITY DOG TRAINING, Koehler Method of	Koehler
VETERINARY HANDBOOK, Dog Owner's Home	Carlson & Giffin

General

COMPLETE DOG BOOK, The	Official Publication of American Kennel Club
DISNEY ANIMALS, World of	Koehler
DOG IN ACTION, The	Lyon
DOG BEHAVIOR, New Knowledge of	Pfaffenberger
DOG JUDGE'S HANDBOOK	Tietjen
DOG JUDGING, Nicholas Guide to	Nicholas
DOG PEOPLE ARE CRAZY	Riddle
DOG PSYCHOLOGY	Whitney
DOG STANDARDS ILLUSTRATED	
DOGSTEPS, Illustrated Gait at a Glance	Elliott
ENCYCLOPEDIA OF DOGS, International	Dangerfield, Howell & Riddle
JUNIOR SHOWMANSHIP HANDBOOK	Brown & Mason
MY TIMES WITH DOGS	Fletcher
OUR PUPPY'S BABY BOOK (blue or pink)	
RICHES TO BITCHES	Shattuck
SUCCESSFUL DOG SHOWING, Forsyth Guide to	Forsyth
TRIM, GROOM AND SHOW YOUR DOG, How to	Saunders
WHY DOES YOUR DOG DO THAT?	Bergman
WILD DOGS in Life and Legend	Riddle
WORLD OF SLED DOGS, From Siberia to Sport Racing	Coppinger